Thomas A. Field
Michelle R. Ghoston

Neuroscience-Informed Counseling with Children and Adolescents

AMERICAN COUNSELING ASSOCIATION
6101 Stevenson Avenue • Suite 600
Alexandria, VA 22304
www.counseling.org

Neuroscience-Informed Counseling with Children and Adolescents

American Counseling Association

6101 Stevenson Avenue, Suite 600 • Alexandria, VA 22304

Associate Publisher • Carolyn C. Baker

Digital and Print Development Editor • Nancy Driver

Senior Production Manager • Bonny E. Gaston

Copy Editor • Beth Ciha

Cover and text design by Bonny E. Gaston

Library of Congress Cataloging-in-Publication Data

Names: Field, Thomas A., author. | Ghoston, Michelle R., author.
Title: Neuroscience-informed counseling with children and adolescents / Thomas A. Field and Michelle R. Ghoston.
Description: Alexandria : American Counseling Association, 2020. | Includes bibliographical references and index.
Identifiers: LCCN 2019053760 | ISBN 9781556203862 (paperback)
Subjects: LCSH: Children—Counseling of. | Youth—Counseling of. | Neurosciences.
Classification: LCC BF636.6 F54 2020 | DDC 158.3083—dc23
LC record available at https://lccn.loc.gov/2019053760

Dedication

This text is dedicated to our shared mentor, Professor Steve Nielsen.

Many years ago, both of us attended the master's-level counseling program at Lynchburg College (now the University of Lynchburg). We were in cohorts a few years apart. Steve served as our mentor throughout our master's program, during our doctoral studies, and beyond. Well known to the Virginia counseling community, Steve is well respected for his intelligence, humor, and commitment to serving the community. Both of us learned from Steve the importance of being involved professionally, remaining curious, and constantly seeking to improve as counselors. We hope to embody the warmth, professional commitment, and seemingly boundless wisdom that Steve epitomized. Although Steve did not contribute to this book formally, his spirit is felt throughout.

Table of

Contents

Preface

We wrote this text with the intention of appealing broadly to new counselors and experienced practitioners. We also intended for this text to be useful to counselors in a variety of settings, such as schools, hospitals and residential facilities, and outpatient clinics. We cover general principles for counseling children and adolescents before moving into more technical information about neurophysiological development across childhood and adolescence and in-depth information about counseling approaches for different developmental stages. We divide the chapters into three sections. The first section provides a background of neuroanatomy and physiology. The second section focuses on neurophysiological development during childhood and relevant counseling approaches. The third section focuses on counseling adolescents. The concluding chapter explores the delivery of neuroscience education to clients utilizing information that is introduced throughout the text. Our intent for each chapter is to present a neuroscience-informed approach to counseling children and adolescents, and thus we often draw from neuroscience findings when presenting information about child and adolescent development and counseling approaches at different developmental stages.

We recognize that terms such as *childhood* and *adolescence* are difficult to define with regard to age, as children may mature earlier or later than others (e.g., secondary sex development). For the sake of clarity, we loosely define *childhood* as ages 0 to 11 and *adolescence* as ages 12 to 18. These are loose definitions, as experts such as Adriana Galván estimate that the range for pubertal onset is 9 to 16 years. We also recognize that adolescence often ends beyond age 18. We have decided not to differentiate middle childhood (i.e., preadolescence) from late childhood in this text because we see clearer distinctions between early childhood (0–11) and adolescence (12–18) when providing counseling. For example, we have led insight-oriented groups with adolescents in which 12 or 13 is the cutoff age for inclusion. We have also successfully used insight-oriented approaches such as cognitive behavior therapy with youth ages 12 and older and have observed that play therapy is less useful with youth after approximately 10 years of age.

Text Features

Each chapter includes several text features that we hope will help you to better comprehend the content. **Key concepts** and **aligned Council for Accreditation of Counseling and Related Educational Programs standards** are identified at the beginning of the chapter to assist you in understanding the content and learning objectives of each chapter. **Quiz questions** are provided at the end of each chapter so you can test your knowledge of key concepts explored in each chapter. **Reflection questions** are embedded at different points in the chapter to prompt your own deep reflection on and processing of the content. **Case vignettes** are used throughout the text to demonstrate how to apply concepts to counseling work. Finally, we have included a comprehensive **neuroscience glossary** at the back of the textbook for you to review when you come across unfamiliar terminology.

Case Vignettes

We use pseudonyms for all of the cases in this text, and we sought to intentionally mask identifying information to preserve the identities of former clients. Often we merge the narratives of several former clients into one composite case. Although we have blinded the identities of the children, adolescents, and families we have previously helped, the specific details of the case information are mostly factually accurate. Most case vignettes are brief, although two cases (those of Brooke and Wayne) are more extended and are explored across several chapters. We wanted to use these elaborated cases to describe an in-depth application of key concepts to case conceptualization and treatment planning.

Integrating Neuroscience Into Counseling Practice

The counseling field is increasingly applying neuroscience to counseling practice and is increasingly in need of training opportunities for learning how to integrate complex information into work with clients. A large concern of ours is overreliance on applied models. These are treated as primary sources by some professionals, yet they are in fact interpretations of basic neuroscience anatomy and physiology. We felt that if we summarized these applied models to counseling practice, we ran the risk of summarizing existing summarizations of neuroscience, which would have led us even further away from the primary source material of neural anatomy and physiology. Thus, you might be surprised to find that we rarely cite commonly known authors such as Daniel Siegel, Louis Cozolino, Allen Schore, and Stephen Porges in the text. We took seriously our charge of using primary sources (i.e., actual neuroscience studies) to provide accurate information about neuroscience and refrained from relying on applied models. We hope this text will increase your knowledge of basic neuroanatomy and physiology, which we believe is fundamental to applying neuroscience in your work.

In our own journeys, we have found that neuroscience has not only supported how we think about counseling but also changed our perspectives entirely. As you read through this text, we encourage you to be open to neuroscience concepts that could change the way you conceptualize and practice counseling. For example, in the text we review the impact of chronic stress and traumatic stress on neurophysiological functioning and its relationship to a host of mental health diagnoses. We also identify strategies for reducing child and adolescent stress, which can be challenging because many of these stressors are not easily reduced and often cannot be removed (e.g., academic requirements, the social environment at school, relationships with parents or guardians). We recognize that the technical nature of the neuroscience terminology might be challenging for some readers. We highly recommend referring back to key terms defined in the glossary at the end of the text to better understand key neuroscience concepts.

Concluding Thoughts

In our favorite textbooks, the personalities of the authors resonate through the pages. We wrote this text with the intention that you will get to know how we think and feel about counseling children and adolescents. At times, our style of writing borders on the informal, to help you understand our own backgrounds and perspectives. At other times, the information is presented in a more formal and technical fashion. We have attempted to balance these two polarities in our writing. We hope that sharing our own experiences with the topic will humanize the neuroscience information and make it more digestible to you.

About the Authors

Thomas A. Field, PhD, is an assistant professor of psychiatry in the Mental Health Counseling and Behavioral Medicine program at Boston University School of Medicine. He has worked as a counselor educator since 2011. He also currently sees clients in private practice. Since 2006, Professor Field has worked with more than 1,000 clients in a variety of settings, including schools, inpatient psychiatric units, and outpatient private practice. He received his doctorate in counseling and supervision from James Madison University. In 2019, he received the Linda Seligman Counselor Educator of the Year Award from the American Mental Health Counselors Association (AMHCA). His primary areas of research are the integration of neuroscience into counseling practice and professional advocacy issues. He is currently the associate editor of the *Journal of Mental Health Counseling*, the coeditor of *Counseling Today*'s neurocounseling column, and chair of the AMHCA Neuroscience Interest Network and Neuroscience Taskforce.

• • •

Michelle R. Ghoston, PhD, is an assistant professor at Wake Forest University. She has been a licensed counselor since 2006 and has worked as a counselor educator in some capacity since 2010. Professor Ghoston has worked with a variety of clients at many different levels and in many settings, including group homes, schools, hospitals, private practice, and intensive in-home treatment. Since entering the world of academia, she has consistently looked back on those early years of working with young people and how they have shaped who she is today. Her primary areas of research are social justice and equity, advocacy, and better understanding how neuroscience influences the work of counselors. Professor

Ghoston currently serves as a member of the editorial board of *Teaching and Supervision in Counseling* (the official journal of the Southern Association for Counselor Education and Supervision) and is on a number of taskforces, including the AMHCA Neuroscience Taskforce.

• • •

Acknowledgments

We are grateful to our colleagues who supported us while we were writing this text and our supervisors from years past who helped us become better counselors. We would like to especially thank Rachel Chaney for her terrific work on several of the graphics used in this book. We also offer the following personal acknowledgments.

Thom: I am grateful for the loving relationships and support of my wife, Selina, and our two children, Elliott and Owen. Being a parent has given me a much richer perspective on child development and strategies for best meeting the needs of children, adolescents, and families.

Michelle: It is with a humble heart that I first give thanks to Thom for inviting me along on this journey. Many thanks to my mother and daughter, who put up with me needing to do a "little" work on this book during our vacation. Mom, you made it clear early on that education was a must—thank you! Lauren, you continue to amaze me with where your life continues to take you. I am beyond thankful and blessed!

We would also like to note that this book was written in the context of our belonging to a community that is dedicated to the integration of neuroscience into counseling. Belonging to this community has helped us over the years to cultivate our understanding of neuroscience-informed counseling. We are grateful for the ongoing impassioned discussions and projects that we share with our colleagues, who include (but are not limited to) Eric Beeson, Ted Chapin, Jamie Crockett, Kathryn Douthit, Mark Gerig, Gary Gintner, Penijean Gracefire, Sean Hall, Allen Ivey, Laura Jones, Chad Luke, Raissa Miller, Yoon Suh Moh, Morgan Riechel, Lori Russell-Chapin, Michael Russo, Eraina Schauss, and Carlos Zalaquett.

• • •

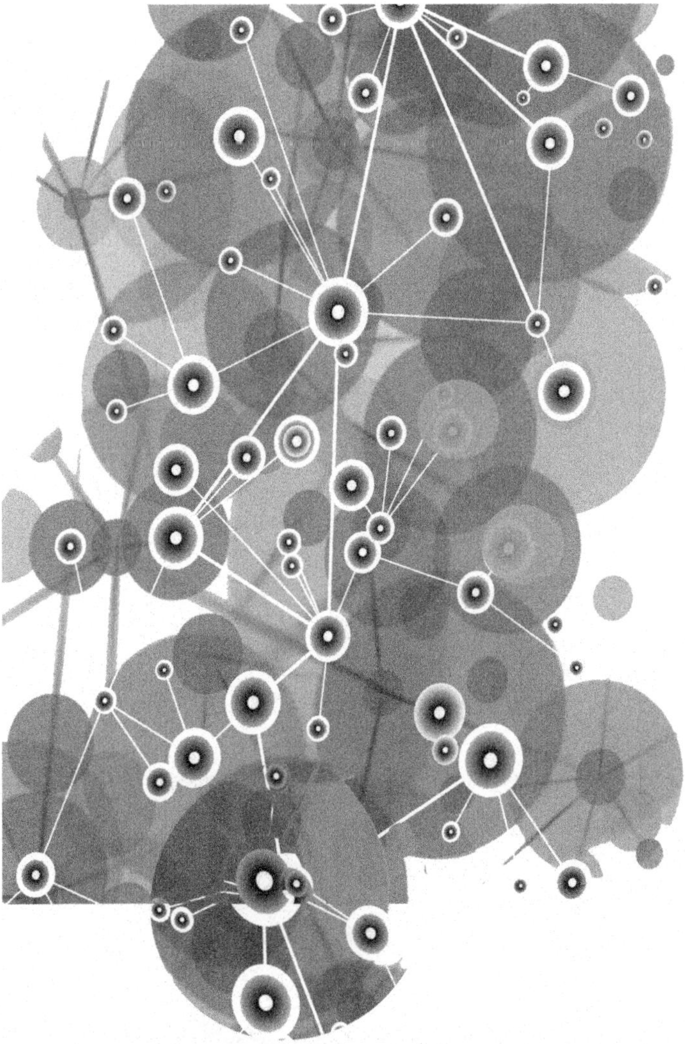

Section I
Foundations

Chapter 1

General Principles for Counseling Children and Adolescents

Key Concepts

- Content and process
- Deficit model of childhood
- Reinforcement association
- Self-efficacy
- Speaker-listener neural coupling

Aligned 2016 CACREP Standards

Standard 2.F.5.f. Counselor characteristics and behaviors that influence the counseling process

Standard 2.F.5.g. Essential interviewing, counseling, and case conceptualization skills

• • •

Both of us began our counseling careers working with children. In this chapter, we describe our background in counseling children and adolescents, discuss the lessons we learned, and propose principles for working effectively with children and adolescents from a neuroscience-informed perspective. These principles are generally consistent across clients.

Thom's Background

I began my counseling career as a behavior specialist at a school for children with severe disabilities. I worked primarily with a late adolescent who had multiple diagnoses, including autism, intellectual disability, Tourette's syndrome, bipolar disorder, and obsessive-compulsive disorder. This person was also taking multiple psychotropic medications, including an antidepressant, antipsychotic, anxiolytic, mood stabilizer, and atypical stimulant (i.e., the five major classifications of psychotropic medications). The experience was formative for me, as I developed a strong relationship with a person who had few words and could barely write their own name legibly. I came to know, respect, and cherish this person and understood who they were beyond their diagnosis or label.

During the 2 years I worked at the school, I volunteered with a local crisis hotline to see whether I would enjoy working with people in more of a counseling capacity (i.e., more active listening, less behavioral intervention). I then took a position as a mental health counselor at an inpatient psychiatric hospital for children and adolescents and worked at that hospital for the next 6 years throughout graduate school. I once did the math and tallied that I provided counseling to more than a thousand children and adolescents during that time period. As a result, I saw the gamut of mental health conditions. I observed the vital role of family and environment in supporting or detracting from a child's mental health. I also became familiar with using formal counseling techniques in individual and group counseling modalities. I had three supervisors, each with decades of experience, who identified with family systems therapy, cognitive behavior therapy (CBT), and psychodynamic therapy. I benefited greatly from that diversity of thought regarding client work.

When I took my first full-time academic job after graduating with my doctorate, I joined a group private practice and continued to work with children and adolescents. The transition from providing short-term counseling in an inpatient setting to providing long-term counseling in a private practice setting was easier than I expected. The issues that children, adolescents, and families faced were quite similar to the ones I saw in the hospital, except perhaps less acute. Many of the adolescents I worked with had strained relationships with their parents and were struggling to forge their own identities. I also often assisted parents and guardians in navigating their own role transition as their children became more independent and needed more support than direction.

During my counseling career, I had several experiences working with younger children. For example, I completed my doctoral internship at an elementary school counseling program. I recently decided to stop providing play therapy to young children in private practice because I noticed that I had less energy for my own kids when I came home after my clinic day. I have learned that I have to take care of myself if I am to be helpful to others. I have found that play therapy with young children requires more energy and attention than regular talk therapy.

Today I see clients in individual private practice 1 day a week in addition to my academic responsibilities. My counseling work is refreshing and often the highlight of my week.

Michelle's Background

I began my career working as an assistant houseparent in a group home for troubled children. I physically lived at the group home Friday through Monday mornings (in my separate quarters). This allowed me to see the young men from the time they entered the group home until their discharge. I was their pseudoparent, administrator, and disciplinarian. These young men were typically between the ages of 12 to 19 (occasionally a young man decided to remain until his 21st birthday, but this was rare). I saw a multitude of diagnoses in this setting, including major depression, anxiety, obsessive-compulsive disorder, reactive attachment disorder, intermittent explosive disorder, attention-deficit/hyperactive disorder, bipolar disorder, substance use and addictions, and conduct disorder. Comorbidity, or having more than one diagnosis, was common. In addition, the young men typically came from dysfunctional homes, had received services in the mental health system for more than half of their young lives, struggled academically, displayed problem behaviors, and were involved with the legal system. They were also often taking psychotropic medication. My time at the group home was challenging yet rewarding. I learned a significant number of things from other mental health professionals, but most important from the young men themselves.

I remained with the group home until I went to work in a temporary emergency shelter for children. I later returned to the group home setting two additional times but in different roles: as a case manager and an independently contracted therapist. In the years that followed, I began to notice the systemic concerns surrounding so many young women and men being in the negative feedback loop of the social systems in which they resided (dysfunctional homes, trouble in school, trouble within the community, and ultimately legal troubles).

As I continued to work in various settings that focused on helping children and adolescents, I realized that I needed and wanted to support this population in a different way. Completing my master's degree while serving as a case manager at the same group home and getting licensed allowed me to take on a more significant role as an intensive in-home therapist. This work brought me face to face with families, extended families, school administrators, probation officers, parole officers, judges, and community leaders. This crystalized for me the need for a holistic approach to meeting the needs of these young people. The levels of trauma, stress, disappointment, and inconsistency they often endured were off the charts. This did not excuse their behaviors, but it helped me understand their current problems rather than solely view them as being defiant and deviant. These experiences helped me develop the holistic approach that I take to the work I continue to do as a licensed professional counselor.

While pursuing my doctorate, I continued to work with young people as an independently contracted therapist. I worked at a residential acute stabilization setting in a hospital and also worked as a counselor at a community college, where I worked with emerging adults.

Today I am licensed in two states and plan to work with children and families in some capacity while continuing my academic responsibilities as a faculty member. If I can help one young person see that their life can change for the better, no matter the systemic barriers that person faces on a daily basis, my heart will rejoice!

Three Primary Principles for Working With Children and Adolescents

From our narratives, you may have already picked up on a few lessons that will become important in your own work with children and adolescents. In this section, we outline three major principles for child and adolescent counseling.

Principle 1: Seek to Know People Beyond Labels

Most master's-level counseling students are very excited to take their psychopathology course and to learn the grisly details of abnormal behavior. If we are honest with ourselves, there is an allure to learning about why people behave in dysfunctional ways. For decades, mental health professionals have relied on the *Diagnostic and Statistical Manual of Mental Disorders* (*DSM;* American Psychiatric Association, 2013) to understand why people experience distress and declines in overall functioning. In today's current practice climate, counselors are required to use diagnostic codes from the *International Classification of Diseases* and the associated *DSM* symptom criteria to bill both public and private party health care reimbursement systems for counseling services. Often counselors are required to make a provisional (i.e., preliminary) diagnosis after only one session with a client to receive insurance reimbursement. The primacy of diagnosis in mental health services can be understood through the lens of the greater medical system. If you see a dentist to get a filling, the dental provider will diagnose the problem (tooth decay) and select an approved intervention that addresses the problem (composite filling). Counselors who bill health care insurance companies for reimbursement of medical procedures must use diagnostic codes.

The use of diagnosis in counseling is often challenging, however, because clients do not present with exact diagnostic criteria. Because biomarkers for mental disorders (e.g., lab tests) have not yet been identified (Field, Beeson, Luke, Ghoston, & Golubovic, 2019), diagnosis can vary between mental health providers and feels subjective at times. For that reason, the National Institute of Mental Health (n.d., 2016) has proposed using a more comprehensive neuroscience-informed model for assessing mental health issues called the *Research Domain Criteria*. The Research Domain Criteria framework encourages the use of multiple physiological assessment methods, such as heart rate, cortisol level, peripheral skin temperature, and so on, in addition to self-reported information. Using such a comprehensive method for assessing children and adolescents is likely out of reach for most practicing counselors today, though it will likely become more feasible as technology and training become more accessible and more guidelines are published and circulated.

Counselors should be discerning and cautious when diagnosing children with mental health issues. Some mental disorders, such as autism and personality disorders, are considered persistent and chronic. Counselors must ethically consider the impact of a diagnosis before assigning it to a client (American Counseling Association, 2014). We recommend gathering significant assessment evidence before making a neurodevelopmental diagnosis such as autism or attention-deficit/hyperactivity disorder.

We have found diagnoses to be, by and large, fairly limited in their usefulness when working with people. Authors such as Sommers-Flanagan and Sommers-Flanagan (2007) and Hansen (2016) have criticized counselors' use of *DSM* diagnoses and their adherence to a mental health culture that stigmatizes clients and reduces their lived experience to diagnostic labels. People are much more than their diagnostic labels. A diagnostic label cannot tell you much about the character, personality, interests, and motivations of the person you are working with. A primary goal of your work as a counselor is to come to deeply know the client. Instead of reducing their clients to their diagnoses, counselors should wonder and inquire about their character and personality. What makes them tick? What do they think about most often? What deeply interests and moves them? Who matters most in their lives, and who are fringe characters? What (if anything) do they want out of counseling? If you can help a child or adolescent figure out the answers to these questions (often they do not know), you will make progress toward forming the kind of relationship that can be transformative. We recommend that counselors intentionally assign diagnoses for reimbursement services but largely refrain from using them to guide their work with clients. There are exceptions to this: Treatment planning can and should be guided by some diagnoses, such as autism. In subsequent chapters, we try to balance the counselor's need to make differential diagnosis with a humanistic counseling approach that transcends diagnosis.

In most instances, there is no compelling evidence that counselors should rely on a diagnosis to identify the treatment approach when providing counseling to children and adolescents (Sommers-Flanagan & Sommers-Flanagan, 2007). The movement to directly address mental disorders with psychological treatments has been heavily criticized in the mental health community. Research teams led by Bruce Wampold (e.g., Wampold & Imel, 2015) have examined multiple studies to look at the overall effect of interventions (e.g., CBT) that directly address a specific diagnosis (e.g., generalized anxiety). Such studies, known as *meta-analyses,* have consistently found that the actual treatment method (i.e., counseling theory and technique) has very little influence on the outcome. People typically improve because of client variables (e.g., motivation) alongside other treatment variables (e.g., the counselor's skill and delivery, the client's relationship with the counselor, the client's belief and expectation that change will occur). Researchers have also failed to find evidence that specific components of an intervention are critical to the success of the overall intervention. For example, trauma-focused CBT places emphasis on the child or adolescent client identifying and retelling a trauma narrative. Yet trauma-focused CBT is just as effective without the trauma narrative being included in the counseling approach (Deblinger, Mannarino, Cohen, Runyon, & Steer, 2011). Therefore, we do not propose one single theoretical approach for working with children in this text, and we attempt to cover several different traditions in our chapters on specific counseling approaches.

Principle 2: Form Effective Working Relationships

Counselors should be flexible in their approach to counseling children and adolescents. You should take the time to get to know the young person you are working with and be flexible in how you allocate time during meetings with them. Children will vary in what they need from the counseling process. In your counseling career, you will work with children, adolescents, and families from a range of backgrounds and cultures. You will work with people whose backgrounds are very different from your own. Even children and adolescents who have comparable backgrounds, cultures, and developmental stages may still need different counseling approaches. To paraphrase Irvin Yalom (2017), be open and willing to create a new counseling approach for each client.

Building effective working relationships with children can require a different approach and skillset than working with adults. We recommend considering the developmental age of the child or adolescent when allocating the amount of time spent in insight-oriented talk therapy.

The prefrontal cortex does not fully mature until approximately 25 years of age (Arain et al., 2013; Casey, Jones, & Hare, 2008), resulting in difficulties with valuing long-term versus short-term benefits and outcomes, limited attention spans, and struggles with verbalizing thoughts and feelings. Although adolescents of high school age are usually capable of sitting through a 50-minute counseling session, it is unrealistic for an elementary school child to do so. Insight-oriented processing with children should be kept to no more than 10 to 20 minutes at a time. For younger children with neurodevelopmental challenges, such as attention deficits or autism, even 5 minutes of talk therapy can overwhelm their frustration tolerance. It is important that the client view counseling as a positive experience, and thus respecting the limits of the child or adolescent is important.

The counselor should consider the child's or adolescent's developmental stage and age when selecting a counseling approach. For example, younger children may prefer play-based work, whereas older adolescents may feel that play therapy is demeaning and prefer more structured talk therapy approaches. In this text, we review counseling approaches by developmental age. Note that some children will be developmentally older or younger than their stated age, and this should be considered when selecting counseling modalities.

Compared to adults, children often have less interest in discussing their life narratives and the meaning of life events in intimate detail. Many adults, even mandated clients, are motivated to address the immediate problems facing them. Adults can appraise time spent discussing tangential topics as distracting from the task at hand. In comparison, children are often motivated to talk about topics of interest to them, such as favorite hobbies or activities. When the counselor talks with a child about a topic of interest and demonstrates a familiarity with the topic, the child is more likely to become interested in the counselor and eventually become more open to discussing other topics. We like to call this *reinforcement association*. To engage in reinforcement association successfully, counselors must often spend time researching topics in popular culture. For example, when working with children and adolescents, we have intentionally sought to keep up on current knowledge of new musical acts, video games, television shows, social media applications, fictional book series, and sports players and teams. In addition to preferred hobbies and activities, adolescents are often motivated to discuss peer relationships that are important to them, especially dating relationships and friendships. We therefore strongly believe that counselors should take an open and flexible approach with children and adolescents. A balance must be struck between discussing these topics of interest and addressing the pressing issues for which counseling was initiated. A brief case example illustrates the importance of flexibility. Thom once worked with a 12-year-old girl named Kelsey and uses first-person narrative to describe the counseling process. See Case Vignette 1.1.

Case Vignette 1.1 Kelsey

Kelsey was a 12-year-old girl who independently asked her mother whether she could attend counseling. In my experience, this was fairly unusual for a child of middle school age. Kelsey struck me as a very mature 12-year-old whom I could have mistaken for a 15- or 16-year-old had I not had the case file. Kelsey had been experiencing symptoms of depression, and her mother had a history of depression. In our first meetings, I often tried to steer the course of the dialogue toward Kelsey's depressive symptoms and her occasional insinuations that she was restricting her eating. Each time I brought these topics up, Kelsey would become annoyed and shut down the conversation. She consistently insisted that she "just wanted to talk." We spent most of the next 18 months discussing topics that spanned friendships, romantic interests, her athletic experiences, and academic work. Very rarely did we address her symptoms directly. Occasionally I would ask her how she was feeling overall. She often reported feeling much better and was grateful that counseling afforded her the space to talk freely about her life experiences with someone who was not a parent or friend. After 18 months, Kelsey reported that her depression had largely subsided and she felt better able to handle her depression when it did occur. We mutually decided to conclude counseling.

• • •

When working with Kelsey, Thom clearly veered toward the extreme end of the spectrum, allowing the child to lead the session with fairly infrequent addressing of the presenting concerns. In Thom's defense, he became convinced early on during the counseling process that Kelsey would stop coming to counseling if he enforced more structure than she was willing to tolerate. Kelsey's story is a helpful example of how a child's developmental age is often different from their actual age, and it highlights the importance of taking a flexible approach to the counseling process when working with youth. Kelsey's need for autonomy and her exploration of identity through discussions of important relationships and activities were more typical of an older adolescent and are fairly unusual for a 12-year-old.

There are several important principles for forming effective counseling relationships with youth in addition to being open and flexible. In particular, it is crucial for the counselor to demonstrate curiosity and bracket assumptions, listen to the underlying meaning and message, respond with genuineness and candor, and demonstrate respect. The following case vignette demonstrates these principles. Thom once worked with a 17-year-old girl named Amber and uses first-person narrative to describe the counseling process. See Case Vignette 1.2.

We can glean a couple of important lessons from this story. When meeting with Amber, it was very important to hold a not-knowing stance and enter into the dialogue with a genuine curiosity about why she thought and felt the way she did. Counselors must work hard to avoid assuming the meaning of a person's statement or behavior. Often there is a deeper meaning and context to *why* people think as they do or behave as they do. Thom could easily have assumed that Amber was being unnecessarily defiant or unreasonable or attempting to provoke her parents' ire as he entered into the dialogue with her. Doing so would have limited his search to understand her thoughts and feelings.

Case Vignette 1.2 Amber

After several years of working in an inpatient psychiatric hospital, I earned my master's degree in counseling and was given additional responsibilities to provide individual, group, and family counseling to a caseload of children and adolescents whose length of stay was approximately 4 to 6 days. The unit had three full-time primary therapists for a total census capacity of 20 children. During one afternoon, a fellow therapist approached me with a dilemma. He was working with an older female adolescent and had reached an impasse. The adolescent had already been in the hospital for longer than our typical length of stay yet was still refusing to go home. She was adamant that she would attempt suicide if she were discharged back to her family.

My colleague had tried many different interventions, none of which had been successful. He approached me with a request that I meet with the adolescent to see if I could provide a helpful perspective and second opinion. I met with Amber that afternoon and explained my reasons for meeting with her. I informed her that I knew she was still suicidal and felt she was not ready to go home. I mentioned that her current therapist had asked me to meet with her. I opened up the dialogue by asking her to describe to me why she felt so suicidal. Amber explained that she felt we were not taking care of the earth, that our natural environment was "going to hell," and that she did not want to live in a world where humans continually degrade the environment.

(Continued)

Case Vignette 1.2 *(Continued)*

I was stunned. Her response was quite unusual and not what I expected. We continued to discuss further why she cared so deeply about the natural world and sustainability. Amber shared that she voraciously read books and articles about pollution, their effect on the ozone layer, the warming of the polar ice caps, and so on. Toward the end of our brief dialogue, I asked her whether she had ever considered doing something about it. She clearly cared deeply about the earth; had she considered how she could be part of the movement to reduce pollution, waste, and carbon emissions? I mentioned in passing that we *needed* people with such a passion.

The meeting concluded, and I did not have a chance to talk with Amber further. Within a few days, she was discharged from the hospital and did not return. In the inpatient world, the staff typically only hear about their patients' outcomes if they are readmitted to the unit. Thus, no news is often good news. In this case, I had the good fortune to run into Amber once more. A few years passed. I was sitting down to dinner at a local Chinese restaurant with my wife. When the server approached, I recognized Amber immediately. The inpatient hospital was in a small town of approximately 75,000 inhabitants, and it was not unheard of to run into old clients in the community. Amber apparently recognized me too and wanted to chat briefly. I walked away from the table, and Amber mentioned to me that she had completed high school and had enrolled in a sustainability program at the local community college. Clearly, our meeting had an impact on her life direction.

• • •

Sharing responses genuinely was important to the outcome of this dialogue. Amber needed to know that Thom was surprised by her response, that it seemed she had a clear reason for living, and that the world needed more people with such convictions about sustainability. Janet Edgette (2002) wrote that using candor is crucial to connecting with adolescents in counseling. Adolescents are particularly sensitive to disingenuous or scripted responses and yearn for more authentic dialogue.

Not all active listening is of the same quality. Optimal active listening involves the counselor attending to the underlying meaning and message that the person is communicating. In listening closely to what Amber was saying, Thom became aware that there was a deeper meaning to her persisting suicidality. It became clear that inside her suicidality was a deep care about the planet and natural preservation.

Uncovering Amber's reasons for living was a crucial component of the intervention. Research teams led by Marsha Linehan (e.g., Linehan, Goodstein, Nielsen, & Chiles, 1983; Osman et al., 1998) have recommended assessing reasons for living when working with suicidal adolescents to detect potential protective factors against a suicide attempt. Linehan created a Reasons for Living Inventory that was subsequently revised for adolescents (Osman et al., 1998) to assist with this assessment. Amber's disgust toward human degradation of the environment and valuing of sustainability were important reasons for living and major protective factors against a future suicide attempt. Although one of the main drivers of suicide attempts is psychological distress and the desire to end psychological suffering (Shneidman, 1998), in this case Amber's suicidal ideation came from desperately wanting things to be different rather than from a desire for nonexistence.

Content and Process

Uncovering the hidden meanings and messages in a child or adolescent's story can be a challenge at first. Beyond the *content* of their verbal communication, we can understand the underlying meaning and message of this communication by attending to the *process* by which this information was communicated. For example, we attend to children's nonverbal communication during the session. Do they become more defensive in body posture? Do they avoid eye contact? We also wonder about the reason for their sharing this information. How might they expect the counselor to respond? And how might they ideally want the counselor to respond? Asking these questions helps to move the conversation to a deeper level.

Imagine that you are working with a defiant child who is intentionally justifying their physical aggression toward a sibling because the sibling "deserved it." If you merely attend to the content of the child's verbal communication, you might get drawn into a power struggle. For example, content-based questions and statements such as "Tell me how you think they deserve it" are likely to be met with unsatisfactory answers, if the child's goal is to elicit a reaction from you. At some point, you will need to address the interpersonal process that is happening to take the dialogue to a deeper level. To illuminate the interpersonal process, you might say, "I feel drawn to counter you, which will get us into conflict. Could we explore that?" or "What reaction are you expecting from me, and what reaction would you ideally want?" You might add later, "How do people typically respond when you justify your aggression? How would you like them to respond?" Addressing the child's attempt to initiate a power struggle will help you avoid playing out the power struggle. It will also help the child realize their own role in their interpersonal conflicts. Later, you can help the child explore whether power struggles result in the child actually satisfying their wants and needs (e.g., needs for attention) and identify more adaptive methods of getting needs met.

If you are new to the counseling process, we highly recommend asking yourself the following questions during dialogues with your clients: (a) Why is this person telling me this? (b) How do I feel compelled to respond? (c) How might this person expect me to respond, and how might they want me to respond? These prompts can help you to attend to the interpersonal process between the speaker and listener, not just the content being spoken.

Principle 3: Address Areas of Personal and Professional Growth as a Counselor

Listening closely to underlying meanings and messages and demonstrating candor and genuineness both require the same underlying attitude. Children and adolescents want to be respected as full people whose thoughts and feelings are important regardless of their age. This might seem like a no-brainer. However, in many communities, adults conceptualize childhood solely as preparation for adulthood. In this conceptual model, children are viewed as half-formed adults who have not yet developed the knowledge, skills, attitudes, beliefs, and behaviors of a fully functioning adult. This deficit model of childhood limits our attempts to prize and cherish the different and unique perspectives of children. Instead, consider that children and adolescents often have a wisdom that is different from that of adults. Children and adolescents are often better able to take risks, be vulnerable, be open, directly communicate their wants and needs, and be genuine in their responses to people. We should value these traits of children and adolescents rather than evaluate their worth using adult standards for behavior.

Countertransference

The society and culture in which children grow up today is different from that of our own childhoods (Sommers-Flanagan & Sommers-Flanagan, 2007). As the saying attributed to Heraclitus goes, we cannot enter into the same river twice. Although it can be tempting for adults to view their own childhood experience as the framework for understanding the experiences of children and adolescents, this is inaccurate and can be unhelpful. Counselors, parents, and guardians should instead try to understand the experiences and perspectives of children and adolescents in a way that brackets their own childhood experiences. Doing so creates the space for them to develop curiosity for their experience. It is also tempting for adults to view their own childhood experiences as superior to the current experiences of youth.

We like to call this the *"good old days" syndrome*. Such perspectives limit the ability of adults to truly understand and respect the lived experiences of today's children and adolescents.

Countertransference is present throughout most of our work as counselors and will show up at times in your work with children. For example, you might have strong reactions to certain parenting styles based on your own childhood. You might overidentify with a child or a parent and attempt to assert your own values. As a counselor, you are charged with intentionally working through countertransference that limits your work with people. In the past, we have processed our own countertransference through journaling, talking with colleagues, and attending personal counseling. Whatever the route, addressing attitudes and biases that could hinder your work is tremendously important to your growth as a counselor.

See Reflection Question 1.1 list, which might be useful for guiding your own journey in reflecting on your attitudes toward children and any known sources of potential countertransference. (We say "known sources," because of course countertransference is typically not consciously known to us until it shows up.)

Counselor Emotional Stability and Self-Regulation

Children and adolescents need the trusted adults in their lives to be emotionally stable and regulated. When an adult is able to listen to their stories and support them without becoming overwhelmed and reactive, children develop confidence that they too can tolerate and manage a situation. To be a holding container for another person's emotional experience, we must intentionally take care of ourselves. Evidence from neuroscience can be instructive here. Lifestyle habits, such as adequate sleep quality and duration (Babson, Trainor, Feldner, & Blumenthal, 2010; Goel, Rao, Durmer, & Dinges, 2009), physical exercise (Bernstein & McNally, 2017), nutrition (Spencer, Korosi, Layé, Shukitt-Hale, & Barrientos, 2017), and mindfulness practice (Guendelman, Medeiros, & Rampes, 2017), give us the ability to respond in an attentive and emotionally regulated fashion. We

Reflection Question 1.1

Write down a brief paragraph for each of the following questions.

1. What was your own childhood like?
2. What legacies might you be carrying forward from your own childhood?
3. How do you conceptualize childhood? In other words, what is the purpose of childhood?
4. What personal attitudes and biases toward children and parenting are you aware of?

are far less able to respond in a regulated manner when we are sleep deprived, hungry, stressed, distracted, and anxious.

If we are listening closely and empathizing, we will experience (to a degree) the same distress and dysregulation as our clients. Neuroscientists have found that listeners tend to experience the same brain activation as the speaker when attending closely. Stephens, Silbert, and Hasson (2010) conducted a study into speaker-listener neural coupling. They used functional magnetic resonance imaging to record the brain activity of a person who told an unscripted and unrehearsed real-life story. The researchers then played this recording to a group of listeners whose own brain activity was also recorded during playback. The researchers found that listeners had the same brain activity as the speaker when participants communicated effectively with each other, albeit with a brief lag. Stephens et al. wrote that verbal communication tends to be a joint activity. This suggests that mirrored brain activity might be a two-way process. If a listener is capable of experiencing the same brain activation as a speaker, it is possible that a speaker may experience the same brain activation as a listener. Thus, our response to children, adolescents, and families as listeners may assist them as speakers to self-regulate.

Stephens et al. (2010) found that listeners at times had brain activation that precipitated the speaker's activation in the same brain regions. When listening closely, listeners could predict and anticipate the responses of the speaker. This deep sense of empathy emerges from close listening and attending. In your journey to being an effective counselor, it is important to not only develop excellent attending skills but also address emotional regulation issues that prohibit you from being an attentive and present listener.

Familiarity With Technology

Familiarity with ever-increasing innovations in technology is also an important ongoing professional development requirement for child and adolescent counselors. When we were growing up, we rarely had contact with friends from school if we were not spending time with them in person. Outside of school, we communicated to friends by telephone (land lines). Today many of our child and adolescent clients communicate with friends throughout the evening when they return home from school using mobile apps and text messaging. In short, they are persistently and deeply engaged with friendships in ways that were not possible before. The benefit of such engagement is the potential for deeper and more lasting friendships. The potential drawback to such engagement is difficulty regulating communication and a need to be continually on with friends. For example, some adolescents struggle not to respond to a text message after they have gone to bed because of fears that their friend will misinterpret their response and think they are ignoring them, which might create a rift in the relationship. Mobile technology can also cause pernicious issues, such as cyberbullying (e.g., Betts, Spenser, & Gardner, 2017), ostracism and exclusion on social media (Schneider et al., 2017), and online predation (Jones, Mitchell, & Finkelhor, 2011). Keeping up with the pace of technology is important to your ongoing relevance as a child and adolescent counselor, as technology is becoming an increasingly important part of the day-to-day experiences of children and families.

Special Considerations

So far, we have outlined principles for counseling children and adolescents. There are a few more special considerations to highlight when counseling children and adolescents regarding the beginning and ending of the counseling process. In this section, we present principles for conducting the intake process and terminating counseling services.

The Intake Process and Informed Consent

The intake process lays the foundation for a successful counseling experience. During the informed consent process, you will likely engage with both the child or adolescent and their parents or guardians. At the least, parents and guardians are regularly involved in crucial logistical considerations, such as transporting children and adolescents to counseling appointments and paying for services. Although some adolescents will initiate counseling without their parent or guardian's knowledge, this is rare. Most often parents and guardians are involved in the decision to initiate counseling. Even in elementary and middle school settings, it is standard practice for school counselors to inform all parents and guardians about small-group counseling that is offered at the school. If the child is younger than the age of consent in the state you are working in, parents can opt them out of school-based counseling services.

When working with clients who are not attending counseling of their own volition (i.e., who are not self-referred), it becomes even more important for counselors to describe the limits of confidentiality. Child and adolescent clients should know with whom information may be shared and under what conditions. For example, parents of elementary school children will likely want periodic updates on their children's progress. Child or adolescent clients who are required to attend counseling by the juvenile justice system (e.g., for truancy violations) should also know that information may be shared with juvenile probation officers. This information helps minor clients make informed decisions about what information to disclose in counseling.

In outpatient settings, we use a different informed consent document and intake procedure for child and adolescent clients than for adult clients. It is important to have all relevant family members attend the first meeting. We recommend discussing confidentiality and parent or guardian rights at the beginning of the first meeting. Children and adolescents will become much more comfortable with self-disclosure if they know that most of the information shared with their counselor will remain private and will not be divulged to their parents or guardians. This means that during the intake process, parents and guardians need to buy into the idea that their child or adolescent will need some degree of privacy during the counseling process. If the parent or guardian wants periodic updates, the content of these updates should be negotiated with the child or adolescent. The parent should understand that the counselor will sometimes refrain from sharing information that the child or adolescent has shared. It is therefore crucial to outline in the informed consent document the types of information that will be cause for notifying the parent or guardian. In most cases, parents or guardians need to be informed if their child or adolescent is suicidal or homicidal and poses a safety risk (i.e., cannot commit to following a safety plan and has an active plan for harming self or others). Incidents of abuse or neglect are also cause for informing parents or guardians in addition to legal authorities such as child protective services. In many other situations, deciding whether to inform the parent or guardian is less clear. Counselors will disagree about whether they would inform parents about the issues below. Pause and reflect on whether you would inform parents or guardians about the following issues depending on the situation. See Reflection Question 1.2 list.

Even if you feel that you would not inform parents about these issues, we recommend including this language in your informed consent as examples of possibilities when you might inform parents or guardians. The child or adolescent should be aware of the parameters of privacy, even if you choose not to divulge information pertinent to any of these issues later in the counseling process.

By now, you may have noticed that we use the term *intake process* instead of *intake session*. We have found that it can take anywhere from two to four sessions to truly understand the full nature of the

Reflection Question 1.2

Consider whether you would notify parents or guardians about the following issues.

- Pregnancy
- High-risk behavior that poses a health risk to self or others, such as drunk driving
- Use of addictive illegal drugs, such as heroin
- Truancy
- Minor illegal behavior, such as petty theft
- Major illegal behavior, such as arson or armed robbery

problem that has brought the child or adolescent into our counseling office. Conducting a full assessment during the intake process can help to determine whether individual counseling or family counseling will eventually be indicated. Do not assume from the initial prescreening phone call that you will know which course of treatment is indicated. Because it can take two to four sessions to fully assess the dynamics in a child and adolescent case, Thom requires at least one parent or guardian to attend the first two to four sessions. Because some parents and guardians are accustomed to dropping off their children for various after-school activities, some may balk at this requirement. If the parent or guardian claims they cannot attend sessions, this is significant information. Usually parents or guardians are willing to make the time commitment if you explain the rationale clearly (i.e., you need to understand the complete picture). In previous marketing materials, Thom has clearly indicated this requirement: "Dr. Field requires parents/guardians to attend the first 2–4 sessions of counseling with child or adolescent clients, so an assessment can be made about whether individual or family therapy is indicated." Not every reader of this text will implement such a strategy. But in Thom's experience, parent/guardian attendance has been invaluable to conducting a full and thorough assessment.

Handling Termination

The typical length of child and adolescent counseling varies greatly by developmental age, setting, presenting issue, and so forth. It is fairly common for children to be referred for counseling toward the beginning of an academic term (i.e., August/September and January) and for counseling to either conclude or take a hiatus during the summer months. The academic environment is a primary stressor for many children, which explains this seasonal variation.

Termination can be a difficult process for many clients. Ending counseling can engender feelings of loss and betrayal. We have seen children refuse to attend their final session out of anger or fear of losing a therapeutic relationship that has been so meaningful to them and literally cling to our leg so they do not have to say goodbye and walk out the door at the end of the final session. The counselor should give the child advance notice of termination and fully process the reasons for concluding counseling. Often the decision to conclude counseling is made between the parent or guardian and the counselor. Children will not necessarily understand the concept of needing to terminate when counseling goals have been reached and will need an explanation that is developmentally appropriate. This explanation should be positive and should highlight achievements that reinforce the child or adolescent's confidence in their abilities, known as *self-efficacy*. For example, "I want to congratulate you! Your mom and I have seen wonderful improvements in [X] areas, and we think it is time for us to take a break from meeting together. You have worked very hard to make those changes."

Young children especially may have relatively little understanding of why counseling is ending. Without adequate information, children are at risk for filling this vacuum with inaccurate beliefs in an attempt to make sense of their situation. We have seen children blame themselves for not being good enough clients. We have also seen children (mistakenly) blame their parents for initiating termination. An explanation to the child or adolescent thus not only can be empowering but also can protect against misinterpretation.

Posttermination relationships with children and adolescents can be quite different from those with adults. We have found that it is common for child clients to need booster sessions after termination. Parents or guardians may also contact you several years later to start another round of counseling and expect you to fit the child into your schedule. In school settings, counselors may meet with children and adolescents at different grade levels. Although you should eventually close the case file after terminating with a child or adolescent client, we recommend keeping those files until the child or adolescent reaches adulthood rather than the standard amount of time for record retention.

There are a variety of reasons why termination might occur prematurely. A child, adolescent, or parent or guardian may not be ready to implement the changes necessary for counseling to be successful. For example, we once worked with a 10-year-old girl who was clearly making no progress toward mastering her obsessive-compulsive tendencies in between sessions. During the eighth session, the mother and daughter acknowledged that they were not ready to follow through on exposure interventions that would reduce the obsessive thoughts and compulsive behaviors and mutually agreed to stop counseling. This termination was a positive outcome. The client should have the autonomy to decide whether they are ready to fully enter into the counseling process. Not every client is ready, and that is okay.

Early terminations can be parent initiated. The parent may feel that the child or adolescent is not improving or that early gains have not been sustained (often this is a marker of a honeymoon phase in treatment). Some parents have good intentions of bringing their children to counseling but struggle to make appointments because of logistical challenges. Life events also cause early termination, such as when a family moves to another geographic location and the child wants to meet in person with a counselor rather than via distance counseling.

The best strategy for avoiding premature termination is to work intentionally to make all parties (child or adolescent, parents or guardians) feel respected, heard, and understood. If a strong alliance and relationship exists by the end of the first session, the risk of premature termination decreases significantly (Yoo, Bartle-Haring, & Gangamma, 2016).

Conclusion

Child and adolescent counseling requires openness, flexibility, candor, and genuineness. Effective working relationships with children are formed when the counselor demonstrates respect and appreciation for the thoughts and feelings of children beyond diagnostic labels. Counselors demonstrate genuine interest and respect through listening attentively to the underlying meanings and messages of the stories and narratives of children and adolescents.

Counselors need to address areas of professional growth to become effective child and adolescent counselors. We recommend that counselors ask themselves tough questions about their own childhoods, their attitudes toward childhood as adults, and areas of countertransference that might show up when counseling children and families. We hope that you, as a counselor, will address the areas in which you need to grow. Your work will be better off for it.

Quiz Questions

1. Parents or guardians should consider attending the first few sessions so that
   a. The child can be observed acting out
   b. The parent can be observed acting out
   c. A determination can be made about individual or family therapy
2. In Stephens et al.'s (2010) speaker-listener neural coupling study, the listener's brain activation
   a. Mirrored that of the speaker
   b. Reduced as the speaker talked
   c. Increased as the speaker was silent
3. *Verbal content* refers to spoken information, whereas *interpersonal process* refers to
   a. Transference and countertransference between counselor and client
   b. Subtle and hidden meanings and messages that are communicated
   c. Obvious and overt needs and wants of the client

References

American Counseling Association. (2014). *ACA code of ethics.* Retrieved from https://www.counseling.org/resources/aca-code-of-ethics.pdf

American Psychiatric Association. (2013). *Diagnostic and statistical manual of mental disorders* (5th ed.). Arlington, VA: Author.

Arain, M., Haque, M., Johal, L., Mathur, P., Nel, W., Rais, A., . . . Sharma, S. (2013). Maturation of the adolescent brain. *Neuropsychiatric Disease and Treatment, 9,* 449–461. doi:10.2147/NDT.S39776

Babson, K. A., Trainor, C. D., Feldner, M. T., & Blumenthal, H. (2010). A test of the effects of acute sleep deprivation on general and specific self-reported anxiety and depressive symptoms: An experimental extension. *Journal of Behavior Therapy and Experimental Psychiatry, 41,* 297–303. doi:10.1016/j.jbtep.2010.02.008

Bernstein, E. E., & McNally, R. J. (2017). Acute aerobic exercise helps overcome emotion regulation deficits. *Cognition & Emotion, 31,* 834–843. doi:10.1080/02699931.2016.1168284

Betts, L., Spenser, R., & Gardner, K. (2017). Adolescents' involvement in cyber bullying and perceptions of school: The importance of perceived peer acceptance for female adolescents. *Sex Roles, 77,* 471–481. doi:10.1007/s11199-017-0742-2

Casey, B. J., Jones, R. M., & Hare, T. A. (2008). The adolescent brain. *Annals of the New York Academy of Sciences, 1124,* 111–126. doi:10.1196/annals.1440.010

Council for Accreditation of Counseling and Related Educational Programs. (2015). *2016 CACREP standards.* Alexandria, VA: Author.

Deblinger, E., Mannarino, A., Cohen, J., Runyon, M., & Steer, R. (2011). Trauma-focused cognitive behavioral therapy for children: Impact of the trauma narrative and treatment length. *Depression and Anxiety, 28,* 67–75. doi:10.1002/da.20744

Edgette, J. S. (2002). *Candor, connection, and enterprise in adolescent therapy.* New York, NY: Norton.

Field, T. A., Beeson, E. T., Luke, C., Ghoston, M., & Golubovic, N. (2019). Neuroscience conceptualizations of depression by counselors. *Journal of Mental Health Counseling, 41,* 260–279. doi:10.17744/mehc.41.3.05

Goel, N., Rao, H., Durmer, J. S., & Dinges, D. F. (2009). Neurocognitive consequences of sleep deprivation. *Seminars in Neurology, 29,* 320–339. doi:10.1055/s-0029-1237117

Guendelman, S., Medeiros, S., & Rampes, H. (2017). Mindfulness and emotion regulation: Insights from neurobiological, psychological, and clinical studies. *Frontiers in Psychology, 8,* 1–23. doi:10.3389/fpsyg.2017.00220

Hansen, J. T. (2016). *Meaning systems and mental health culture: Critical perspectives on contemporary counseling and psychotherapy.* Lanham, MD: Lexington Books.

Jones, L. M., Mitchell, K. J., & Finkelhor, D. (2011). Trends in youth internet victimization: Findings from three youth internet safety surveys 2000–2010. *Journal of Adolescent Health, 50,* 179–186. doi:10.1016/j.jadohealth.2011.09.015

Linehan, M. M., Goodstein, J. L., Nielsen, S. L., & Chiles, J. A. (1983). Reasons for staying alive when you are thinking of killing yourself: The Reasons for Living Inventory. *Journal of Consulting and Clinical Psychology, 51,* 276–286. doi:10.1037/0022-006X.51.2.276

National Institute of Mental Health. (n.d.). *Research Domain Criteria (RDoC).* Retrieved from https://www.nimh.nih.gov/research-priorities/rdoc/index.shtml

National Institute of Mental Health. (2016). *NIMH strategic plan for research.* Bethesda, MD: Author. Retrieved from https://www.nimh.nih.gov/about/strategic-planning-reports/index.shtml

Osman, A., Downs, W. R., Kopper, B. A., Barrios, F. X., Baker, M. T., Osman, J. R., . . . Linehan, M. M. (1998). The Reasons for Living Inventory for Adolescents (RFL-A): Development and psychometric properties. *Journal of Clinical Psychology, 54,* 1063–1078. doi:10.1002/(SICI)1097-4679(199812)54:8<1063::AID-JCLP6>3.0.c0;2-Z

Schneider, F., Zwillich, B., Bindl, M., Hopp, F., Reich, S., & Vorderer, P. (2017). Social media ostracism: The effects of being excluded online. *Computers in Human Behavior, 73,* 385–393. doi:10.1016/j.chb.2017.03.052 0747-5632

Shneidman, E. S. (1998). *The suicidal mind.* New York, NY: Oxford University Press.

Sommers-Flanagan, J., & Sommers-Flanagan, R. (2007). *Tough kids, cool counseling: User-friendly approaches with challenging youth* (2nd ed.). Alexandria, VA: American Counseling Association.

Spencer, S. J., Korosi, A., Layé, S., Shukitt-Hale, B., & Barrientos, R. M. (2017). Food for thought: How nutrition impacts cognition and emotion. *NPJ Science of Food, 1,* 1–8. doi:10.1038/s41538-017-0008-y

Stephens, G. J., Silbert, L. J., & Hasson, U. (2010). Speaker-listener neural coupling underlies successful communication. *Proceedings of the National Academy of Sciences, USA, 107,* 14425–14430. doi:10.1073/pnas.1008662107

Wampold, B., & Imel, Z. E. (2015). *The great psychotherapy debate: The evidence for what makes psychotherapy work* (2nd ed.). New York, NY: Routledge.

Yalom, I. D. (2017). *The gift of therapy: An open letter to a new generation of therapists and their patients.* New York, NY: Harper Perennial.

Yoo, H., Bartle-Haring, S., & Gangamma, R. (2016). Predicting premature termination with alliance at sessions 1 and 3: An exploratory study. *Journal of Family Therapy, 38,* 5–17. doi:10.1111/1467-6427.12031

Chapter 2

Structure and Function of the Nervous System

Key Concepts

- Central nervous system
- Neurons: soma, nucleus, dendrites, receptors, axon, axon terminal buttons
- Glia
- Synaptic cleft
- Excitatory and inhibitory neurotransmitters
- Neurotransmission process
- Monoamine and amino acid neurotransmitters
- Brain stem
- Cerebellum
- Cerebrum
- Frontal, occipital, parietal, and temporal lobes
- Subcortical and cortical structures
- Peripheral nervous system
- Autonomic nervous system
- Sympathetic and parasympathetic branches of the autonomic nervous system
- Homeostasis
- Enteric nervous system
- Gut microbiota

- Inflammation
- Cytokines
- Endocrine system

Aligned 2016 CACREP Standards

Standard 2.F.3.e. Biological, neurological, and physiological factors that affect human development, functioning, and behavior

• • •

Neuroscience is fundamental to our understanding of child and adolescent development. In this chapter, we review fundamental information about the structure and function of the nervous system to prepare you for subsequent information about childhood development and problems or disorders that occur during the developmental process. This chapter has strong connections to the next chapter, on genetics, epigenetics, and neuroplasticity. Several concepts mentioned in this chapter are further explored in Chapter 3, such as the role of the stress response system in a child's overall functioning. This chapter was informed by several sources, including *Neuroscience: Exploring the Brain* (4th ed.) by Bear, Connors, and Paradiso (2015); *From Neuron to Brain* (5th ed.) by Nicholls and colleagues (2011); *Neuroscience* (5th ed.) by Purves and colleagues (2011); and *Principles of Neural Science* (5th ed.) by Kandel, Schwartz, Jessell, Siegelbaum, and Hudspeth (2012). We encourage you to explore these textbooks if you would like more grounding in the basic anatomy and physiology of the nervous system.

The terminology used in this chapter might be challenging to you. In writing the chapter, we attempted to fully describe each scientific term that we used, knowing that the experience can feel like learning a new language! To help you digest this information, we recommend consulting the glossary at the end of this text to clarify unfamiliar terms.

Before we begin, we want to emphasize an important principle in understanding the function of the brain and body. The systems of the brain and body are intricately connected and often work synchronously with each other. Although we often study isolated brain regions, the reality is that all sections of the brain and body work in an interconnected rather than an isolated manner (Field, 2019; Jasanoff, 2018). This is crucial to emphasize, because we tend to divide and separate the functioning of the brain and body, which limits our exploration of the linkages between mental and physical health (Field, 2019; Jasanoff, 2018). Throughout this text, we emphasize the interconnected nature of the brain and body.

We now explore the systems of the brain and body, giving special attention to the central nervous system (CNS) and peripheral nervous system (PNS). We also briefly examine the endocrine system. The divisions and branches of the CNS and PNS are depicted in Figure 2.1.

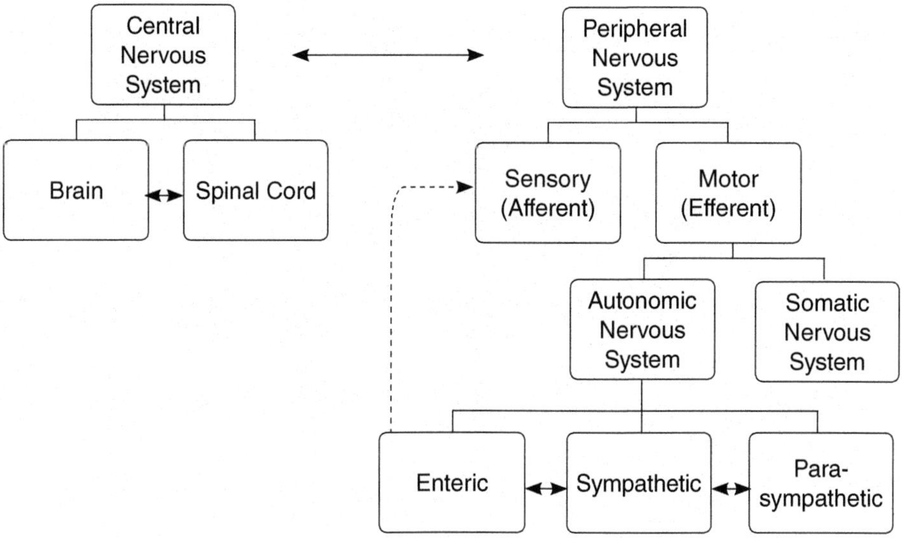

FIGURE 2.1

Nervous System

CNS

The CNS comprises the brain and the spinal cord (Bear et al., 2015). The brain processes incoming sensory information and sends signals down the spinal cord to communicate with the rest of the body. The spinal cord also transmits information to the brain from the body. This system is called the *central* nervous system because of the brain and spinal cord's ability to influence and coordinate the rest of the body (Bear et al., 2015). The CNS is composed of several cells, most notably nerve cells called *neurons* and glial cells. The purpose of neurons is to receive and transmit electrical messages (Nicholls et al., 2011). The neurons in the brain are largely pyramidal neurons, whereas the neurons in the PNS are largely sensory and motor neurons (more about this later).

The purpose of glial cells is to support the functioning of a neuron by transporting nutrients to neurons, holding neurons in place, and cleaning up debris and waste from areas of injury and cell death—in particular during sleep (Nicholls et al., 2011). There are multiple types of glia, such as astrocytes, oligodendrocytes, and microglia. Microglia have important roles in inflammatory responses. Figure 2.2 provides a basic diagram of neurons and glia.

Neurons have several different structures that are essential to their functioning. Each of these structures is displayed in Figure 2.3. A neuron's functioning is directed by the cell body (also called *soma*), which contains the cell's nucleus. As we explore in Chapter 3, the

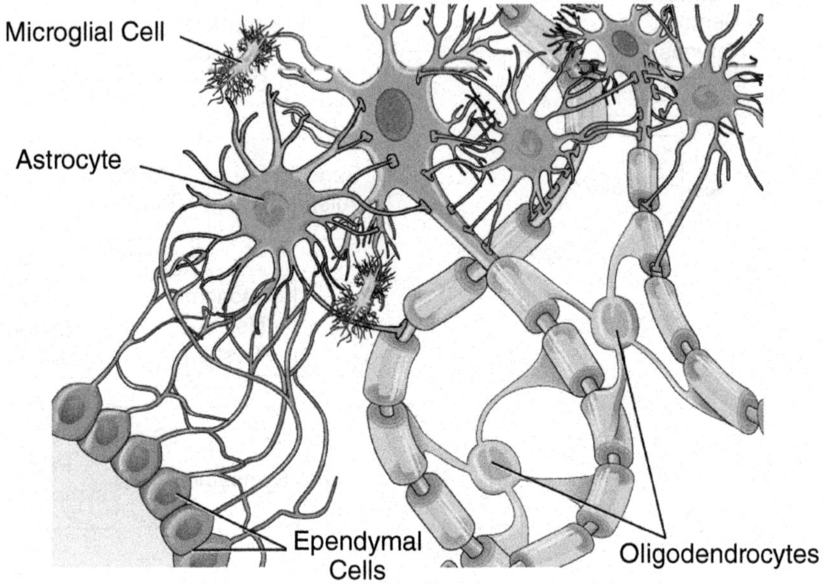

FIGURE 2.2

Glial Cells of the Central Nervous System

Note. From Openstax, 2016. In Wikimedia Commons, used under Creative Commons Attribution 4.0 International License.

nucleus produces and stores DNA and enzymes that are crucial to the cell's function. Each neuron also contains structures for receiving information (dendrite receptors) and sending information (axon terminal buttons) via chemical signaling. Each part of the cell has an important role in the communication of information from one neuron to another, known as *neurotransmission.*

The neurotransmission process begins when two neurons are in close proximity. An electrical signaling occurs when a neuron comes into close proximity to another neuron. The first neuron moves neurotransmitters from repositories known as *vesicles* to the axon terminal buttons, where they are released into the synaptic cleft between the two neurons (Bear et al., 2015). Many of these neurotransmitters are received by the next neuron through dendrite receptors. Some of the neurotransmitters are reabsorbed back into the original axon through a process known as *reuptake.* The rest of the released neurotransmitters remain in the synaptic cleft, where they are broken down by enzymes. When neurotransmitters bind to the receptors of the next neuron, it opens the neuron's ion channels. If enough ions enter a cell, it creates a polarized electrical charge known as an *action potential.* If enough of a charge is created, the neuron will fire an electrical impulse from the dendrites to the neuron's axon terminal buttons via the axon. The axon plays a critical role in conducting the

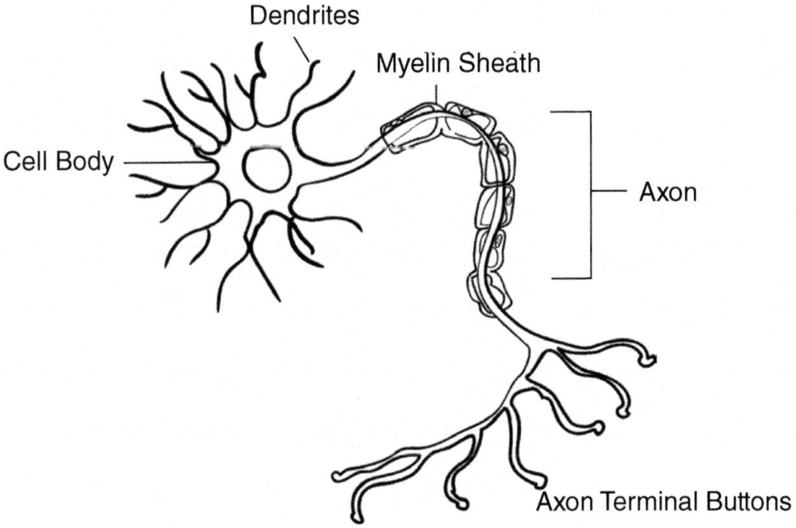

FIGURE 2.3

The Nerve Cell

Note. From National Institute on Drug Abuse, 2005. In Wikimedia Commons.

electrical current and carrying it to the axon terminal buttons. When conduction occurs, this neuron then signals to another nearby neuron and releases neurotransmitters from its own axon terminal buttons into the next synaptic cleft. This process continues, sending messages from neuron to neuron throughout the nervous system. The collective series of synaptic connections are known as *neural pathways.* A visual diagram of this process is provided in Figure 2.4. Note that even at the cellular level (i.e., that of neurons), the structure and function of the CNS only makes sense when we examined interconnected relationships (i.e., neurons to neurons). In other words, the function of a neuron can only be fully understood by examining its relationship to other neurons (Nicholls et al., 2011).

The CNS is composed of gray matter and white matter (Kandel et al., 2012). Both gray matter and white matter consist of neurons and glia. The major difference between gray matter and white matter is that gray matter consists largely of neurons that have unmyelinated axons, whereas white matter consists largely of neurons with myelinated axons (Kandel et al., 2012). Myelination is a process whereby a plasma membrane extension, known as a *myelin sheath,* is wrapped around the axon to form a tight membrane and insulate the cell (Nicholls et al., 2011). This fatty sheath of myelin allows for improved electrical conduction and transportation throughout the cell. For example, an unmyelinated axon needs a diameter approximately 500 times the size of a myelinated axon to conduct electricity at the same speed

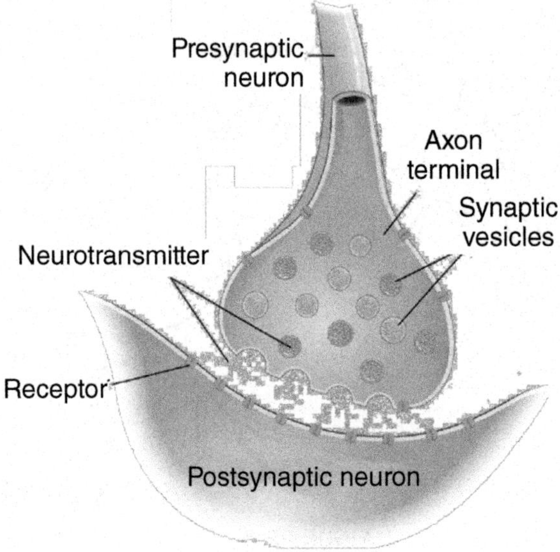

FIGURE 2.4

Neurotransmission

Note. Image modified from "The synapse," by OpenStax College, Anatomy and Physiology. Used under Creative Commons Attribution 3.0 Unported License.

and requires 5,000 times more energy (Snaidero & Simons, 2014). The color differs because the fatty myelin sheath is white, whereas the unmyelinated cell bodies of neurons are light gray with pinkish tints from blood vessel capillaries. Disruption or deterioration of myelin leaves the axon exposed to damage. Thus, disruption in myelination can result in a host of maladies, such as a disturbance of gene transcription in the cell nucleus (see Chapter 3 for more information about gene transcription). Problems with myelination are also associated with multiple sclerosis (Duncan & Radcliff, 2016).

Neurotransmitters

Multiple types of neurotransmitters are released from a neuron's axon terminal buttons. Some commonly known neurotransmitters are the monoamines, also known as *catecholamines* (e.g., dopamine, norepinephrine, serotonin). Amino acids, such as glutamate and gamma-aminobutyric acid (GABA), are another form of neurotransmitter. Neurotransmitters can have excitatory and inhibitory effects. An excitatory effect increases the likelihood that postsynaptic neurons will experience an action potential, whereas an inhibitory effect reduces the likelihood (Nicholls et al., 2011). The major excitatory neurotransmitter in the CNS is glutamate. Glutamate helps to balance out the major inhibitory neurotransmitter, GABA (Shabel, Proulx, Piriz, & Malinow, 2014).

Each neuron has thousands of receptors per cell and many receptor types (Nicholls et al., 2011). Because neurotransmitters can bind to multiple types of receptors, they can have different effects based on the receptor type. Ligand-activated ionotropic receptors change in shape when a neurotransmitter binds, resulting in the opening of calcium ion channels. When ion channels open, a positive or negative charge is created in the cell, depending on the type of ion (positive or negative) that enters the cell. Metabotropic receptors do not directly open ion channels. Instead, these receptors trigger another signaling pathway that may indirectly open or close an ion channel. As you can see, the process of neurotransmission is quite complex and not always predictable. A list of neurotransmitters and their effect on receptors is included in Table 2.1.

Each neurotransmitter has multiple functions. Dopamine is associated with motivation and reward prediction alongside voluntary movement of muscles (Kandel et al., 2012). Norepinephrine is related to dopamine and is associated with attention and arousal (Kandel et al., 2012). It has important roles in activating the PNS following the detection of threat, resulting in increased heart rate, among other physiological responses. Norepinephrine is also related to other important neurotransmitters and hormones, such as epinephrine and adrenaline. Serotonin has important roles in the sleep cycle, appetite and temperature regulation, as well as mood (Kandel et al., 2012). Melatonin is related to serotonin and has important roles in preparing the body for sleep. Melatonin secretion is influenced by exposure of the eyes to light and has an established role in circadian rhythm (Bear et al., 2015). Humans are diurnal creatures, and darkness prompts our bodies to prepare for sleep. Glutamate is the most common neurotransmitter and is associated with synaptogenesis (the growth of new synapses; Kandel et al., 2012). GABA is a metabolite of glutamate and has a role in sleep and in moderating anxiety (Kandel et al., 2012).

Brain Structures

Now that we have learned how messages are communicated throughout the CNS, we explore the different and interconnected regions

TABLE 2.1

Neurotransmitter Functioning

Neurotransmitter	Type	Activates Ionotropic Receptors	Activates Metabotropic Receptors
Dopamine (DA)	Monoamine/Catecholamine	Yes (excitatory)	Yes
Gamma-aminobutyric		No	Yes
acid (GABA)	Amino acid	Yes (inhibitory)	Yes
Glutamate (Glu)	Amino acid	Yes (excitatory)	Yes
Norepinephrine (NE)	Monoamine/Catecholamine	No	Yes
Serotonin (5-HT)	Monoamine/Catecholamine	Yes (inhibitory)	Yes

and structures of the brain. We describe these from the framework of which brain regions developed first evolutionarily. Although we describe functions of these regions and structures, it is important to emphasize that each works in a connected and synchronous fashion with other regions and structures.

The brain is a large, sponge-like mass that has three central parts: the brain stem, the cerebellum, and the cerebrum (Bear et al., 2015). The cerebrum fills most of the skull, though it is largely believed to be the last of the three brain areas to have developed fully (Hofman, 2014). Figure 2.5 depicts the different brain structures that we explore in each of these three areas.

Brain Stem and Spinal Cord

The brain stem is located at the bottom of the brain and connects the brain to the spinal cord (Bear et al., 2015). It also connects parts of the cortex to the PNS. It is composed of structures that include the medulla oblongata, midbrain, and pons. The brain stem is associated with basic survival functions. The medulla oblongata is involved in cardiac functioning (e.g., blood pressure, heart rate) and respiratory functioning (e.g., breathing). The midbrain regulates body temperature alongside sleep and wake cycles and motor movement. It also has an important role in hearing and vision. The pons relays sensory signals to the thalamus and has a role in balance, bladder control, body posture, eye movement, and facial expressions and sensations. Damage to areas of the brain stem can result in difficulties with motor coordination, dizziness, disturbances in hearing and vision, and problems with speech production (Bear et al., 2015).

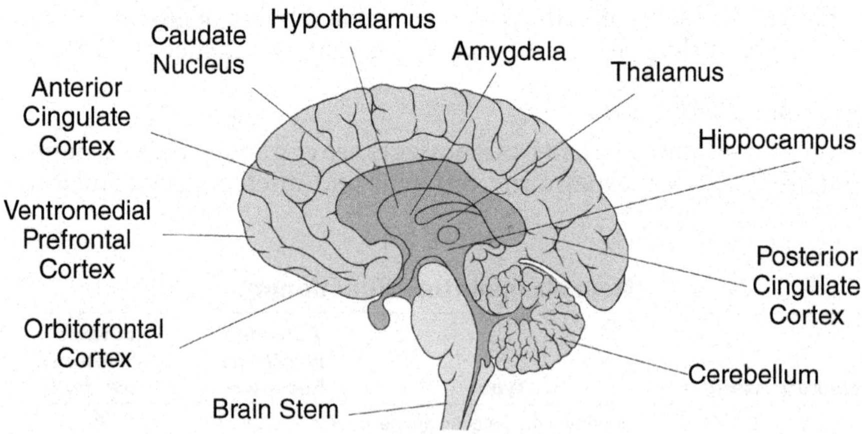

FIGURE 2.5

Brain Structures

Note. From Patrick J. Lynch, medical illustrator and C. Carl Jaffe, MD, cardiologist. Used under Creative Commons Attribution 2.5 License, 2006.

Two sets of nerves connect the brain and body. Cranial nerves begin at the brain, whereas spinal nerves emerge from segments of the spinal cord (Bear et al., 2015). There are 12 cranial nerves (CN I to CN XII), such as the olfactory nerve (CN I), which is associated with smell; the optic nerve (CN II), which is associated with vision; and the vagus nerve (CN X), which is associated with parasympathetic activation (more about this later).

The spinal cord is made of nerve fibers that run down the center of the spine. The bones of the spine (i.e., vertebrae) protect the spinal cord. Spinal nerves have an important role in sending messages throughout the body. Cerebrospinal fluid provides nutrients to the brain and spinal cord and removes waste and debris. Upper motor neurons reside within the spinal cord to send messages up and down the cord, whereas lower motor neurons are found in spinal nerves that branch out from the spinal cord. Damage to the spinal cord can result in loss of communication between the brain and body, resulting in serious sensory and mobility issues such as loss of sensation, numbness, and paralysis (Bear et al., 2015).

Cerebellum

The *cerebellum,* Latin for "little cerebrum," is a fascinating structure that is located close to the brain stem and below the cerebrum. The cerebellum contains more than half of the total neurons in the brain, despite its relatively small size (only 10% of brain volume; Klein, Ulmer, Quinet, Mathews, & Mark, 2016). The cerebellum plays important roles in motor movement and coordination by receiving motor commands and making movements more accurate and adaptive to the situation. For example, the cerebellum has an important role in motor learning through trial and error, such as learning to balance on a bike or calibrating a baseball swing to hit the ball. It also has roles in cognition and emotion, such as attention, executive functioning (or planned behavior), working memory, and pain (Strick, Dum, & Fiez, 2009).

Cerebrum

The cerebrum consists of several important regions, such as the subcortex, limbic region, and cerebral cortex (Bear et al., 2015). The various regions and structures of the cerebrum work in concert to send messages both within the cerebrum and to different areas of the brain and nervous system.

The subcortex is located dorsal to (i.e., above) the cerebellum and brain stem though still ventral to (i.e., below) the surface of the cerebral cortex (Bear et al., 2015). The limbic region of the subcortex contains several important structures for processing sensory information. The thalamus is known as the central relay center of the cerebrum and sends messages to various parts of the subcortex and cortex. The hippocampus has an important role in memory formation and consolidation and is involved in the processing of new memories, the storage of long-term memories, and memory retrieval. Memory is essential to social functioning in terms of being able to remember relational histories with people, remembering their preferences, remembering whether information has already been shared with certain people, and even making predictions based on prior knowledge (e.g., What activity might my friend want to play with me? Rubin, Watson, Duff, & Cohen, 2014). Recent studies have also found that the hippocampus has an important role in mediating sensory processing throughout the brain (Chan et al., 2017).

The amygdala is a complex structure composed of several parts (or nuclei) and is known for its role in processing emotions (Bear et al., 2015). The amygdala has an important function in threat detection and fear processing alongside the hippocampus, hypothalamus, and prefrontal cortex. When threats are detected in the environment, the amygdala communicates with the hypothalamus to send messages to the pituitary gland, the master hormone gland of the brain (Bear et al., 2015). The pituitary gland then sends messages to the adrenal glands, comprising the adrenal cortex and medulla, located above the kidneys (Bear et al., 2015). The adrenal glands release stress hormones such as adrenaline and cortisol. The hypothalamic-pituitary-adrenal (HPA) axis therefore includes structures of the subcortex and parts of the endocrine system. The endocrine system is composed of glands that release hormones (e.g., the pituitary gland).

The subcortex contains other structures that are located between the cortex and the limbic region, such as the basal ganglia, cingulate cortex, and insula. The basal ganglia is located near the limbic region and contains several structures, such as the caudate nucleus, putamen, globus pallidus, and striatum. These structures are associated with smooth motor movement and planning. The striatum and its structures (e.g., the nucleus accumbens) is associated with motivation, aversion, and conditioned learning and has an important role in addiction processes (Bear et al., 2015).

The insula is also located close to the limbic region and has a variety of functions, including emotional and sensory processing and higher order cognition, such as empathy (Uddin, Nomi, Hébert-Seropian, Ghaziri, & Boucher, 2017). It is activated when children become aware of internal bodily sensations (known as *interoception*) and the emotional experiences of self and others. For these reasons, it has been dubbed the visceral part of the brain (Stephani, Fernandez-Baca Vaca, Maciunas, Koubeissi, & Lüders, 2011). It has connections to the anterior cingulate cortex and ventromedial prefrontal cortex.

The anterior (frontal) and posterior (rear) cingulate cortexes work together and have somewhat different functions. The anterior cingulate cortex is involved in emotional processing and regulation, with linkages to both the limbic regions and prefrontal cortex. The anterior cingulate cortex is implicated in conditioned learning, especially related to emotions, such as when a child experiences pain on touching a sharp or hot object (Stevens, Hurley, & Taber, 2011). Over- or underregulation of affect is problematic. For example, overregulation of affect can result in less conditioned learning in response to emotional experiences (Stevens et al., 2011). The posterior cingulate cortex (PCC) is believed to be crucial to information processing, with linkages to the ventromedial area of the prefrontal cortex (Leech & Sharp, 2014). It has a key role in the default mode network (DMN), which we review later in this chapter. The PCC becomes activated when retrieving autobiographical memories. It is also associated with regulating attention. The PCC is therefore active when a child is reflecting and processing their experiences. Abnormal functioning of the PCC has been connected to cognitive impairment.

Cortex

The cortex is the outer layer of tissue that covers most of the brain. It covers the subcortex and is dorsal to the brain stem and cerebellum. There are thought to be four lobes of the cerebral cortex: the frontal lobe, the temporal lobe, the occipital lobe, and the parietal lobe (Bear et al., 2015). Before we describe the lobes of the cerebrum, it can be helpful to review basic terminology pertaining to location. *Dorsal* means "above," whereas *ventral* means "below." *Anterior* means "toward the front," whereas *posterior* means "toward the back." These terms are displayed around the periphery of the diagram in Figure 2.6.

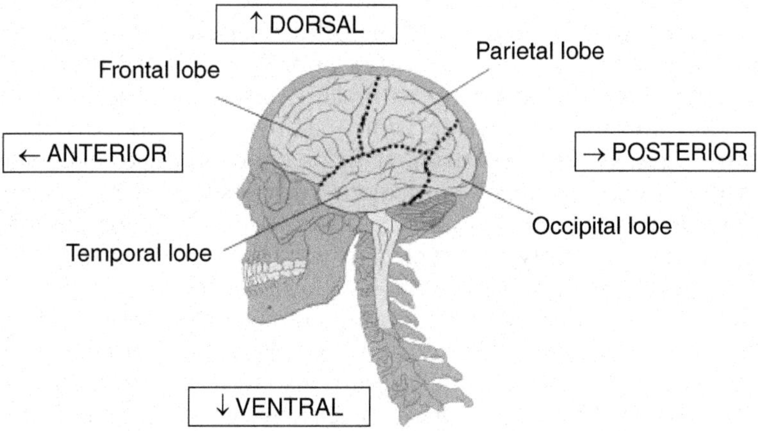

FIGURE 2.6

Lobes of the Cerebrum

Note. From Patrick J. Lynch, medical illustrator and C. Carl Jaffe, MD, cardiologist. Used under Creative Commons Attribution 2.5 License, 2006.

The frontal lobe has several regions, such as the primary motor cortex, the premotor cortex, the prefrontal cortex, and the orbitofrontal cortex. The primary motor cortex and premotor cortex send messages to the brain stem and spinal cord to direct voluntary movements. They receive information from the somatosensory area and thalamus regarding movement positioning, timing, and coordination.

The functions of the prefrontal cortex are often described by their location to the skull (Bear et al., 2015). The medial prefrontal cortex is located toward the midline of the forehead. The dorsal area of the medial prefrontal cortex is associated with self-referential thought (Raichle, 2015). We often understand information in our environment through our own frame of reference. For example, when asked to identify tasks that their parents or friends enjoy, young children often respond by identifying activities that they themselves personally enjoy (which may not be the preference of their parent or friend). As children mature, they are better able to understand the perspectives of others, known as *mentalization* or *theory of mind*. The ventral area of the medial prefrontal cortex (vmPFC) is located just above the orbitofrontal cortex and is associated with emotional regulation. It has an especially strong connection to the amygdala and has an important role in the regulation of anxiety and fear responses (Motzkin, Philippi, Wolf, Baskaya, & Koenigs, 2015). For example, if a child is frightened by a loud sound in the environment, the vmPFC will be activated during their cognitive processing of the potential threat (e.g., "It was just a door slamming shut, no need to worry"). The vmPFC is also a key structure in the DMN (more on this later) and is believed to be one of the main regions damaged in the famous case of Phineas Gage (Raichle, 2015).

The lateral prefrontal cortex comprises the largest portion of the frontal lobe and is located above the orbitofrontal cortex. The dorsal area of the lateral prefrontal cortex appraises sensory information (e.g., from the eyes and ears) to make decisions and is thought to be responsible for rational decision making and planned behavior, known as *executive functioning*. It helps children make decisions in unscripted, unpredictable, and open-ended situations (Collins & Koechlin, 2012). It receives and sends information throughout the brain and has especially strong circuits with the thalamus and caudate nucleus of the basal ganglia.

The orbitofrontal cortex has connections to the limbic and olfactory systems and alongside the vmPFC plays an important role in emotional processing and regulation. It also functions to discriminate between smells. The orbitofrontal cortex helps children to inhibit their impulses to adhere to social norms and conventions. For example, the orbitofrontal cortex is activated when a child controls their impulses to inappropriately snatch a desired object from another person.

Broca's area, which is associated with both speech production (i.e., spoken words) and language comprehension (Rodd, Davis, & Johnsrude,

2005), is also located in the frontal lobe. When children communicate verbally to their parents or counselor, Broca's area is likely active. Underactivity in Broca's area can result in problems such as stuttering and aphasia (i.e., knowing what to say but being unable to form the words).

The other three lobes of the brain are the occipital, parietal, and temporal lobes. The occipital lobe is located posterior to the skull (i.e., at the back of the head) and contains the primary visual cortex. It processes visual stimuli and sensory information. It can be implicated in seizures that are triggered by flicker stimulations of flashing colors or lights. The parietal lobe is located behind the frontal lobe, in front of the occipital lobe, and above the temporal lobe. It contains the somatosensory cortex and is implicated in awareness of oneself in space and navigation (proprioception). It is also the main area of the brain that receives input from the skin, such as touch sensors. The temporal lobe is located beneath the parietal lobe. It houses structures (e.g., the hippocampus) that play an important role in the consolidation, storage, and retrieval of long-term memories, known as *declarative memory*. Wernicke's area, which alongside Broca's area is associated with language comprehension, is located in the temporal lobe. The temporal lobe is also associated with visual object recognition.

DMN

Earlier we briefly mentioned the DMN. After learning about the cortex and subcortex, it is worth revisiting the different structures involved in a child's ability to engage in defocused and wandering thought. The DMN is active when a person is in a resting state and not actively engaged in attention-demanding tasks (Raichle, 2015). The brain structures involved in the DMN are the ventromedial prefrontal cortex, the dorsal medial prefrontal cortex, and the PCC. You may remember that the vmPFC is involved in emotional processing, the dorsal area of the medial prefrontal cortex is involved in self-referential thought, and the PCC is involved in autobiographical memories and regulating attention. When connected during DMN activity, these structures help people to process their experiences and emotions, make sense of them, and relate them to their sense of self. Such activity helps children to learn from their experiences. Reduced DMN activity has been associated with depression, juvenile conduct problems and impulsivity, and schizophrenia (Raichle, 2015).

PNS

Like the CNS, the PNS is composed of neurons. These neurons are often bunched together into fibers, and multiple fibers form a nerve. Each nerve also contains tissue and blood vessels. The nerves of the PNS connect the CNS (brain and spinal cord) with the body's various glands, limbs, muscles, organs, and skin (Nicholls et al., 2011).

PNS nerves are classified as afferent and efferent (Nicholls et al., 2011). Afferent nerves carry messages *from* muscles, glands, and the senses, whereas efferent nerves carry messages *to* muscles, glands, and the senses (e.g., touch sensors, eyes). These nerves often transmit information that is not known to us consciously but is crucial to our body's overall functioning. For example, afferent nerves transfer information about the current inner state of the body's organs, such as the organ's current energy intake, need for blood supply and oxygen, and so on.

The neurons involved in these functions differ from the neurons of the CNS. Motor neurons and sensory neurons have a different structure than CNS neurons. As their name suggests, motor neurons are associated with muscles and muscle movement, whereas sensory neurons are associated with the body's sensory systems (e.g., touch, sight, smell).

For example, if the hand touches a painfully hot object, sensory neurons in PNS send rapid messages to the brain in the CNS. The brain then sends messages from CNS neurons to PNS motor neurons. The transfer of information from CNS neurons to motor neurons occurs in the spinal cord. The motor neurons are instructed to move the hand away from the hot object. The motor neurons then transmit information across the neuromuscular junction, where PNS nerves connect to muscles, and the hand moves. This example demonstrates how the CNS and PNS often function in concert to carry out important functions.

The PNS is organized into three primary divisions: the sensory, autonomic, and enteric systems. The sensory nervous system contains afferent nerves composed of sensory neurons that transfer information from our five senses to the CNS. It also contains efferent nerves made of motor neurons that carry information from the CNS to the muscles to initiate voluntary movement required for activities such as reaching and grabbing an object.

The autonomic nervous system (ANS) is more complex and has important implications for child development and mental health. In the following section, we describe the function of the three branches of the ANS.

ANS

The ANS controls involuntary functions related to heart functioning, respiration, and other reflexes such as vomiting (Bear et al., 2015). It is self-regulatory, which means that the ANS can increase or reduce the amount of energy, blood flow, and so forth to the organs of the body without a person being consciously aware of these regulatory actions. The ANS is divided into three separate branches: the sympathetic, parasympathetic, and enteric branches (Rao & Gershon, 2016). The first two branches (sympathetic and parasympathetic) have opposing actions and function to help a person maintain a balance of activation and recovery, known as *homeostasis*. The third branch (enteric) has a close relationship to the other two branches, though it is considered an independent system (Rao & Gershon, 2016).

Sympathetic and Parasympathetic Branches

During sympathetic activation, the sympathetic-adrenal-medullary axis and the HPA axis become activated, and stress hormones such as adrenaline and cortisol are released (Bear et al., 2015). Adrenaline functions to prepare a person for action by increasing heart rate, dilating the pupils, and slowing digestion. Cortisol assists with controlling blood sugar and blood pressure levels, regulates metabolism, and reduces inflammation. Hormone release involves structures from the CNS, PNS, and endocrine system (otherwise known as the body's hormonal system, which is described later in this chapter). The process of sympathetic activation was described by Smith and Vale (2006) and is summarized here. In response to an event in a person's environment, structures in the limbic region, in particular the amygdala, hippocampus, and thalamus, evaluate sensory information. These subcortical structures evaluate the sensory stimulus relative to prior knowledge and memories. If a threat is detected, a message is sent to the hypothalamus, which in turn triggers the release of corticotropin-releasing hormone. Corticotropin-releasing hormone sends a message to the pituitary gland, which releases adrenocorticotropic hormone (ACTH). ACTH is carried down to the adrenal cortex and medulla, which are located above the kidneys. ACTH stimulates the release of glucocorticoid hormones, such as cortisol, at the adrenal cortex. It can also activate the release of adrenaline (also called *epinephrine*) and noradrenaline (also called *norepinephrine*) by the adrenal medulla. Eventually, glucocorticoids such as cortisol provide feedback to the pituitary gland and hypothalamus to stop the release of cortisol. This is the stress response system's negative feedback loop.

The release of these hormones prompts physiological activation in response to the detection of threat (Smith & Vale, 2006). Adrenaline and cortisol prepare a person for action, such as by increasing heart rate and saving energy by reducing the energy consumption of other organs such as the stomach and digestive system. The function of this activation is to prepare the person to take action to address the potential threat in the environment. Because the person needs to respond fairly quickly to the threat, the process of sympathetic activation can happen very quickly and does not necessarily involve the frontal lobe. Instead, subcortical systems, such as the limbic structures, are mostly active. This means that the process of initial sympathetic activation is more reflexive and less associated with higher order, rational, and conscious thinking (Field, Beeson, & Jones, 2015). If a person were to pause and process their options rather than immediately respond, the person may place their survival at risk (Field et al., 2015). Thus, the reflexivity of sympathetic activation is believed to have evolutionary origins. A person's ability to prevent sympathetic activation and immediately engage parasympathetic recovery is limited, because the body responds automatically to perceived threats. Therefore, asking children to think before acting is often a tall order because their bodies are priming them for a quick, reflexive response to a threat in their environment (Field et al., 2015). See Reflection Question 2.1.

Children's behavioral response to sympathetic activation can vary. They might demonstrate an approach response to the perceived threat and become agitated and aggressive. They may demonstrate an avoidance response to the perceived threat by withdrawing from interpersonal contact or leaving the situation. They may also demonstrate a motionless response and feel unable to verbalize thoughts and feelings. Böhnke, Bertsch, Kruk, and Naumann (2010) found that nonacute activation of the HPA axis and cortisol secretion provokes avoidance responses, whereas acute activation prompts aggressive responses. It is believed that acute HPA axis activation might activate the negative feedback loop and reduce cortisol secretion, enabling approach rather than avoidance responses (Montoya, Terburg, Bos, & van Honk, 2012).

Once a person's sympathetic branch of the ANS has become activated, the person can eventually initiate recovery through parasympathetic activation, which results in reduced heart rate, increased digestion, and so forth. Actions associated with parasympathetic activation include engaging in diaphragmatic breathing and relaxing muscle tension. Research by Ma et al. (2017) found that diaphragmatic breathing activates parasympathetic recovery and reduces cortisol levels compared to a control condition. There is therefore research that supports the importance of children using deep, diaphragmatic breathing to activate the parasympathetic branch of the ANS. Note that parasympathetic activation can also occur when a person is in a relaxed state, not just when the person is recovering from sympathetic activation.

Because of these activating and recovery functions, neurons in the sympathetic branch of the ANS often transmit excitatory neurotransmitters (e.g., noradrenaline, which eventually triggers the release of adrenaline), whereas neurons in the parasympathetic branch of the ANS largely transmit inhibitory neurotransmitters (e.g., acetylcholine, GABA). Note that the neurotransmitter acetylcholine has an excitatory effect in the sensory nervous system yet an inhibitory effect on the ANS (i.e., it stimulates parasympathetic activation).

Reflection Question 2.1

Why might we, as a society, place such an emphasis on thinking before acting during sympathetic activation, even when it is rarely achievable for children?

The ANS is always activated in either a sympathetic or a parasympathetic state. Situational variables and environments can activate either branch of the ANS, and thus the ANS is crucial to the body's dynamic adaptation to the environment. For example, an elementary-age child might have minor sympathetic activation during school, especially when facing a mildly anxiety-provoking test like an exam, which helps with attention and concentration. The child might have parasympathetic activation when relaxing in the evening and at bedtime as they prepare for sleep. As the Yerkes-Dodson theory goes, a moderate and balanced amount of activation (e.g., cortisol secretion) is important for daily functioning (Yerkes & Dodson, 1908). It is when hormones such as cortisol are excreted at chronically high levels that it becomes problematic and causes dysfunction in systems of the brain and body. See Reflection Question 2.2.

Enteric Nervous System (ENS)

The ANS has a third branch, the ENS. The ENS is a division of the ANS that functions to send and receive messages related to the gastrointestinal system. For example, the ENS regulates the secretion of gastric acid, the release of hormones in the gut, and changes in blood flow. The ENS also contains neurons related to afferent (sensory) and efferent (motor) functions and operates autonomously from the CNS. It does, however, have strong connections to the CNS and PNS, with nerve strands that communicate to and from the rest of the body, including the brain and spinal cord. One of these nerves is the vagus nerve (CN X), which connects the brain stem to the gastrointestinal tract. In addition to performing other functions, such as modulating heart rate, the vagus nerve regulates the contraction and stretching of the gut, known as *gut motility*. The ENS also has connections to the ANS, perhaps most obvious when one considers that the digestive system slows down to preserve energy during sympathetic activation. Knowledge of ENS function is perhaps lesser known compared to knowledge of the sensory nervous system and ANS.

The gastrointestinal tract contains trillions of microorganisms that are collectively called *gut microbiota* (also *gut flora*). The collective unit of gut microbiota is known as the *gut microbiome*. Most microbiota are located in the colon, with some microbiota located in the stomach. (Intense acids and enzymes of the stomach make it less hospitable to microbiota than the colon; Dieterich, Schink, & Zopf, 2018.) These gut microbiota function to metabolize foods and nutrients and maintain the immune system (Tremaroli & Bäckhed, 2012). Gut bacteria also

Reflection Question 2.2

How might you introduce the concept of healthy and unhealthy stress to a child? What information would you share, and what information would you exclude?

care for cells within the gastrointestinal system, such as neurons and even glia in the intestines (Kabouridis et al., 2015). The relationship between microbiota and the brain is believed to be bidirectional. The brain sends messages to the microbiota regarding metabolism and the functioning of the immune system (e.g., absorption, secretion, blood flow). In addition, gastrointestinal functioning can impact brain functioning. For example, celiac disease can have impacts on cognition, such as impaired concentration and "brain fog" (Yelland, 2017, p. 90). The strong relationship between the CNS and ENS has been called the *microbiota gut-brain axis* (Mittal et al., 2017). Microbiota have an important role in producing metabolites during metabolism, such as fatty acids, which affect the release and modulation of neurotransmitters (Mittal et al., 2017). Neurotransmitters have a role in influencing the absorption of nutrients, activation of the immune system, and gut motility (Mittal et al., 2017). Neurotransmitters (e.g., acetylcholine, norepinephrine) are also intricately involved in the stress response system, which itself has a strong relationship to gut functioning.

Although most microbiota are important to our overall health, some microbiota are pathogenic and cause health problems. You are likely familiar with microbiota that cause illness, such as salmonella. In part because of the linkage between stress and gut function, there is emerging evidence of the role of gut microbiota in the development of mental health conditions (Kim, Yun, Oh, & Choi, 2018). Alzheimer's disease, autism, depression, and Parkinson's disease all have correlates with alterations in gut microbiota composition (Kim et al., 2018).

Immune System

When a body fights an infection (i.e., a foreign microbial invasion of a bacterial pathogen such as a virus) or initiates repair of an injury to cells or tissue, white blood cells (sometimes called *leukocytes* or *immune cells*) are activated. There are several types of white blood cells. These cells take on several different functions to protect the organism against infection. The gastrointestinal system contains a large concentration of white blood cells and is a crucial part of immune response.

There are two forms of immune system response: innate and adaptive (or acquired) immunity. *Innate immunity* refers to the immune system's identification of known pathogens such as bacteria and viruses (National Institute of Allergy and Infectious Diseases, 2014). Once a pathogen has been identified, white blood cells work to neutralize and eradicate it. Types of white blood cells associated with innate immunity include basophils, eosinophils, monocytes, and neutrophils. Basophils are active during allergic responses, when they release histamines that dilate blood vessels. This dilation enhances blood flow to the site of infection or injury, sometimes resulting in swelling. Monocytes become macrophages, which also engulf (i.e., eat) invading bacteria by phagocytosis. Like lymphocytes, monocytes also create cytokines (more about this later). Neutrophils are first responders to microbial infection. They also engulf invading bacteria, though they are less effective at phagocytosis than macrophages, because they are smaller cells and thus engulf fewer microorganisms. In addition to these cells, natural killer cells have a role in identifying and destroying virus-infected and tumorous cells through apoptosis. They form holes in target cells that result in cell death (National Institute of Allergy and Infectious Diseases, 2014).

Adaptive immunity is the body's ability to respond to new and unknown pathogens and problems (National Institute of Allergy and Infectious Diseases, 2014). Adaptive immunity involves a type of white blood cell called a *lymphocyte*. B-cells and T-cells are types of lymphocytes that divide and multiply rapidly to address the identified infection. Once dispersed, B-cells make antibodies that neutralize pathogenic bacteria. T-cells create cytokines that help to coordinate immune system response. T-cells also recognize prior infectious bacteria and initiate an antibody response, thus serving as the memory of the immune system.

Vaccination trains the immune system to respond to a strain of pathogen. During vaccination, dead cells are entered into the body. This creates T-cell memory for the pathogen so that the body is more prepared for later infections by the same bacteria or virus.

Gut Inflammation

The microbiota in the gut often have a role in the inflammation process when the immune system becomes activated (Dieterich et al., 2018). Inflammation is crucial to overall immune system functioning, as this process enhances blood flow to the site of infection or injury so that white blood cells can address the pathogen. Cytokines are proteins that have a crucial role in inflammatory responses, as they draw and recruit white blood cells to the site of infection or injury. Those white blood cells then engulf the pathogen, destroy degraded cells, and dilate blood vessels to increase the amount of white blood cells flowing into the area. Proinflammatory cytokines promote inflammation, whereas antiinflammatory cytokines inhibit inflammation. Gut microbiota can provoke pro- and antiinflammatory cytokines (Dieterich et al., 2018).

Acute inflammation is useful for controlling infection and repairing cells and tissue. Yet if inflammation persists for a prolonged period, it becomes harmful and will damage cells and tissue. Cytokines are able to cross the blood-brain barrier (a blood vessel lining that protects the brain from infection) and activate the HPA axis. In the brain, proinflammatory cytokines can alter neurotransmitter metabolism and reduce brain-derived neurotrophic factor and glutamate, resulting in fatigue and mood changes, including depression (Farooq, Asghar, Kanwal, & Zulqernain, 2017; Felger & Lotrich, 2013). High numbers of cytokines have been especially associated with manic states in bipolar disorder (Bai et al., 2014; Brietzke et al., 2009). It also appears that higher amounts of circulating cytokines have been associated with nonresponse to antidepressants (Fitzgerald et al., 2006). High numbers of circulating cytokines are also associated with physical health conditions such as cardiovascular disease and diabetes (Farooq et al., 2017).

The stress response system has an important bidirectional relationship with the immune system (Farooq et al., 2017). Cytokines can activate the HPA axis, resulting in the release of cortisol. In addition, high levels of cortisol can cause immunosuppression (i.e., reduce the responsiveness of the immune system) to reduce overactivation of the immune system and inflammatory damage to cells and tissue. Thus, the CNS, PNS, ENS, and endocrine systems are all intricately connected in their function and communication, especially during stress response.

To summarize, the ENS has an essential role in not only digestion and metabolism but also the immune system and stress response system. In subsequent chapters, we further explore the complex interrelationship between the CNS, PNS, ENS, and endocrine system, especially in relationship to the chronic stress response pathway and psychoneuroimmunology.

Endocrine System

Earlier in the chapter, we mentioned the endocrine system when describing the stress response system. Although not a formal nervous system, the endocrine system has many linkages to the CNS and PNS, evidenced by descriptions of sympathetic activation. For example, structures of the subcortex (i.e., the CNS) send messages to the adrenal cortex to release hormones (i.e., the endocrine system) via the ANS division of the PNS. Because of the endocrine system's importance to the stress response system and to sexual development and maturation (which we describe in subsequent chapters), it is worth briefly summarizing the function of the endocrine system here.

Figure 2.7 depicts components of the endocrine system. The endocrine system comprises the glands of the brain and body that release hormones to regulate the activity of cells and organs. Hormones have a role in energy metabolism and in the body's growth and development. When multiple glands signal one another in sequence, they are referred to as an *axis* (e.g., the HPA axis).

There are several important glands in the endocrine system. The pituitary gland is located in the brain and is considered the master hormone gland of the brain and body, as it sends messages to several other glands to secrete hormones (Nicholls et al., 2011). For example, you may remember from earlier that the hypothalamus sends

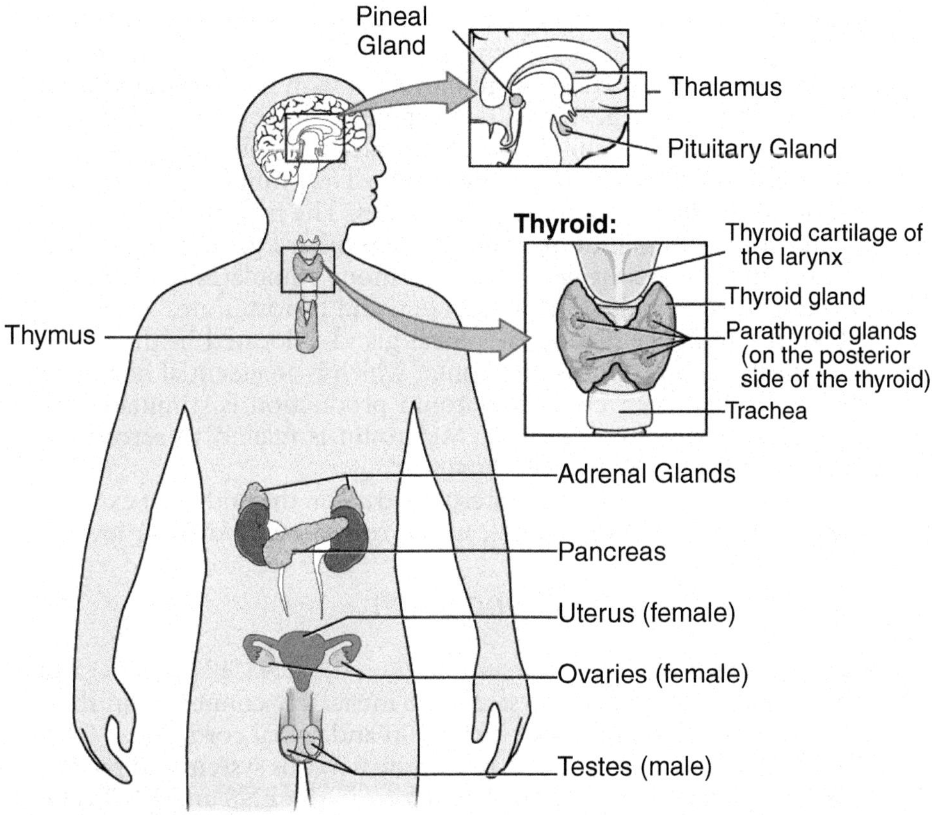

FIGURE 2.7

The Endocrine System

Note. From OpenStax College, 2013. In Wikimedia Commons. Used under Creative Commons Share Alike Attribution 3.0 Unported License.

corticotropin-releasing hormone to the pituitary gland, which then secretes ACTH. When ACTH reaches the adrenal medulla, located above the kidneys, it releases adrenaline and cortisol. Adrenaline and cortisol are hormones that assist with the regulation of metabolism and blood pressure. Because adrenaline and cortisol are also stress hormones, they tend to raise blood pressure, elevate heart rate, and constrict metabolism when they are released when the body is prepared to respond to perceived threat.

The thyroid gland is located in front of the neck. The pituitary gland releases thyroid-stimulating hormone to the thyroid gland, which in turn releases hormones such as thyroxine and triiodothyronine. These hormones control metabolism (i.e., how the body uses energy). The ovaries and testes are also considered glands, as they contain sex hormones (e.g., estrogen, progesterone, testosterone). These hormones are responsible for sexual development and are essential to reproduction. The ovaries excrete estrogen and progesterone, whereas the testes excrete testosterone. These hormones assist with the development of sex characteristics (e.g., breast development, pubic hair, and genital development) during childhood and adolescence. In addition, progesterone has a key role during pregnancy. The pituitary gland plays a key role in the secretion of these hormones. The hypothalamus sends gonadotropin-releasing hormone to the pituitary gland, which then excretes luteinizing hormone. This hormone stimulates ovulation in females and the production of estrogen and testosterone.

Like the pituitary gland, the pineal gland is located in the brain. The pineal gland produces melatonin, which is an essential hormone involved in the sleep cycle. Melatonin production is stimulated by darkness and inhibited by light. Melatonin is related to serotonin, which itself has a role in sleep function.

Finally, the pancreas is another crucial gland in the body that excretes glucagon and insulin hormones, which regulate blood sugar levels.

Conclusion

The brain and body's nervous systems (i.e., the CNS, PNS, ENS) and endocrine (i.e., hormonal) systems are intricately connected in their function and communication. The brain and spinal cord of the CNS often direct the activities of the rest of the nervous system and receive messages about the body's functioning from the PNS and ENS. The endocrine system has an important role in the stress response system and in maturation and development.

When working with children and adolescents, it can be helpful to understand the structure and function of their brain and body. Children's behavior (both verbal and nonverbal) is often strongly impacted by their neurophysiological development. The information in this chapter provides a foundation for subsequent chapters about how and why children develop and which counseling approaches are helpful at various stages of development. You may find it helpful to return to this chapter as you explore further chapters to better understand the interconnected functioning between systems.

Quiz Questions

1. Nerve cells in the PNS have different functions. Afferent cells send messages _____ the CNS, whereas efferent cells send messages _____ the CNS.
    a. From, to
    b. To, from
    c. Inside, outside

2. The structures involved in the stress response system include
   a. Hippocampus, prefrontal cortex, insula
   b. Hypothalamus, pineal gland, amygdala
   c. Hypothalamus, pituitary gland, adrenal cortex
3. During inflammation, white blood cells produce an important chemical known as _____ that directs the inflammatory process.
   a. Cortisol
   b. Cytokines
   c. Cytoplasm

References

Bai, Y., Su, T., Tsai, S., Wen-Fei, C., Li, C., Pei-Chi, T., & Mu-Hong, C. (2014). Comparison of inflammatory cytokine levels among type I/type II and manic/hypomanic/euthymic/depressive states of bipolar disorder. *Journal of Affective Disorders, 166,* 187–192. doi:10.1016/j.jad.2014.05.009

Bear, M. F., Connors, B. W., & Paradiso, M. A. (2015). *Neuroscience: Exploring the brain* (4th ed.). Philadelphia, PA: Wolters-Kluwer.

Böhnke, R., Bertsch, K., Kruk, M. R., & Naumann, E. (2010). The relationship between basal and acute HPA axis activity and aggressive behavior in adults. *Journal of Neural Transmission, 117,* 629–637. doi:10.1007/s00702-010-0391-x

Brietzke, E., Stertz, L., Fernandes, B. S., Kauer-Sant'anna, M., Mascarenhas, M., Escosteguy Vargas, A., . . . Kapczinski, F. (2009). Comparison of cytokine levels in depressed, manic and euthymic patients with bipolar disorder. *Journal of Affective Disorders, 116,* 214–217. doi:10.1016/j.jad.2008.12.001

Chan, R. W., Leong, A. T. L., Ho, L. C., Gao, P. P., Wong, E. C., Dong, C. M., . . . Wu, E. X. (2017). Low-frequency hippocampal-cortical activity drives brain-wide resting state functional MRI connectivity. *Proceedings of the National Academy of Sciences, USA, 114,* E6972–E6981. doi:10.1073/pnas.1703309114

Collins, A., & Koechlin, E. (2012). Reasoning, learning, and creativity: Frontal lobe function and human decision-making. *PLoS Biology, 10,* e1001293. doi:10.1371/journal.pbio.1001293

Council for Accreditation of Counseling and Related Educational Programs. (2015). *2016 CACREP standards.* Alexandria, VA: Author.

Dieterich, W., Schink, M., & Zopf, Y. (2018). Microbiota in the gastrointestinal tract. *Medical Sciences, 6,* 116–131. doi:10.3390/medsci6040116

Duncan, I. D., & Radcliff, A. B. (2016). Inherited and acquired disorders of myelin: The underlying myelin pathology. *Experimental Neurology, 283*(Pt B), 452–475. doi:10.1016/j.expneurol.2016.04.002

Farooq, R. K., Asghar, K., Kanwal, S., & Zulqernain, A. (2017). Role of inflammatory cytokines in depression: Focus on interleukin-1β. *Biomedical Reports, 6,* 15–20. doi:10.3892/br.2016.807

Felger, J. C., & Lotrich, F. E. (2013). Inflammatory cytokines in depression: Neurobiological mechanisms and therapeutic implications. *Neuroscience, 246,* 199–229. doi:10.1016/j.neuroscience.2013.04.060

Field, T. A. (2019). Bridging the brain and body divide: A commentary and response to Wilkinson. *The Journal of Humanistic Counseling, 58,* 108–118. doi:10.1002/johc.12100

Field, T. A., Beeson, E. T., & Jones, L. K. (2015). The new ABCs: A practitioner's guide to neuroscience-informed cognitive-behavior therapy. *Journal of Mental Health Counseling, 37,* 206–220. doi:10.17744/1040-2861-37.3.206

Fitzgerald, P., O'Brien, S. M., Scully, P., Rijkers, K., Scott, L. V., & Dinan, T. G. (2006). Cutaneous glucocorticoid receptor sensitivity and pro-inflammatory cytokine levels in antidepressant-resistant depression. *Psychological Medicine, 36,* 37–43. doi:10.1017/S003329170500632X

Hofman, M. A. (2014). Evolution of the human brain: When bigger is better. *Frontiers in Neuroanatomy, 8,* 1–12. doi:10.3389/fnana.2014.00015

Jasanoff, A. (2018). *The biological mind: How brain, body, and environment collaborate to make us who we are.* New York, NY: Basic Books.

Kabouridis, P. S., Lasrado, R., Mccallum, S., Chng, S. H., Snippert, H. J., Clevers, H., . . . Pachnis, V. (2015). Microbiota controls the homeostasis of glial cells in the gut lamina propria. *Neuron, 85,* 289–295. doi:10.1016/j.neuron.2014.12.037

Kandel, E. R., Schwartz, J. H., Jessell, T. M., Siegelbaum, S. A., & Hudspeth, A. J. (2012). *Principles of neural science* (5th ed.). New York, NY: McGraw-Hill.

Kim, N., Yun, M., Oh, Y., & Choi, J. (2018). Mind-altering with the gut: Modulation of the gut-brain axis with probiotics. *Journal of Microbiology, 56,* 172–182. doi:10.1007/s12275-018-8032-4

Klein, A. P., Ulmer, J. L., Quinet, S. A., Mathews, V., & Mark, L. P. (2016). Nonmotor functions of the cerebellum: An introduction. *American Journal of Neuroradiology, 37,* 1005–1009. doi:10.3174/ajnr.A4720

Leech, R., & Sharp, D. J. (2014). The role of the posterior cingulate cortex in cognition and disease. *Brain, 137,* 12–32. doi:10.1093/brain/awt162

Ma, X., Yue, Z. Q., Gong, Z. Q., Zhang, H., Duan, N. Y., Shi, Y. T., . . . Li, Y. F. (2017). The effect of diaphragmatic breathing on attention, negative affect and stress in healthy adults. *Frontiers in Psychology, 8,* 1–12. doi:10.3389/fpsyg.2017.00874

Mittal, R., Debs, L. H., Patel, A. P., Nguyen, D., Patel, K., O'Connor, G., . . . Liu, X. Z. (2017). Neurotransmitters: The critical modulators regulating gut-brain axis. *Journal of Cell Physiology, 232,* 2359–2372. doi:10.1002/jcp.25518

Montoya, E. R., Terburg, D., Bos, P. A., & van Honk, J. (2012). Testosterone, cortisol, and serotonin as key regulators of social aggression: A review and theoretical perspective. *Motivation and Emotion, 36,* 65–73. doi:10.1007/s11031-011-9264-3

Motzkin, J. C., Philippi, C. L., Wolf, R. C., Baskaya, M. K., & Koenigs, M. (2015). Ventromedial prefrontal cortex is critical for the regulation of amygdala activity in humans. *Biological Psychiatry, 77,* 276–284. doi:10.1016/j.biopsych.2014.02.014

National Institute of Allergy and Infectious Diseases. (2014, January). *Immune cells.* Retrieved from https://www.niaid.nih.gov/research/immune-cells

Nicholls, J. G., Martin, A. R., Brown, D. A., Diamond, M. E., Weisblat, D. A., & Fuchs, P. A. (2011). *From neuron to brain* (5th ed.). Sunderland, MA: Sinauer Associates.

Purves, D., Augustine, G. J., Fitzpatrick, D., Hall, W. C., LaMantia, A., & White, L. E. (2011). *Neuroscience* (5th ed.). Sunderland, MA: Sinauer Associates.

Raichle, M. E. (2015). The brain's default mode network. *Annual Review of Neuroscience, 38,* 433–447. doi:10.1146/annurev-neuro-071013-014030

Rao, M., & Gershon, M. D. (2016). The bowel and beyond: The enteric nervous system in neurological disorders. *Nature Reviews Gastroenterology & Hepatology, 13,* 517–528. doi:10.1038/nrgastro.2016.107

Rodd, J. M., Davis, M. H., & Johnsrude, I. S. (2005). The neural mechanisms of speech comprehension: fMRI studies of semantic ambiguity. *Cerebral Cortex, 15,* 1261–1269. doi:10.1093/cercor/bhi009

Rubin, R. D., Watson, P. D., Duff, M. C., & Cohen, N. J. (2014). The role of the hippocampus in flexible cognition and social behavior. *Frontiers in Human Neuroscience, 8,* 1–15. doi:10.3389/fnhum.2014.00742

Shabel, S. J., Proulx, C. D., Piriz, J., & Malinow, R. (2014, September 19). GABA/glutamate co-release controls habenula output and is modified by antidepressant treatment. *Science, 345,* 1494–1498.

Smith, S. M., & Vale, W. W. (2006). The role of the hypothalamic-pituitary-adrenal axis in neuroendocrine responses to stress. *Dialogues in Clinical Neuroscience, 8,* 383–395.

Snaidero, N., & Simons, M. (2014). Myelination at a glance. *Journal of Cell Science, 127,* 2999–3004. doi:10.1242/jcs.151043

Stephani, C., Fernandez-Baca Vaca, G., Maciunas, R., Koubeissi, M., & Lüders, H. O. (2011). Functional neuroanatomy of the insular lobe. *Brain Structure & Function, 216,* 137–149. doi:10.1007/s00429-010-0296-3

Stevens, F., Hurley, R., & Taber, K. (2011). Anterior cingulate cortex: Unique role in cognition and emotion. *Journal of Neuropsychiatry and Clinical Neurosciences, 23,* 121–125. doi:10.1176/appi.neuropsych.23.2.121

Strick, P. L., Dum, R. P., & Fiez, J. A. (2009). Cerebellum and nonmotor function. *Annual Review of Neuroscience, 32,* 413–434. doi:10.1146/annurev.neuro.31.060407.125606

Tremaroli, T., & Bäckhed, F. (2012, September 12). Functional interactions between the gut microbiota and host metabolism. *Nature, 489,* 242–249. doi:10.1038/nature11552

Uddin, L. Q., Nomi, J. S., Hébert-Seropian, B., Ghaziri, J., & Boucher, O. (2017). Structure and function of the human insula. *Journal of Clinical Neurophysiology, 34,* 300–306. doi:10.1097/WNP.0000000000000377

Yelland, G. (2017). Gluten-induced cognitive impairment ("brain fog") in coeliac disease. *Journal of Gastroenterology and Hepatology, 32,* 90–93. doi:10.1111/jgh.13706

Yerkes, R. M., & Dodson, J. D. (1908). The relation of strength of stimulus to rapidity of habit-formation. *Journal of Comparative Neurology and Psychology, 18,* 459–482. doi:10.1002/cne.920180503

Chapter 3

Cellular Function and Epigenetics

Key Concepts

- Cell structures (nucleus, cytoplasm, cytoskeleton, mitochondria, ribosomes)
- DNA, chromosomes, telomeres, genome
- Gene transcription, gene translation, RNA, mRNA, tRNA
- Epigenetics, gene expression, methylation, epigenome
- Neurogenesis, synaptogenesis, synaptic pruning, neuroplasticity
- Brain-derived neurotrophic factor
- Long-term potentiation and depression
- Apoptosis
- Cortisol, hypercortisolism, attenuation hypothesis, metaplasticity hypothesis

Aligned CACREP 2016 Standards

Standard 2.F.3.c. Theories of normal and abnormal personality development

Standard 2.F.3.e. Biological, neurological, and physiological factors that affect human development, functioning, and behavior

Standard 2.F.3.f. Systemic and environmental factors that affect human development, functioning, and behavior

Standard 2.F.3.g. Effects of crisis, disasters, and trauma on diverse individuals across the life span

• • •

In this chapter, we explore important fundamental questions about childhood and adolescent development: What is the role of heredity and environment in child and adolescent development? To what extent do genetics inform the development of personality traits, character, and mental health conditions? To answer complicated questions like these, we have to explore the basics of cellular biology, gene transcription, and several landmark studies from a field known as *epigenetics.* This information is quite technical, and we recommend that you consult the glossary to better understand unfamiliar terminology. The information below was informed by sources that include the National Human Genome Research Institute (n.d.), the National Institutes of Health's (NIH) genetics home reference institute, and the sixth edition of *Molecular Biology of the Cell* by Alberts and colleagues (2014).

Cellular Structure and Function

The central and peripheral nervous systems are composed of nerve cells and fluid. Cells perform different functions, which they complete by receiving nutrients and converting them into energy. The basic structure of a cell is depicted in Figure 3.1.

At the heart of the cell is its nucleus. The nucleus directs the cell's functioning, such as to grow, divide, separate, or die (Alberts et al., 2014; NIH, 2019). The nucleus contains an essential molecule known as *deoxyribonucleic acid* (DNA). The nucleus is surrounded

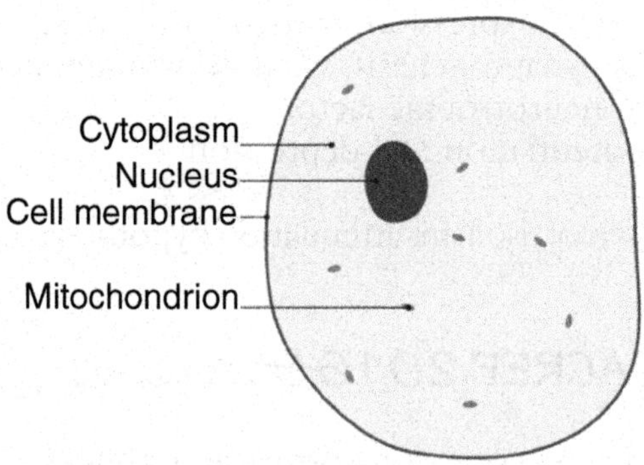

FIGURE 3.1

Basic Structure of the Human Cell

Note. From domdomegg, 2016. In Wikimedia Commons. Used under Creative Commons Attribution 4.0 International License.

by a fluid known as *cytoplasm,* which is encased in the plasma membrane. The frame of the cell is known as the *cytoskeleton.* Cells contain several organelles that carry out the nucleus's directions, most notably lysosomes and peroxisomes, mitochondria, and ribosomes. Lysosomes and peroxisomes rid the cell of foreign bacteria and recycle parts of the cell. Mitochondria convert nutrients into energy for the cell to use and have their own DNA separate from that of the nucleus. Ribosomes create proteins by processing genetic information (more on this later).

Almost every cell in the human body has the same DNA (NIH, 2019). DNA is a molecule made from hereditary material that is passed down from a person's parents. When an egg is fertilized by a sperm, genetic material from both parents join to form an embryo, first called a *zygote.* Nucleus DNA is evenly distributed between parents, whereas mitochondrial DNA is only derived from egg cells (not from sperm cells). Some health conditions are associated with mitochondrial DNA, such as diabetes. Thus, diabetes is typically only inherited if the mother transmits DNA associated with diabetes (NIH, 2019).

DNA contains instructions essential to an organism's survival. It also contains instructions for developing new proteins. These instructions are known as *genes.* Only 1% of DNA contains genetic information (i.e., protein coding; Alberts et al., 2014). The DNA sequences that code proteins are known as *exons,* whereas the DNA sequences that do not code proteins are known as *introns.* The remainder of DNA (i.e., introns) regulates information about protein production, such as when protein coding occurs, how it occurs, and how much protein is produced.

DNA is composed of four main chemicals: adenine (A), guanine (G), cytosine (C), and thymine (T). These four chemicals pair up. Adenine (A) almost always pairs with guanine (G), and cytosine (C) almost always pairs with thymine (T). The sequence order of these chemical pairings informs which information is available when creating new cells or maintaining cells. The entirety of genetic instructions in one's DNA is called the *genome* (NIH, 2019). The size of a gene can vary greatly, from hundreds to millions of A, G, C, and T chemicals. Humans share 99% of the same genes (NIH, 2019).

Cells have many DNA molecules. To fit into the nucleus of a cell, histone proteins coil around DNA molecules to make tight packages known as *chromosomes.* Without being tightly packaged, DNA would never fit into the nucleus of a cell. The DNA molecules in a single nucleus would reach 6 feet in length if placed end to end (Alberts et al., 2014)!

A person's cells must divide into two identical cells to replace older cells (NIH, 2019). There are two processes of cell division known as *mitosis* and *meiosis.* In mitosis, each divided cell has identical DNA. In meiosis, DNA is split between the divided cells. Reproductive cells known as *gametes* are formed by meiosis. In mitosis, the structure of chromosomes is essential to preventing DNA from being unevenly distributed.

Human cells typically contain 23 pairs of chromosomes (46 total). Reproductive cells called *gametes* are the only cells that do not contain pairs of chromosomes. When cells split via meiosis, chromosomes are split between the divided gamete cells. Gametes thus contain a single set of 23 chromosomes rather than a double set (i.e., 23 pairs or 46 chromosomes). The sperm and egg each have a set of 23 chromosomes that combine into 46 chromosomes during fertilization. Twenty-two of these 23 chromosomal pairs are similar in sperm and eggs. One of the 23 chromosomal pairs, known as the *sex chromosome,* is different. This special type of chromosome plays an important role in DNA heredity. Female cells have two X sex chromosomes (XX), whereas male cells have one X and one Y sex chromosome (XY). The inheritance of certain X and Y chromosomes can result in problems such as Kleinfelter syndrome in males, which is caused by an extra X sex chromosome (i.e., XXY).

Any changes in the number or type of chromosomes can cause significant problems (NIH, 2019). For example, Down syndrome is caused when cells have three copies of chromosome 21 rather than two, known as *trisomy 21* (NIH, 2019). Turner syndrome is caused when children have only one copy of a chromosome rather than two. Figure 3.2 shows the three copies of chromosome 21 in Down syndrome.

Telomeres are made of DNA and are found at the ends of chromosomes (NIH, 2019). They tie up genetic material and stop it from unravelling. When cells divide, a small amount of telomeres are lost. Eventually all of the telomere DNA will be lost. When this occurs,

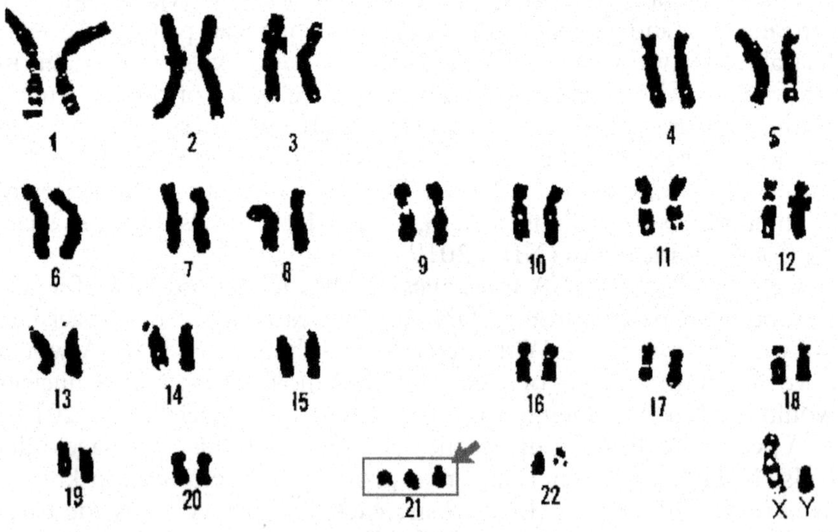

FIGURE 3.2

Trisomy 21 Karyotype

Note. From U.S. Department of Energy Human Genome Program, 2006. In Wikimedia Commons.

the cell can no longer replicate before dividing and it dies. Cells that divide frequently, such as white blood cells, can have special enzymes that prevent a chromosome from losing telomere DNA. This protective function allows these cells to survive longer. It is interesting that cancer cells do not lose telomeres, which can lead to rapid proliferation of cancer cells (NIH, 2019).

Sometimes cells encounter a DNA error that cannot be repaired. In such cases, *apoptosis* can occur, whereby the cell intentionally breaks apart and dies. This helps the body remove cells that are not needed and reduces the risk of diseases such as cancer. Mitochondria have a role in programmed cell death.

Gene Transcription and Translation

Most genes contain information for creating proteins, though a small percentage of genes produce ribonucleic acid (RNA) instead (Alberts et al., 2014). RNA is a molecule related to DNA. RNA codes, decodes, and regulates the expression of DNA. Like DNA, RNA is a nucleic acid found in the nucleus of a cell. RNA can also be found in a cell's cytoplasm. During gene transcription, RNA polymerase binds to DNA, and DNA unwinds so it can be copied.

There are two steps to creating proteins from DNA instructions (Alberts et al., 2014; NIH, 2019). These steps are depicted in Figure 3.3. In the first step of this process, enzymes called *RNA* read DNA information about protein development and copy it onto messenger RNA (mRNA) molecules. This process is known as *gene transcription.* Once the DNA instructions for creating proteins have been copied onto mRNA, mRNA leaves the nucleus of the cell and enters the cytoplasm. In the cytoplasm, ribosomes read the precise chemical

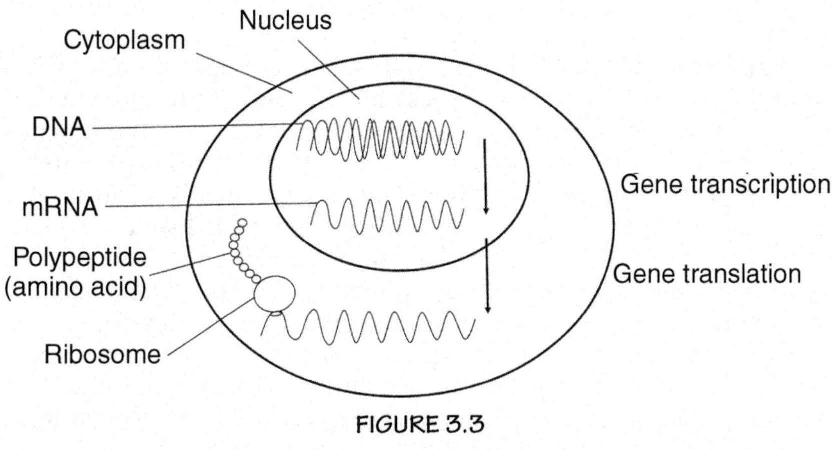

FIGURE 3.3

Gene Transcription and Translation

sequence that was copied earlier from DNA that mRNA is carrying. This is known as *gene translation*. Transfer RNA (tRNA) then builds the amino acids in the exact order specified in the instructions. Chains of these amino acids collectively form proteins.

There are many different kinds of proteins, all of which have essential functions. Antibodies are proteins that protect the body by binding to viruses and bacteria. Enzymes are proteins that read genetic information in DNA and are responsible for chemical reactions within cells. Messenger proteins, such as hormones (e.g., growth hormones), coordinate processes between cells and tissue, such as creating new synapses.

Cells express only a small number of genes. The transcription of genetic material is influenced by transcription factor proteins, which bind to a gene to increase or reduce transcription. This influences the amount of proteins that are developed from genetic material.

Epigenetics

Other chemical compounds can attach to segments of DNA to influence whether genes are able to be transcribed (i.e., expressed) or not (i.e., silenced; Alberts et al., 2014). For example, methyl groups (one carbon atom, three hydrogen atoms) can bind to a segment of DNA and are known to stop the production of proteins from that segment of DNA (i.e., gene silencing). This ability of other chemical compounds to affect protein production by impacting gene transcription is referred to as *epigenetics*. The entirety of the genome and the chemical compounds that influence gene expression make up the epigenome.

Some children are born with genetic predispositions for certain traits and health problems based on DNA that was passed to them in the mother's egg and father's sperm. Genetic factors such as mutations, as well as a person's environment, can influence which traits or health problems emerge (Alberts et al., 2014).

Epigenetics provides helpful insights into the age-old discussion about the role of nature (genetics) and nurture (environment) in child development. Environmental events influence whether chemical compounds such as methyl groups will attach to segments of DNA (Alberts et al., 2014). This means that a person's environment has a strong impact on which genes are expressed. Even studies of monozygotic twins (i.e., twins that share the same DNA, known as *identical twins*) have found that epigenetic changes might explain why identical twins differ in some traits (Fraga et al., 2005).

Epigenetics also complicates the discussion of nature versus nurture, because research has found that these epigenetic modifications to gene expression and subsequent protein production remain even after cells divide and can be inherited similar to DNA. This is referred to as *transgenerational epigenetic inheritance* (Heard & Martienssen,

2014). This means, in practicality, that a person's environment can affect not only their current functioning but the later functioning of their offspring as well (Heard & Martienssen, 2014).

Epigenetic Studies Into the Stress Response System

Meaney and Szyf (2005) conducted a famous experiment that sought to clarify whether heredity (genetics) or environment (epigenetics) has a greater role in the stress response system of rat pups. You may recall that in Chapter 2 we described the stress response system of the autonomic nervous system (both the sympathetic and parasympathetic branches). Stress hormones, such as cortisol and adrenaline, have been the focus of research for quite some time, as overproduction of these hormones has been strongly associated with both physical and mental health problems.

In their experiment, Meaney and Szyf (2005) selected two sets of rat mothers based on behavioral observations. One set of mothers were attentive to their young and demonstrated nurturance through licking and grooming, whereas the other set of mothers did not provide the same licking and grooming behaviors to their young. The researchers impregnated each set of mothers and switched the offspring at birth, so that rat pups born to nurturing mothers were switched with rat pups from non-nurturing mothers. They then tracked the rat pups for several weeks and measured whether genes associated with the control of stress hormone production were actively creating proteins or silenced via methylation (i.e., gene silencing). The researchers believed that stressful environments would impair the stop system for cortisol production, resulting in a dysregulated stress response system that overproduced and oversecreted cortisol. At the end of the experiment, the researchers compared rat pups by the amount of glucocorticoid receptor methylation, which is associated with cortisol release.

Pause for a moment. Which set of rat pups do you think had a dysregulated stress response system? Rat pups with possible genetic predispositions toward a greater stress response (i.e., those born to mothers who were non-nurturing) who were raised in a nurturing rather than stressful environment? Or rat pups who did not seem to have genetic predispositions (i.e., those born to mothers who were nurturing) but were raised in a stressful environment?

The Meaney and Szyf (2005) experiment is so often cited because the researchers found that only the rat pups who were raised in the stressful environment developed increased sensitivity to stress. The rat pups who were raised in the nurturing environment did not develop increased methylation of genes associated with glucocorticoid receptors. See Reflection Question 3.1.

The Meaney and Szyf (2005) experiment has important implications for child development. The experiment suggests that an organism's

Reflection Question 3.1

Do the results of the Meaney and Szyf study regarding the greater role of the environment than genetics in the development of heightened sensitivity to stress surprise you? Why or why not?

genetic predispositions have less of a role in its development than the environment in which it is raised. This means that parents with higher stress hormone production who might potentially pass on genetic predispositions can shield their offspring from developing an overactive stress response system if they work intentionally to create an attentive and nurturing environment for their children.

Subsequent studies in humans have also found greater sensitivity to stress in children who are raised in stressful environments (Romens, McDonald, Svaren, & Pollak, 2015). Romens and colleagues (2015) compared children who had been physically maltreated and children who had not. Children with histories of abuse had greater methylation (i.e., gene silencing) of exon 1F located in the genetic region *NR3C1*. The *NR3C1* region is associated with control over stress production, and silencing gene transcription and subsequent protein production from this region results in greater production of cortisol.

Similar research has been conducted by Yehuda and colleagues (2016), who studied the heredity of cortisol overproduction in Holocaust survivors, focusing on the *FKBP5* region of the genetic sequence. Like *NR3C1, FKBP5* is associated with control of cortisol production, and methylation (silencing) of *FKBP5* results in increased cortisol production. Parents who were Holocaust survivors had increased methylation of *FKBP5* compared to a control group of parents who were not survivors of the Holocaust. Despite this increased methylation of *FKBP5* in parents who were Holocaust survivors, *FKBP5* methylation was actually lower in children of Holocaust survivors compared to children in the control condition. We can conclude from this study that a child's current environment has a greater role in whether they develop an overactive stress response system than genetics and heredity.

One of the limitations of these studies is that they do not address how stress hormone overproduction develops over the course of a child's life. Trickett, Noll, and Putnam (2011) conducted one of the few longitudinal studies into the relationship between environmental trauma, epigenetics, and stress overproduction. Trickett et al. studied children who were exposed to early childhood trauma over the course of 23 years. The researchers included two groups in the study: female children who had experienced sexual abuse during childhood, and female children who had not experienced sexual abuse (to the extent known). The study had a high retention rate (almost 90%) over several decades. The sample was diverse, with African American children making up approximately half of the participants. To understand the impacts of abuse on the hypothalamic-pituitary-adrenal (HPA) axis and stress response system, the researchers gave all participants a chemical that stimulated corticotropin-releasing hormone (CRH). Like *NR3C1* and *FKBP5,* CRH is a gene sequence associated with cortisol release. CRH stimulates secretion of adrenocorticotropic hormone (ACTH) from the pituitary gland, which sends messages to the adrenal gland to release cortisol.

Trickett et al. (2011) found that in early childhood, females with histories of abuse had increased ACTH production in response to CRH compared to the control group. Yet in early adulthood, the opposite was true. Females with histories of abuse had reduced ACTH production compared to the control group. Trickett et al. believed that this finding supported the attenuation hypothesis of Susman (2006). The attenuation hypothesis proposes that people who experience extreme and chronic early childhood stress develop an asymmetrical stress response marked by initially increased cortisol excretion during childhood and then subsequently blunted cortisol excretion during adulthood. Susman and Trickett et al. proposed that this asymmetrical response is caused by the attenuation and breakdown of the HPA axis, which means that the brain and body become used to chronically high levels of stress and secrete less cortisol as a way to maintain *homeostasis.* Although this might seem adaptive, the authors argued that low levels of circulating cortisol are associated with a series of issues, including posttraumatic stress (Miller, Chen, & Zhou, 2007), depression (Shenk, Noll, Putnam, & Trickett, 2010), antisocial behavior (Shenk et al., 2010), and impaired immune and cardiovascular function (Raison & Miller, 2003; Trickett et al., 2011).

Alongside CRH, *FKBP5,* and *NR3C1,* overproduction of stress hormones such as cortisol has been linked to gene sequences associated with arginine vasopressin, ACTH and its precursor (pro-opiomelanocortin), and the *HSD11β1/2* enzyme that degrades cortisol once secreted (Argentieri, Nagarajan, Seddighzadeh, Baccarelli, & Shields, 2017). As mentioned in Chapter 2, overproduction of cortisol has a host of negative effects. In a review of 32 studies, Argentieri et al. (2017) found that DNA methylation of *FKBP5* and *NR3C1* was associated with posttraumatic stress, *FKBP5* was associated with Alzheimer's disease, *NR3C1* was associated with breast and lung cancer, and *HSD11β1/2* was associated with hypertension. Jokinen et al. (2017) found that methylation of genes associated with CRH was associated with adolescent suicide attempts.

In addition to dysregulation and attenuation of the HPA axis, Trickett et al. (2011) observed a host of negative psychosocial outcomes for children who had been abused compared to controls. Females with histories of abuse had more than double the rates of teen pregnancy, sexual assault and retraumatization in adulthood, and domestic violence in adulthood (Trickett et al., 2011). They also had 4 times the incidence of suicidal ideation and self-injurious behavior; had higher rates of preterm delivery in adulthood; and experienced impaired cognitive functioning, measured by the Woodcock–Johnson IV (Trickett et al., 2011). Furthermore, significantly more females with histories of abuse met the criteria for obesity (42% vs. 28%). The authors believed that obesity may have been impacted by increased cortisol production during childhood. Trickett et al. cited prior studies that found that high levels of circulating cortisol during childhood influenced the development of adipose tissue, which is associated with abdominal fat (Rosmond, 2003). Finally, females with histories of abuse also experienced accelerated pubertal development and began stages of hormonal and sexual maturation 6 to 8 months earlier on average.

Chronic Stress Pathway

To better understand how cortisol can be so deleterious when overproduced and excreted, we must expand our exploration of epigenetics to now examine the long-term effects of the chronic stress pathway to negative health outcomes. In this section of the chapter, we cover important processes by which the body replaces degraded and dying cells with new ones. We also explore the role of cortisol in this long-term process of nervous system regulation.

DNA methylation has a direct impact on neuronal growth (i.e., the birth of new neurons) and neurotransmission. For the nervous system to function, it must develop new cells to replace old degraded cells that eventually die. The body produces new nerve cells (i.e., neurons) through a process called *neurogenesis.* For those cells to thrive across their life spans, new synaptic connections must be forged as well. The growth of new synaptic connections is known as *synaptogenesis.* Synaptic connections that are underutilized may be winnowed through a process called *synaptic pruning.* Growth factors such as the protein brain-derived neurotrophic factor (BDNF) stimulate the continual growth of new neurons (neurogenesis), whereas the amino acid neurotransmitter glutamate assists in the creation of synaptic connections. The continual growth of new neurons and synapses over time is known as *long-term potentiation* (LTP). The ability of the nervous system to create new synaptic connections is called *neuroplasticity.*

In the absence or reduction of these growth factors, a cell will decay and/or reduce its synaptic connections to the extent that an insufficient number of new cells replace the number of degraded cells. This process is known as *long-term depression* (LTD). Note that LTD is a different term than *persisting major depression* and pertains more to cellular function than to mental health (though, as we shall see, LTD does have a role in mental disorders).

Our environment plays an important role in LTP and LTD processes. Chronic stress has an especially important impact on LTD. When a child experiences a persisting stressor in the environment, such as abuse or neglect or bullying, DNA sequences associated with control of the stress response system are methylated (silenced). This can result in chronically high levels of circulating cortisol (known as hypercortisolism; Guerry & Hastings, 2011). This chronically high cortisol can cause a series of changes that have damaging effects. Hypercortisolism overstimulates and degrades cells, leading to apoptosis (programmed cell death; Sapolsky, 2000a). It also inhibits neurogenesis by inhibiting glutamate receptors and downregulating BDNF (Numakawa, Odaka, & Adachi, 2017). This process has LTD effects, such as fewer action potentials, less receptor signaling, and fewer synaptic connections. Over time, neurons and glia are destroyed more quickly than they can be replaced, which results in a reduction in volume in brain density. For example, amygdala and hippocampal volume is reduced by hypercortisolism (Malykhin & Coupland, 2015; Pagliaccio et al., 2014; Sapolsky, 2000a). Because structures like the amygdala and hippocampus have regulatory control over the stress response system, chronically high levels of cortisol will impair the negative feedback system over time. When this occurs, the brain and body have even less control over the HPA axis, and cortisol production becomes even further dysregulated (Sapolsky, 2000b). This eventually leads to shifting the baseline set point for cortisol secretion, resulting in lasting changes to the homeostatic balance of the autonomic nervous system. Because of these lasting changes to baseline cortisol secretion, researchers have termed this relationship between DNA methylation, chronic stress, downregulated glutamate and BDNF, and LTD the *metaplasticity hypothesis* (Hulme, Jones, & Abraham, 2013; Vose & Stanton, 2017).

The gastrointestinal system is strongly impacted by overproduction of cortisol. Chronic stress is associated with metabolic problems such as obesity (van der Valk, Savas, & van Rossum, 2018) and type 2 diabetes (Harris et al., 2017). Furthermore, almost all immune cells have receptors for cortisol, and chronic cortisol prohibits their functioning in response to infection. This immunosuppression can result in susceptibility to bacterial and viral illness and even increased risk of cancer cell development and promulgation (Dhabhar, 2009). Inflammation also becomes more intense, resulting in cell death and degradation. Chronic inflammation can also cause nerve damage, increasing susceptibility to arthritis, autoimmune diseases (e.g., Crohn's disease, ulcerative colitis), and fibromyalgia.

Major Depression

Experts such as Guerry and Hastings (2011) have argued that the linkage between dysregulation of the HPA axis and major depression is "the most consistent and robust biological finding in psychiatry to date" (p. 137), with an estimated 50% of major depressive episodes linked to chronic stress and HPA hyperactivity. In children, chronic stress is a risk factor for subsequent first episodes of depression (Pagliaccio et al., 2014).

Exposure to chronic stress and DNA methylation of gene sequences associated with BDNF and *NR3C1* appear to influence the development of depressive symptoms and diagnoses (Chen, Meng, Pei, Zheng, & Leng, 2017; Li et al., 2019). Depression results in an 8% to 10% reduction in hippocampal volume and may thus be a risk factor for conditions such as Alzheimer's disease (Malykhin & Coupland, 2015). High circulating cortisol may be the root cause of reductions in hippocampal volume, as cortisol can overstimulate and destroy hippocampal cells. Hypercortisolism also causes persisting inflammatory responses, and proinflammatory cytokines can overstimulate and degrade neurons in the brain. When brain structures are impaired, it further weakens central nervous system inhibitory control over the HPA axis (Sapolsky, 2000b), resulting in even more progressive hypercortisolism. This metaplasticity hypothesis has been used to explain the development of depressive symptoms (Vose & Stanton, 2017).

In summary, the eventual outcomes of a hyperactive HPA axis and chronically high secretion of cortisol are physical and mental health problems. A graphic depiction that summarizes this chronic stress pathway is depicted in Figure 3.4.

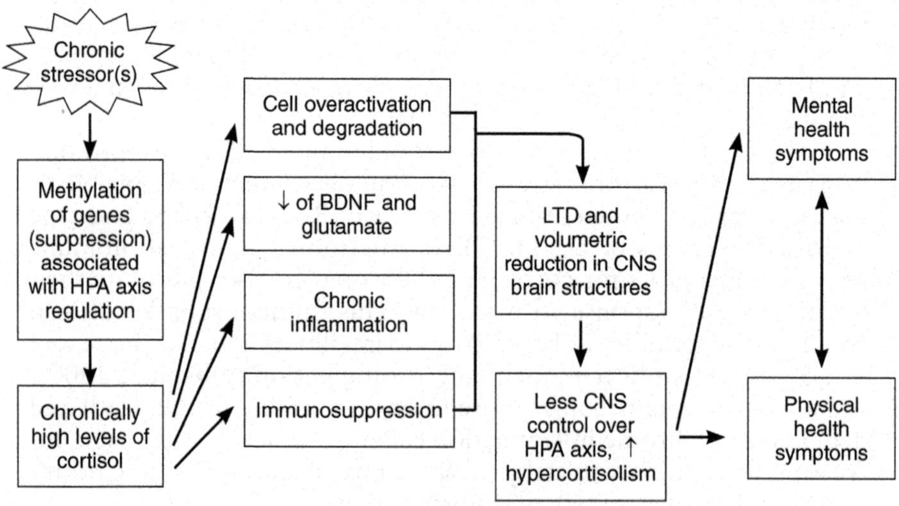

FIGURE 3.4

Chronic Stress Pathway

Note. HPA = hypothalamic-pituitary-adrenal; BDNF = brain-derived neurotropic factor; LTD = long-term depression; CNS = central nervous system.

Sources of Chronic Stress in Childhood

Persisting stressors for children and adolescents include abuse and neglect, bullying, and high-conflict households (e.g., volatile relationships between parents and guardians, domestic violence), to name a few. Felitti and colleagues (1998) explored the impact of adverse childhood experiences on health status and subsequent adult outcomes. The researchers surveyed nearly 10,000 adults, who responded to a survey about their exposure to seven major stressors: (a) psychological abuse, (b) physical abuse, (c) sexual abuse, (d) substance use by household member, (e) depression or suicide attempt by household member, (f) violence toward mother or stepmother, and (g) imprisonment of household member (Felitti et al., 1998).

Nearly two thirds of respondents reported having been exposed to one of the major stressors during childhood, and one quarter reported having been exposed to two or more (Felitti et al., 1998). Several major stressors were relatively common. One in four children had experienced physical abuse (28%), lived in a household with a family member engaging in substance use (27%), and/or lived through parental separation/divorce (23%). One in five children had experienced sexual abuse (21%) or lived in a household with a family member who had a significant mental disorder (19%). A further 15% had experienced emotional neglect, 11% had experienced emotional abuse, and 10% had experienced physical neglect.

The researchers found that childhood experiences of four or more major stressors greatly increased (doubled or even tripled) the risk for alcohol and drug addiction, depression, obesity, sexual promiscuity (i.e., 50 or more sexual partners), sexually transmitted diseases, and suicide attempts. The authors also found a "dose-response" relationship (p. 250) between the number of major stressors and the development of cardiovascular disease and cancer, which means that accumulated major stressors further increased the risk of health conditions (Felitti et al., 1998). The researchers did not find significant differences in exposure to adverse childhood experiences by demographics such as age, sex or gender, race or ethnicity, or education level.

Researchers have proposed a separate diagnostic category for early childhood exposure to chronic stress, arguing that the condition differs from posttraumatic stress (van der Kolk, Ford, & Spinazzola, 2019). A diagnosis of posttraumatic stress requires a traumatic event, in which a person is exposed to serious injury, threatened or actual death, or sexual violence. The stressor categories above would not meet criteria for a traumatic event yet are clearly major stressors that have the potential to trigger chronic stress responses. To better capture the diagnosis of early childhood exposure to chronic stress, researchers such as Bessel van der Kolk have proposed the term *developmental trauma disorder* (van der Kolk et al., 2019).

Implications for Counseling

It is clear from the research that chronic and traumatic stress is a significant risk factor for a series of epigenetic changes that can have profound health consequences. You might be wondering how counselors can intervene. From the studies mentioned in this chapter, several implications can be extracted that could inform counseling practice.

First and foremost, chronic and traumatic stress needs to be reconceptualized as a core issue that can induce presenting symptomatology for clients. When conceptualizing cases and planning counseling interventions, counselors should consider how to intervene to reduce chronic stress, which might be underlying other symptomatology. Chapter 12 provides an overview of a case conceptualization that conceptualizes chronic stress as a root problem.

To examine the potential presence of chronic stress, counselors need to assess for environmental stressors that have the potential for harmful effects beyond questions about traumatic events and abuse or neglect. Counselors should also inquire about ongoing major stressors, including household member depression, substance use, and suicidality; violence toward parents or guardians; and imprisonment of household members (Felitti et al., 1998).

When sources of chronic stress are detected, counselors need to intervene early to prevent problems from occurring. Family intervention and referrals to social supports in the community might be crucial. In the Trickett et al. (2011) study, the researchers noted a concerning trend regarding the intergenerational association of sexual abuse. The females in the study with histories of sexual abuse were far more likely to have mothers with their own histories of sexual abuse (45% vs. 16%). Most of their mothers' sexual abuse (85%) was reported to be interfamilial and to have a similar age of onset (8–9 years of age). The researchers noted that mothers with histories of sexual abuse themselves experienced low social support from their families (Trickett et al., 2011). Thus, counselors should consider additional resources such as support groups for mothers who report low social support. Parent education seems less pressing, as no differences existed in parenting style between mothers who had and had not experienced abuse (Trickett et al., 2011).

When working with children and adolescents with existing stressor-related problems, counselors should consider interventions that are known to actually target dysregulation of the HPA axis and ameliorate its effects. Although counseling itself does not seem to reliably reduce cortisol (Fischer & Cleare, 2017), counselors can integrate lifestyle interventions into counseling, such as improving sleep quality and engaging in aerobic exercise (see Chapter 11 for more information about therapeutic lifestyle change). Researchers have found that a single bout of physical exercise increases BDNF (Venezia, Quinlan, & Roth, 2017) and that sleep is also related to

BDNF production (Schmitt, Holsboer-Trachsler, & Eckert, 2016). Physical exercise increases gray matter volume in the frontal lobe and hippocampus (Erickson et al., 2011) and improves white matter integrity in children (Chaddock-Heyman et al., 2014). See Reflection Question 3.2.

One further consideration is important to mention. Counselors cannot always adequately intervene to assist a client who is facing major stressors without being willing to advocate for changes to the systems that are causing the stressors. For example, children with minority statuses (e.g., racial, ethnic, gender identity, sexual orientation, disability) are more likely than those from majority backgrounds to encounter stressors, such as discrimination, prejudice, oppression, or other forms of social injustice. Counselors will therefore need to consider how to press for changes to systems that best support the growth of children. This is particularly important in regard to the school system, which is the primary system with which all children interact. To assist you in understanding areas of potential advocacy and how best to respond, we provide a case study of advocating in a school setting. See Case Vignette 3.1.

Case Vignette 3.1 Terrence

You are working with an African American first-grade boy named Terrence, who was recently expelled from his elementary school for throwing a chair at a teacher. This was Terrence's first anger incident at school. Terrence feels sad because he misses his twin brother, who is still in the same classroom from which Terrence was expelled. The antecedent to Terrence's aggression was his being forced to sit at another table, away from his twin brother. You learn that Terrence and his twin brother have multiple family members in prison and have lived with multiple extended family members since they were born. The school had only suspended a second-grade boy of Euro-American background a year earlier for similar behavior.

• • •

In this instance, a clear act of injustice occurred. Not only was the expulsion likely inappropriate for a first-time incident, the school chose different responses for students from different ethnic backgrounds.

Reflection Question 3.2

How might this information about hypercortisolism inform your practice as a counselor? Which aspects of your counseling approach might you change?

An expulsion at such a young age can have long-term consequences. Terrence will likely have to attend an alternative school and be permanently separated from his twin brother during the school day. Terrence is experiencing multiple stressors and likely finds some degree of comfort in being close to the only stable person in his life, his twin brother. As the counselor, it would be important for you to contact Terrence's parents or guardians and plan to advocate to the school board for a reconsideration of the expulsion. The teachers at the school may also need some brief information about why Terrence became aggressive that day and his need for closeness with his brother in the school setting.

We recognize that advocacy can be a challenge and takes additional time that is not spent in direct client contact. This time commitment can feel overwhelming to counselors working in community mental health or private practice settings. Advocacy can also be complicated for employees of the school, such as the school counselor, who might feel conflicted about advocating in opposition to the decision of their principal. We recommend consulting with other counselors and professionals when making decisions about complicated situations such as these.

Conclusion

The human body is an incredible organism, capable of adjusting to the demands of the environment at the cellular level. Each cell contains instructions for manufacturing new proteins, which support cell function. A child's environment has a strong influence on which genes are transcribed and translated and which proteins are produced. Methylation (silencing) of certain genetic sequences associated with regulation of the HPA axis creates a multitude of problems that are self-perpetuating. In this chapter, we referred to this process as the *chronic stress pathway.* The outcomes of this pathway permeate into adulthood. Because of the apparent centrality of stress in physical and mental health issues, we proposed in this chapter that chronic stress (hypercortisolism) should be considered a root cause of symptomatology. We described a counseling approach to address these stressors, with consideration for advocacy actions.

Quiz Questions

1. During gene transcription, _____ copies instructions from DNA regarding how to manufacture proteins.
   a. mRNA
   b. tRNA
   c. Ribosome

2. During gene translation, _____ interprets transcribed DNA instructions that will eventually be used to manufacture amino acids (polypeptides).
   a. mRNA
   b. tRNA
   c. Ribosome
3. The chronic stress pathway involves
   a. Methylation, ↓ BDNF, LTD, hypercortisolism
   b. Methylation, ↑ BDNF, LTP, hypercortisolism
   c. Methylation, ↑ DNA, ↓ RNA, immunosuppression

References

Alberts, B., Johnson, A. D., Lewis, J., Morgan, D., Raff, M., Roberts, K., & Walter, P. (2014). *Molecular biology of the cell* (6th ed.). New York, NY: Norton.

Argentieri, M. A., Nagarajan, S., Seddighzadeh, B., Baccarelli, A. A., & Shields, A. E. (2017). Epigenetic pathways in human disease: The impact of DNA methylation on stress-related pathogenesis and current challenges in biomarker development. *EBioMedicine, 18,* 327–350. doi:10.1016/j.ebiom.2017.03.044

Chaddock-Heyman, L., Erickson, K. I., Holtrop, J. L., Voss, M. W., Pontifex, M. B., Raine, L. B., . . . Kramer, A. F. (2014). Aerobic fitness is associated with greater white matter integrity in children. *Frontiers in Human Neuroscience, 8,* 584. doi:10.3389/fnhum.2014.00584

Chen, D., Meng, L., Pei, F., Zheng, Y., & Leng, J. (2017). A review of DNA methylation in depression. *Journal of Clinical Neuroscience, 43,* 39–46. doi:10.1016/j.jocn.2017.05.022

Council for Accreditation of Counseling and Related Educational Programs. (2015). *2016 CACREP standards.* Alexandria, VA: Author.

Dhabhar, F. S. (2009). Enhancing versus suppressive effects of stress on immune function: Implications for immunoprotection and immunopathology. *Neuroimmunomodulation, 16,* 300–317. doi:10.1159/000216188

Erickson, K., Voss, M. W., Prakash, R. S., Basak, C., Szabo, A., Chaddock, L., . . . Kramer, A. F. (2011). Exercise training increases size of hippocampus and improves memory. *Proceedings of the National Academy of Sciences, USA, 108,* 3017–3022. doi:10.1073/pnas.1015950108

Felitti, V. J., Anda, R. F., Nordenberg, D., Williamson, D. F., Spitz, A. M., Edwards, V., . . . Marks, J. S. (1998). Relationship of childhood abuse and household dysfunction to many of the leading causes of death in adults: The adverse childhood events study. *American Journal of Preventive Medicine, 14,* 245–258. doi:10.1016/S0749-3797(98)00017-8

Fischer, S., & Cleare, A. J. (2017). Cortisol as a predictor of psychological therapy response in anxiety disorders: Systematic review and meta-analysis. *Journal of Anxiety Disorders, 47,* 60–68. doi:10.1016/j.janxdis.2017.02.007

Fraga, M. F., Ballestar, E., Paz, M. F., Ropero, S., Setien, F., Ballestar, M. L., . . . Esteller, M. (2005). Epigenetic differences arise during the lifetime of monozygotic twins. *Proceedings of the National Academy of Sciences, USA, 102,* 10604–10609. doi:10.1073/pnas.0500398102

Guerry, J. D., & Hastings, P. D. (2011). In search of HPA axis dysregulation in child and adolescent depression. *Clinical Child and Family Psychology Review, 14,* 135–160. doi:10.1007/s10567-011-0084-5

Harris, M. L., Oldmeadow, C., Hure, A., Luu, J., Loxton, D., & Attia, J. (2017). Stress increases the risk of type 2 diabetes onset in women: A 12-year longitudinal study using causal modelling. *PLoS ONE, 12,* e0172126. doi:10.1371/journal.pone.0172126

Heard, E., & Martienssen, R. A. (2014). Transgenerational epigenetic inheritance: Myths and mechanisms. *Cell, 157,* 95–109. doi:10.1016/j.cell.2014.02.045

Hulme, S. R., Jones, O. D., & Abraham, W. C. (2013). Emerging roles of metaplasticity in behaviour and disease. *Trends in Neurosciences, 36,* 353–362. doi:10.1016/j.tins.2013.03.007

Jokinen, J., Boström, A. E., Dadfar, A., Ciuculete, D. M., Chatzittofis, A., Åsberg, M., & Schiöth, H. B. (2017). Epigenetic changes of the CRH gene are related to severity of suicide attempt and a general psychiatric score for adolescents. *EBioMedicine, 27,* 123–133. doi:10.1016/j.ebiom.2017.12.018

Li, M., D'Arcy, C., Li, X., Zhang, T., Joober, R., & Meng, X. (2019). What do DNA methylation studies tell us about depression? A systematic review. *Translational Psychiatry, 9,* 68. doi:10.1038/s41398-019-0412-y

Malykhin, N. V., & Coupland, N. J. (2015). Hippocampal neuroplasticity in major depressive disorder. *Neuroscience, 309,* 200–213. doi:10.1016/j.neuroscience.2015.04.047

Meaney, M. J., & Szyf, M. (2005). Environmental programming of stress responses through DNA methylation: Life at the interface between a dynamic environment and fixed genome. *Dialogues in Clinical Neurosciences, 7,* 103–123.

Miller, G. E., Chen, E., & Zhou, E. S. (2007). If it goes up, must it come down? Chronic stress and the hypothalamic-pituitary-adrenocortical axis in humans. *Psychological Bulletin, 133,* 25–45. doi:10.1037/0033-2909.133.1.25

National Human Genome Research Institute. (n.d.). *Introduction to genomics.* Retrieved from https://www.genome.gov/About-Genomics/Introduction-to-Genomics

National Institutes of Health. (2019, July). *Genetics home reference.* Retrieved from https://ghr.nlm.nih.gov/

Numakawa, T., Odaka, H., & Adachi, N. (2017). Actions of brain-derived neurotrophic factor and glucocorticoid stress in neurogenesis. *International Journal of Molecular Sciences, 18,* 2312. doi:10.3390/ijms18112312

Pagliaccio, D., Luby, J. L., Bogdan, R., Agrawal, A., Gaffrey, M. S., Belden, A. C., . . . Barch, D. M. (2014). Stress-system genes and life stress predict cortisol levels and amygdala and hippocampal volumes in children. *Neuropsychopharmacology, 39,* 1245–1253. doi:10.1038/npp.2013.327

Raison, C. L., & Miller, A. H. (2003). When not enough is too much: The role of insufficient glucocorticoid signaling in the pathophysiology of stress related disorders. *American Journal of Psychiatry, 160,* 1554–1565. doi:10.1176/appi.ajp.160.9.1554

Romens, S. E., McDonald, J., Svaren, J., & Pollak, S. D. (2015). Associations between early life stress and gene methylation in children. *Child Development, 86,* 303–309. doi:10.1111/cdev.12270

Rosmond, R. (2003). Stress induced disturbances of the HPA axis: A pathway to type 2 diabetes? *Medical Science Monitor, 9,* 35–39.

Sapolsky, R. M. (2000a). Glucocorticoids and hippocampal atrophy in neuropsychiatric disorders. *Archives of General Psychiatry, 57,* 925–935. doi:10.1001/archpsyc.57.10.925

Sapolsky, R. M. (2000b). The possibility of neurotoxicity in the hippocampus in major depression: A primer on neuron death. *Biological Psychiatry, 48,* 755–765. doi:10.1016/S0006-3223(00)00971-9

Schmitt, K., Holsboer-Trachsler, E., & Eckert, A. (2016). BDNF in sleep, insomnia, and sleep deprivation. *Annals of Medicine, 48,* 42–51. doi:10.3109/07853890.2015.1131327

Shenk, C. E., Noll, J. G., Putnam, F. W., & Trickett, P. K. (2010). A prospective examination of the role of childhood sexual abuse and physiological asymmetry in the development of psychopathology. *Child Abuse & Neglect, 34,* 752–761. doi:10.1016/j.chiabu.2010.02.010

Susman, E. J. (2006). Psychobiology of persistent antisocial behavior: Stress, early vulnerabilities and the attenuation hypothesis. *Neuroscience & Biobehavioral Reviews, 30,* 376–389. doi:10.1016/j.neubiorev.2005.08.002

Trickett, P. K., Noll, J. G., & Putnam, F. W. (2011). The impact of sexual abuse on female development: Lessons from a multigenerational, longitudinal research study. *Development and Psychopathology, 23,* 453–476. doi:10.1017/S0954579411000174

van der Kolk, B., Ford, J. D., & Spinazzola, J. (2019). Comorbidity of developmental trauma disorder (DTD) and post-traumatic stress disorder (PTSD): Findings from the DTD field trial. *European Journal of Psychotraumatology, 10,* 1562841. doi:10.1080/20008198.2018.1562841 van der Valk, E. S., Savas, M., & van Rossum, E. (2018). Stress and obesity: Are there more susceptible individuals? *Current Obesity Reports, 7,* 193–203. doi:10.1007/s13679-018-0306-y

Venezia, A. C., Quinlan, E., & Roth, S. M. (2017). A single bout of exercise increases hippocampal BDNF: Influence of chronic exercise and noradrenaline. *Genes, Brain, and Behavior, 16,* 800–811. doi:10.1111/gbb.12394

Vose, L. R., & Stanton, P. K. (2017). Synaptic plasticity, metaplasticity, and depression. *Current Neuropharmacology, 15,* 71–86. doi:10.2174/1570159X14666160202121111

Yehuda, R., Daskalakis, N. P., Bierer, L. M., Bader, H. N., Klengel, T., Holsboer, F., & Binder, E. B. (2016). Holocaust exposure induced intergenerational effects on FKBP5 methylation. *Biological Psychiatry, 80,* 372–380. doi:10.1016/j.biopsych.2015.08.005

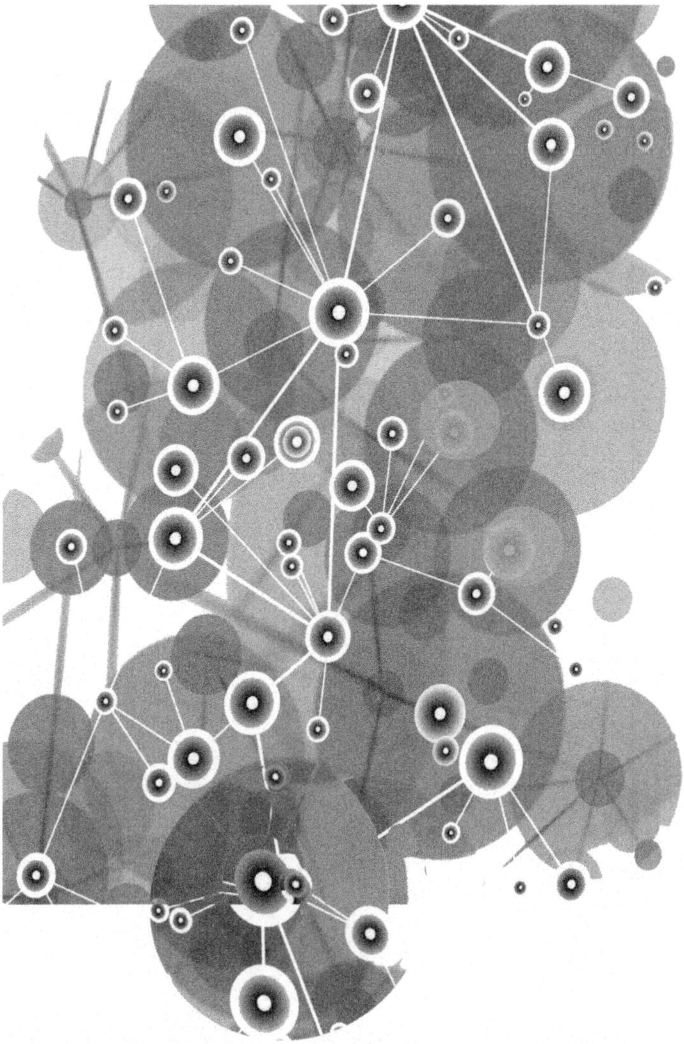

Section II
Childhood

Chapter 4

Neurophysiological and Social Development During Childhood

Key Concepts

- Fetal and infant development
- Congenital problems
- Oxytocin and bonding
- Myelination during childhood
- Synaptic pruning during childhood
- Play behavior

Aligned 2016 CACREP Standards

Standard 2.F.3.b. Theories of learning
Standard 2.F.3.c. Theories of normal and abnormal personality development
Standard 2.F.3.e. Biological, neurological, and physiological factors that affect human development, functioning, and behavior
Standard 2.F.3.f. Systemic and environmental factors that affect human development, functioning, and behavior

• • •

In prior chapters, we reviewed the nervous system and cellular function. A next step in learning foundational information about childhood and adolescence is examining the developmental process with regard to neurophysiological and social development. In this chapter, we build on prior information from Chapters 2 and 3 to understand this developmental process, starting at conception (i.e., fertilization) and extending through the elementary years. We thus adhere to our definition of *childhood* stated in the Preface as encompassing 0 to 11 years of age, although we also want to recognize that some children mature to adolescence earlier than age 11.

Human growth and development is a large topic area, and we were selective in the information we decided to cover in this chapter. Because this text is focused on applied and practical information pertinent to counseling, we chose to focus on neurodevelopmental information that would be useful to the counseling process and inform subsequent chapters. We do not cover typical theories of human development (e.g., Erik Erikson, Jean Piaget) in this chapter. We also note that although identity development begins in childhood, we cover ethnic, gender, and sexual identity development in Chapter 8, on adolescent development.

As with prior chapters, we recommend that you consult the glossary to clarify the meaning of unfamiliar terminology. In writing this chapter, we aquired information from the National Institute of Child Health and Human Development (2017) and the Centers for Disease Control and Prevention (CDC; 2018a, 2018b, 2019). We also consulted the following texts when writing this chapter: *Developmental Neuroscience* by Fahrbach (2013), *Developmental Cognitive Neuroscience: An Introduction* (4th ed.) by Johnson and de Haan (2015), and *Fundamentals of Human Neuropsychology* (7th ed.) by Kolb and Whishaw (2015). We recommend these texts if you want to learn more about child neural development.

Fetal Development

During the embryonic period, a special organ forms in the uterus called the *placenta*. The placenta not only provides the fetus with oxygen and nutrients via the umbilical cord and attempts to filter out harmful substances but also secretes estrogens, progesterone, and human chorionic gonadotropin hormone. This latter hormone reduces the mother's immune function so that the fetus is not rejected as a foreign organism. In addition, human chorionic gonadotropin secretes human placental lactogen, which prepares the mother's breasts for lactation.

The development of the nervous system is one of the first processes to begin upon fertilization and one of the last to be completed following delivery. By the third week of gestation, the neural plate folds to form a neural groove before transitioning into the neural tube. Within the neural tube, neurons and glia begin to form. The neural tube will eventually become the brain and spinal cord (i.e., the central nervous system). By Week 5, several important neural tube structures have developed that will eventually become important structures in the adult brain. The telencephalon will become major structures of the cerebrum, including the amygdala, hippocampus, frontal cortex, hypothalamus, and pituitary gland; the diencephalon will become the thalamus and pineal gland; the mesencephalon will become the cerebellum; and the myelencephalon will become the medulla oblongata. These neural tube structures and others are depicted in Figure 4.1.

During the second trimester, a few significant developments occur. By Week 20, the hypothalamic-pituitary-adrenal axis is established. The thyroid hormonal system soon follows, which assists with the development of the fetus's metabolism. The baby's muscular system develops to the extent that the mother can feel kicks from the fetus. In the third trimester, the brain increases fourfold in size, and brain tissue volume likewise increases in a steady linear fashion as new neurons and glia (i.e., gray matter) are generated (Glass et al., 2015).

Congenital Problems

Fetal, newborn, and infant development are critical periods because events during these stages of development can have profound and lasting impacts. Multiple factors can result in congenital problems, such as the age of the parents, nutritional and vitamin deficiencies, infections, the presence of toxins, and side effects of medication.

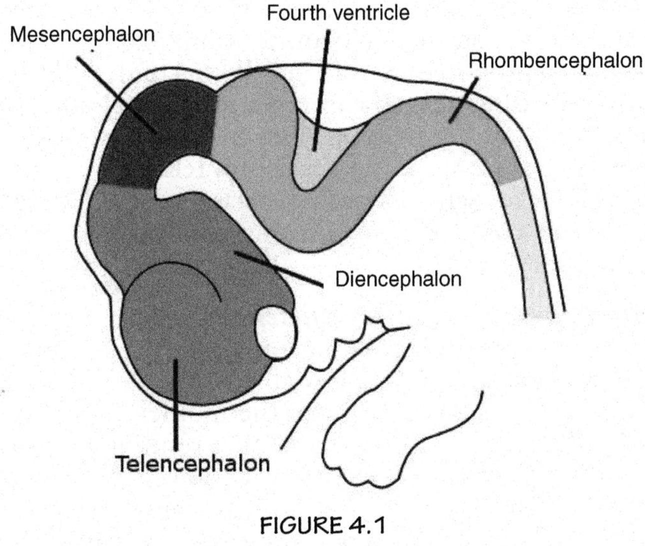

FIGURE 4.1

Neural Tube at Six Weeks' Gestation

Note. From Kurzon, 2007. In Wikimedia Commons.

Age of the Parents

Parental age has been associated with risk for congenital problems. Parents in the United States are conceiving children at older ages. The birth rate for women 40 to 44 years of age has more than doubled since 1990 (Matthews & Hamilton, 2014). This increase in age is associated with a greater risk for congenital problems in the fetus. In an older study from 2002, a mother's risk of conceiving a child with Down syndrome increased fourfold between 35 and 40 years of age and tenfold between 35 and 45 years of age (Morris, Mutton, & Alberman, 2002). In a large study of 5.8 million children from five countries that examined the relationship between parental age and a child's development of autism, fathers older than 50 were 66% more likely to conceive a child with autism compared to fathers ages 20 to 29 (Sandin et al., 2016). A 15% increase in risk was observed for mothers older than 50, and an 18% increase in risk was found for mothers younger than 20 years old. These risk ratios were found when the researchers controlled for confounding factors and even the age of the other parent. In the study, it appeared that risk did not increase significantly until parents were older than 40 years of age. Note that other hypothesized factors (e.g., vaccinations) show no evidence of a causal link to these developmental disabilities (Hviid, Hansen, Frisch, & Melbye, 2019).

The exact mechanism of the effect of parental age on congenital problems is unknown. Several hypotheses have been proposed. First, the effect of parental age could be caused by DNA copy errors. Sperm cells will have copied 600 times by age 40 compared to 200 times at age 20 (Malaspina, Gilman, & Kranz, 2015). Similar copy errors have been proposed in ovarian cells. Second, DNA mutations occur with increasing age. For example, sperm telomeres increase in length with age rather than decrease in length as is true of other cells (Sharma et al., 2015). Longer sperm telomere length appears to be a risk factor for schizophrenia (Malaspina et al., 2014). Third, epigenetic errors could account for this age effect (Perrin, Brown, & Malaspina, 2007).

Nutritional and Vitamin Deficiencies

In utero, fetal growth and development is influenced by the mother's diet and nutrition. Folic acid is essential to the development of the brain and spinal cord, and deficits in the mother's folate intake can result in significant neural tube defects that result in paralysis, vision and hearing loss, intellectual disability, and even death in the baby (CDC, 2018b). The fetus also needs other vitamins to develop, such as iron, vitamin B12, and so on. For these reasons, a prenatal vitamin supplement is often recommended (National Institute of Child Health and Human Development, 2017).

Infections

Viral infections such as rubella, toxoplasmosis, and Zika virus can cause a reduction in head size known as *microcephaly*, which is associated with severe neurodevelopmental abnormalities and intellectual disability (CDC, 2018a). Zika virus gained attention because no vaccine exists, and it can be transmitted through mosquito bites and through sexual intercourse.

Toxins

Lead is a known neurotoxin. Exposure to lead in utero can increase the risk of miscarriage, low birth weight, stillbirth, and premature birth. It can also cause intellectual impairment, developmental disorders, and impulse control problems. At the cellular level, lead is able to cross the blood-brain barrier rapidly and has neurotoxic actions that include apoptosis (programmed cell death) and interference with myelination during early childhood (Sanders, Liu, Buchner, & Tchounwou, 2009). Pregnant mothers and children may be exposed to lead through corroded water pipes or lead paint in their environment.

Exposure of the fetus or newborn to alcohol via breastfeeding can lead to fetal alcohol spectrum issues, such as intellectual and developmental disabilities, abnormal facial features, and problems with organ function. Current research indicates that no amount of exposure to alcohol during pregnancy is safe for the fetus. Although brain damage is dose dependent (i.e., it worsens as alcohol consumption increases), even a small amount of exposure to alcohol can cause changes to brain structure (Eckstrand et al., 2012). Research has found that exposure to alcohol during pregnancy reduces gray matter volume in the cingulate cortex, frontal lobe, temporal lobe, and caudate nucleus (Eckstrand et al., 2012). As we learned in Chapter 2, these brain regions are associated with executive functioning, attention, and memory.

Smoking or consuming tobacco and cannabis can also have significant negative effects on the fetus, such as doubling the risk of stillbirth. Even passive exposure to tobacco (i.e., exposure to secondhand smoke) doubles the risk of stillbirth and increases the risk of premature birth and low birth weight (Khader, Al-Akour, Alzubi, & Lataifeh, 2011). Nicotine readily crosses the placenta, and concentrations of nicotine can be 15% higher in the placenta than in the mother (Wickström, 2007). Nicotine is also excreted through breastmilk, so the baby will be exposed even if the mother smokes or consumes tobacco away from the newborn. Cannabis use has been associated with low birth weight alongside lasting deficits in attention, impulse control, and memory (Grant, Petroff, Isoherranen, Stella, & Burbacher, 2018). Inhalation of tobacco and cannabis smoke is problematic given the other toxins involved, such as carbon monoxide.

Labor and Delivery

Several complications can occur during pregnancy, labor, and delivery. Detailing the full extent of these is beyond the scope of this chapter, but a few are worth mentioning. Preterm birth is fairly common in the United States, affecting 11.5% of all births (Glass et al., 2015). Expected birth terms are typically 37–42 weeks' gestation. Births before 37 weeks' gestation are considered premature. *Extremely premature birth* is defined as birth before 28 weeks' gestation. The estimated age of viability, defined as an approximately 50% likelihood of survival, is considered to be birth at 23 to 24 weeks (Glass et al., 2015). Neonatal care is continually improving, and the age of viability has reduced over time.

Although newborns are better able to survive and thrive at earlier ages of premature delivery, extremely premature birth is associated with increased risk of persisting cognitive deficits. In a large study of nearly 900 children, approximately one quarter of children who were born at or before 28 weeks had significant cognitive deficits at 10 years of age (Kuban et al., 2016). Males appear to be at greatest risk (Kuban et al., 2016). Extremely premature infants are more likely to have impairments in executive function with regard to impulse control, cognitive flexibility, planning and organizational ability, and working memory (Luu, Ment, Allan, Schneider, & Vohr, 2011). These impairments resemble core symptoms of attention-deficit/hyperactivity disorder (ADHD), and the incidence of ADHD is 3 times higher in extremely premature infants than children born at term (Franz et al., 2018). These neurological impairments are believed to be caused by missed opportunities for brain development in the third trimester (remember, the brain increases fourfold in size in the third trimester).

Infant Development

During the first 3 months after delivery, a series of developmental changes occur as the newborn adjusts to the external world. The infant period is proposed to last from birth to 24 months after delivery, with the first month called the *neonate stage*. During this time, the immune system develops and the cerebellum triples in size, associated with rapid growth in motor abilities. The hippocampus also develops during the first 4 months, resulting in improvements to facial recognition (Farroni, Massaccesi, Menon, & Johnson, 2007). At approximately 3 years of age, gut microbiota stabilize. At this stage of development, the bacterial composition of the child's gut resembles that of the adult gut (Bokulich et al., 2016).

Attachment

During the first years of life, infants largely learn via their relationships with their caregivers. For example, infants learn to mimic vocal sounds and tones from their parents and guardians. Because their environment is new and fraught with potentially threatening stimuli, infants also learn to navigate and explore their environment while relying on their caregivers to provide protection and support. Attachment to caregivers is thus an essential survival mechanism during early childhood.

The neuropeptide oxytocin has an important role in the bonding of parents or caregivers and children during pregnancy and the first year of life. It is broadly thought of as a bonding chemical that facilitates close relationships and associated feelings of trust, intimacy, and empathy (Feldman, Gordon, & Zagoory-Sharon, 2011; Hurlemann et al., 2010). Oxytocin is also involved in parent-infant synchrony (or attuned emotional behaviors), such as gaze, facial expression, and touch (Feldman et al., 2011). It seems that physical touch, such as being held and breastfeeding, are particularly important antecedents to oxytocin release (Feldman et al., 2011).

Oxytocin is produced by the hypothalamus and projects to (i.e., has directional neural pathways with) the nucleus accumbens and the pituitary gland (Ross & Young, 2009). Oxytocin receptors are also located in the amygdala, which is important given the calming and soothing effect of oxytocin in response to anxiety and fear (Kirsch et al., 2005; Knobloch et al., 2012). Oxytocin inhibits the release of adrenocorticotropic hormone by the pituitary gland and thus can downregulate the stress response in the hypothalamic-pituitary-adrenal axis. When infants are upset or frightened, it is fairly common for them to seek the comfort of their parents. A child's bonding with their caregiver results in the release of oxytocin, which can help assuage fear activation and stress response. It is interesting that the secretion of oxytocin seems to be influenced by novel interactions. Oxytocin levels are higher in mothers who interact with other unfamiliar children than in mothers who interact with their own children (Bick & Dozier, 2010).

Sex differences exist in response to the secretion of oxytocin. Females seem to have greater activation of the amygdala on receiving oxytocin compared to males, which is believed to be caused by oxytocin's interaction with estrogen (Lischke et al., 2012). Estrogen enhances the secretion of oxytocin and binding to receptors in the amygdala (Lischke et al., 2012). In males, testosterone suppresses oxytocin (Okabe, Kitano, Nagasawa, Mogi, & Kikusui, 2013). Okabe et al. (2013) proposed that testosterone's suppression of oxytocin is a function of evolution, as oxytocin is associated with empathy responses that may compromise activities such as hunting and attacking threats in the environment.

Animal studies have found that low secretion of oxytocin has profound effects on social behavior. Studies that have replaced genes associated with oxytocin receptors with nongenetic DNA in mice (sometimes referred to as ***knockout studies***) have found impaired recognition of others, increased aggression, and impaired interaction between rat offspring and their mothers (Nishimori et al., 2008). Although it is unethical to replace human genetic sequences, these behaviors are also observed in humans who have oxytocin deficits. For example, a meta-analysis of 16 studies found significant changes and mutations to oxytocin receptor genes in children with autism compared to controls (LoParo & Waldman, 2015). Social impairments are a central symptom cluster of autism, and thus oxytocin receptor dysfunction might be a potential biomarker of the disorder (LoParo & Waldman, 2015). Oxytocin also appears to have antidepressant effects in animal studies, and some researchers have proposed that a lack of parental bonding and oxytocin might be a pathway to clinical depression later in life (McQuaid, McInnis, Abizaid, & Anisman, 2014). See Reflection Question 4.1.

Neural and Cognitive Development During Infancy and Early Childhood

The brain develops at a rapid pace during the first years of life. By approximately 2 years of age, all of the major brain structures (e.g., structures of the subcortex and cerebral cortex) resemble those of the adult brain (Johnson & de Haan, 2015). Neuronal growth (i.e., neurogenesis) is fastest during the fetal stage (Johnson & de Haan, 2015). After birth, the brain experiences tremendous growth in synaptic connections (synaptogenesis). In addition, there is substantial growth in the myelination of these neurons. You may recall that the fatty myelin sheath assists with electrical conduction, or the speed with which electrical messages can be passed within cells. As a result of synaptogenesis and myelination, the connections between neurons become more numerous and messages are passed more quickly. Dendrites also begin to branch out and develop more receptors. Figure 4.2 depicts this neural developmental process.

Neural development during early childhood helps us understand why infants become more adept at a number of tasks over time. In regard to motor neurons and motor movement, infants become able to grab objects, move their facial muscles to make sounds and words, crawl, and walk on two feet. In regard to sensory development, infants become better able to see longer distances as they develop and differentiate sensory input, such as identifying different smells. Children also begin to develop more complicated higher order cognitive functions, such as learning sequences (e.g., bedtime routines), developing

Reflection Question 4.1

How might oxytocin play a role in the counseling relationship?

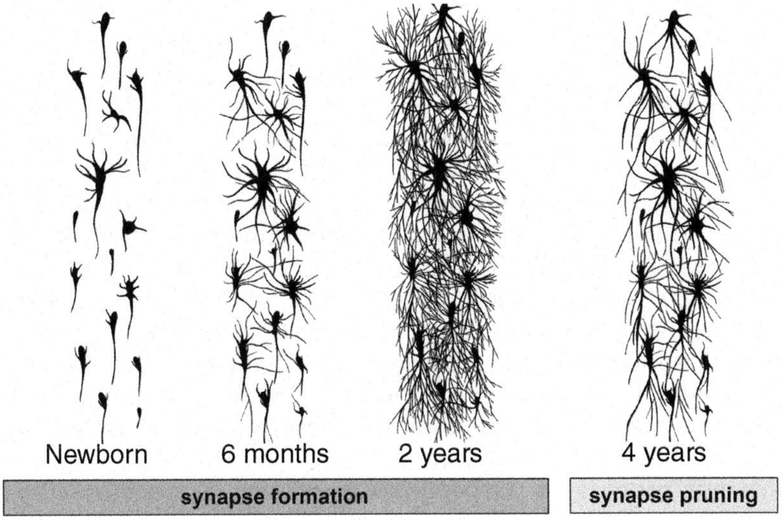

FIGURE 4.2

Synapse Formation and Pruning

Note. From Rachel Chaney, illustrator. Used by permission.

and expressing language, and using declarative memory retrieval (e.g., requesting objects they played with several days before).

Not all areas of the central nervous system myelinate at the same rate. Myelination in the brain tends to develop in a back-to-front direction, with neurons associated with sensory and motor functions myelinating more quickly than areas of the brain associated with prefrontal function (Casey, Tottenham, Liston, & Durston, 2005; Johnson & de Haan, 2015). Myelination of the sensorimotor cortex is largely complete by the second year, whereas myelination of the prefrontal cortex lasts through early adulthood (i.e., until a person is in their 20s). This slow development of the prefrontal cortex and associated executive functioning helps us understand why young children have difficulty with frustration tolerance and impulse control.

The sensorimotor cortex develops before the prefrontal cortex because infants must learn to communicate when they are hungry and need to feed, among other functions. The infant's cry for nourishment is an essential survival function and does not require primary activation of the prefrontal cortex. In contrast, imagine an infant who has an adult-like cognitive ability for rational thought at birth but is unable to see their caregiver, unable to call out when hungry, and so on. The infant's survival would be under threat! Thus, it is important that the parts of the nervous system that are associated with basic sensorimotor function develop first.

Synaptic Pruning

By approximately the end of the second year, the child has the most synaptic connections they will ever have during their lifetime (Johnson & de Haan, 2015). The high number of synaptic connections enable the child to learn tasks at a rapid pace. Children at this age have more synaptic connections than they functionally need. Synaptic connections are therefore eliminated (pruned). The number of neurotransmitters that are produced and excreted also reduces during this period (Johnson & de Haan, 2015). By the time a child reaches 10 years of age, 50% of their synapses will have been eliminated (Kolb & Whishaw, 2015). Synaptic pruning is experience dependent, which means that synaptic connections that are not activated through a child's interactions with the environment are pruned (Kolb & Whishaw, 2015). Thus, the synapses that are eliminated will differ between individual children based on their experiences. Microglia have an important role in synaptic pruning, as they engulf synapses via phagocytosis (Shafer et al., 2012). Figure 4.2 visualizes the developmental trajectory of synaptic pruning.

Autism has been associated with reductions in synaptic pruning and an increase in the density of dendritic spines (i.e., more receptors; Tang et al., 2014). In a study by Tang and colleagues (2014), typically developing adolescents had 41% fewer synapses than typically developing infants, whereas adolescents with autism had only 16% fewer synapses than infants with autism. It appears that synaptic pruning is essential to healthy functioning of the central nervous system, and a preponderance of synapses can result in overcommunication between brain structures, which creates confusion and noise within the brain (Tang et al., 2014). In the study, children with autism also appeared to have higher than average numbers of degraded and older neurons, a marker of problems with glia function (Tang et al., 2014).

Childhood

After infancy, children continue to seek nurturance, protection, and support from their parents and guardians as they further explore the world around them and yearn for some degree of independence. Children lean on early attachment bonds that they forged with their caregivers during infancy. At this stage, children develop cooperative play skills and enjoy playing with caregivers and peers. Even during independent activity, children will often seek attention from their caregivers. Caregivers at this stage often balance attentively supporting their child's independent activities with intervening to address problems that the child cannot resolve without assistance. Because children continue to need guidance and direction at times, parents and guardians take a fairly active role during early childhood. For example, a child might be unable to clean up a spill without assistance or might need guidance in resolving a peer conflict.

The needs of the child will change with age, as the child matures and develops. In this section, we review key factors in early child development, such as the role of play, sibling relationships, and early school experiences.

The Role of Play in Child Development

During early childhood, play behavior has a central role in child development (Ginsberg & Committee on Communications, 2007). In rats, play behavior activates the prefrontal cortex and striatum, which are associated with cognition, motivation, and conditioned reward responses (Van Kerkhof, Damsteegt, Trezza, Voorn, & Vanderschuren, 2013). Play also facilitates transcription of brain-derived neurotrophic factor in the amygdala and dorsolateral prefrontal cortex (Gordon, Burke, Akil, Watson, & Panksepp, 2003). Accordingly, young children often process their emotional experiences through play. Children benefit most from unstructured and self-directed play, which facilitates creativity and mental processing (Ginsberg & Committee on Communications, 2007). In school settings, play helps children transition into a more structured environment and develop academic readiness skills (Blanco, Ray, & Holliman, 2012). Play with other children also facilitates social skills such as sharing, negotiation, conflict resolution, and self-advocacy (Blanco et al., 2012). Play with caregivers also grants an opportunity for the adult caregiver to gain insights into the child's inner world (Ginsberg & Committee on Communications, 2007). Playing together is a healthy method of communicating to children that their caregivers are attentive to them and care about their perspectives. Play is so crucial to child development that Ginsberg and Committee on Communications (2007) cautioned parents and guardians to limit access to technology (e.g., screen time) and to structure the daily household routine so that adult caregivers have ample time for unstructured play with their children.

Impairments in play skills have important effects on the overall development of social skills and communication (Lang et al., 2010). For example, children with autism often experience deficits in symbolic or imaginative play while also engaging in repetitive and self-stimulatory behavior that can interrupt their ability to fully engage in play (Lang et al., 2010). Children with autism may need assistance developing play skills, which may serve as a building block for scaffolding subsequent social skills, such as attending to and learning social cues. Early intervention seems critical, as play behavior seems to be associated with the quality of the interaction between the caregiver and the child with autism (Naber et al., 2008). Play skills are best taught through behavioral techniques (Wong et al., 2015), which are examined in a subsequent chapter.

Sibling Relationships

More than 80% of children live in households with other siblings, slightly higher than the percentage of children who live in a household with a father figure (McHale, Updegraff, Whiteman, 2012). Younger siblings often learn from their older siblings, who serve as social role models (McHale et al., 2012). A child's interaction with their siblings can have an important role in their development of self-regulation. Padilla-Walker, Harper, and Jensen (2010) found that positive sibling perceptions were associated with longitudinal self-regulation and prosocial behavior and were a protective factor against externalizing behavior problems (e.g., aggression). In contrast, sibling hostility has been associated with internalizing problems, such as anxiety and depression (Campione-Barr, Greer, & Kruse, 2013; Padilla-Walker et al., 2010). Siblings of children with developmental disabilities such as autism appear to be at heightened risk for social and behavioral problems (Orsmond & Seltzer, 2007). Counselors will at times work with child adjustment issues related to sibling relationships. It can sometimes be helpful to include siblings in the counseling process to work through relational conflict. In-home counseling can be especially facilitative in this regard.

Academics and School Experiences

School serves a variety of functions for children. Not only does school assist children in developing linguistic, mathematics, and science knowledge and skills, it can also serve as a facilitator of peer interaction and social skills development. In school, children learn to work cooperatively, develop patience, and navigate difficult relationships (Ginsberg & Committee on Communications, 2007).

Elementary school can also bring attention to problems that are less pronounced in the home environment, such as difficulty attending to tasks for extended periods and trouble sitting still. Elementary school is often the time when neurodevelopmental issues such as ADHD are first assessed. In the next chapter, we explore controversies related to the diagnosis of ADHD in children. Some children may need accommodations to reach their academic potential, and we recommend that counselors have sound knowledge of the special education system and eligibility process in the state where they are practicing. In our experience, families often need guidance in accessing school-based services and advocating for their child. We recommend that counselors in clinical settings develop relationships with school counselors to better understand the services provided in schools and the eligibility process. See Reflection Question 4.2.

Reflection Question 4.2

What do you currently know about eligibility for special education services and the types of services that are provided in schools? What gaps in your knowledge are you aware of?

Conclusion

Counselors can benefit from a working knowledge of neurophysiological and social development to comprehensively conceptualize early childhood experiences and problems that arise. In this chapter, we learned that children will likely benefit from play-based activities, need an approach that affirms and strengthens caregiver bonds and attachments, and require the counselor's understanding that they will not have developed the prefrontal functioning to benefit from traditional insight-oriented talk therapy that requires substantial frustration tolerance. We also learned that preventing congenital problems (to the extent possible) is important, as many congenital issues persist throughout childhood into adulthood if acquired. In subsequent chapters, we introduce several counseling approaches for working with children, including play-based creative approaches and behavioral interventions.

Quiz Questions

1. How much exposure to alcohol is safe (i.e., has no risk of harmful effects) for a fetus and newborn?
   a. None
   b. 1 unit during the third trimester only
   c. 1 unit during breastfeeding only
2. Oxytocin is most likely to be excreted during which of the following activities?
   a. Cooing at the infant
   b. Playing peek-a-boo with the infant
   c. Holding and cuddling the infant
3. Autism is associated with
   a. Reductions in synaptic pruning and greater density of dendritic spines
   b. Dysfunction in oxytocin receptors
   c. Both a and b

References

Bick, J., & Dozier, M. (2010). Mothers' and children's concentrations of oxytocin following close, physical interactions with biological and non-biological children. *Developmental Psychobiology, 52,* 100–107. doi:10.1002/dev.20411

Blanco, P. J., Ray, D. C., & Holliman, R. (2012). Long-term child centered play therapy and academic achievement of children: A follow-up study. *International Journal of Play Therapy, 21,* 1–13. doi:10.1037/a0026932

Bokulich, N. A., Chung, J., Battaglia, T., Henderson, N., Jay, M., Li, H., . . . Blaser, M. J. (2016). Antibiotics, birth mode, and diet shape microbiome maturation during early life. *Scientific Translations of Medicine, 8,* 343ra82. doi:10.1126/scitranslmed.aad7121

Campione-Barr, N., Greer, K. B., & Kruse, A. (2013). Differential associations between domains of sibling conflict and adolescent emotional adjustment. *Child Development, 84,* 938–954. doi:10.1111/cdev.12022

Casey, B. J., Tottenham, N., Liston, C., & Durston, S. (2005). Imaging the developing brain: What have we learned about cognitive development? *Trends in Cognitive Sciences, 9,* 104–110. doi:10.1016/j.tics.2005.01.011

Centers for Disease Control and Prevention. (2018a, January). *Facts about microcephaly.* Retrieved from https://www.cdc.gov/ncbddd/birthdefects/microcephaly.html

Centers for Disease Control and Prevention. (2018b, January). *Planning for pregnancy.* Retrieved from https://www.cdc.gov/preconception/planning.html

Centers for Disease Control and Prevention. (2019, March). *Basics about FASDs.* Retrieved from https://www.cdc.gov/ncbddd/fasd/facts.html

Council for Accreditation of Counseling and Related Educational Programs. (2015). *2016 CACREP standards.* Alexandria, VA: Author.

Eckstrand, K. L., Ding, Z., Dodge, N. C., Cowan, R. L., Jacobson, J. L., Jacobson, S. W., & Avison, M. J. (2012). Persistent dose-dependent changes in brain structure in young adults with low-to-moderate alcohol exposure in utero. *Alcoholism, Clinical and Experimental Research, 36,* 1892–1902. doi:10.1111/j.1530-0277.2012.01819.x

Fahrbach, S. E. (2013). *Developmental neuroscience: A concise introduction.* Princeton, NJ: Princeton University Press.

Farroni, T., Massaccesi, S., Menon, E., & Johnson, M. H. (2007). Direct gaze modulates face recognition in young infants. *Cognition, 102,* 396–404. doi:10.1016/j.cognition.2006.01.007

Feldman, R., Gordon, I., & Zagoory-Sharon, O. (2011). Maternal and paternal plasma, salivary, and urinary oxytocin and parent–infant synchrony: Considering stress and affiliation components of human bonding. *Developmental Science, 14,* 752–761. doi:10.1111/j.1467-7687.2010.01021.x

Franz, A. P., Bolat, G. U., Bolat, H., Matijasevich, A., Santos, I. S., Silveira, R. C., . . . Moreira-Maia, C. R. (2018). Attention-deficit/hyperactivity disorder and very preterm/very low birth weight: A meta-analysis. *Pediatrics, 141,* e20171645. doi:10.1542/peds.2017-1645

Ginsberg, K. R., & Committee on Communications, Committee on Psychological Aspects of Child and Family Health. (2007). The importance of play in promoting healthy child development and maintaining strong parent–child bonds. *Pediatrics, 119,* 182–191. doi:10.1542/peds.2006-2697

Glass, H. C., Costarino, A. T., Stayer, S. A., Brett, C., Cladis, F., & Davis, P. J. (2015). Outcomes for extremely premature infants. *Anesthesia and Analgesia, 120,* 1337–1351. doi:10.1213/ANE.0000000000000705

Gordon, N. S., Burke, S., Akil, H., Watson, S. J., & Panksepp, J. (2003). Socially-induced brain "fertilization": Play promotes brain derived neurotrophic factor transcription in the amygdala and dorsolateral frontal cortex in juvenile rats. *Neuroscience Letters, 341,* 17–20. doi:10.1016/S0304-3940(03)00158-7

Grant, K. S., Petroff, R., Isoherranen, N., Stella, N., & Burbacher, T. M. (2018). Cannabis use during pregnancy: Pharmacokinetics and effects on child development. *Pharmacology & Therapeutics, 182,* 133–151. doi:10.1016/j.pharmthera.2017.08.014

Hurlemann, R., Patin, A., Onur, O. A., Cohen, M. X., Baumgartner, T., Metzler, S., . . . Kendrick, K. M. (2010). Oxytocin enhances amygdala-dependent, socially reinforced learning and emotional empathy in humans. *Journal of Neuroscience, 30,* 4999–5007. doi:10.1523/JNEUROSCI.5538-09.2010

Hviid, A., Hansen, J. V., Frisch, M., & Melbye, M. (2019). Measles, mumps, rubella vaccination and autism: A nationwide cohort study. *Annals of Internal Medicine, 170,* 513–520. doi:10.7326/M18-2101

Johnson, M. H., & de Haan, M. (2015). *Developmental cognitive neuroscience: An introduction* (4th ed.). Hoboken, NJ: Wiley-Blackwell.

Khader, Y. S., Al-Akour, N., Alzubi, I. M., & Lataifeh, I. (2011). The association between second hand smoke and low birth weight and preterm delivery. *Maternal Child Health, 15,* 453–459. doi:10.1007/s10995-010-0599-2

Kirsch, P., Esslinger, C., Chen, Q., Mier, D., Lis, S., Siddhanti, S., . . . Meyer-Lindenberg, A. (2005). Oxytocin modulates neural circuitry for social cognition and fear in humans. *Journal of Neuroscience, 25,* 11489–11493. doi:10.1523/JNEUROSCI.3984-05.2005

Knobloch, H. S., Charlet, A., Hoffmann, L. C., Eliava, M., Khrulev, S., Cetin, A. H., . . . Grinevich, V. (2012). Evoked axonal oxytocin release in the central amygdala attenuates fear response. *Neuron, 73,* 553–566. doi:10.1016/j.neuron.2011.11.030

Kolb, B., & Whishaw, I. Q. (2015). *Fundamentals of human neuropsychology* (7th ed.). Boston, MA: Worth.

Kuban, K. C., Joseph, R. M., O'Shea, T. M., Allred, E. N., Heeren, T., Douglass, L., . . . Extremely Low Gestational Age Newborn (ELGAN) Study Investigators. (2016). Girls and boys born before 28 weeks gestation: Risks of cognitive, behavioral, and neurologic outcomes at age 10 years. *Pediatrics, 173,* 69–75.e1. doi:10.1016/j.jpeds.2016.02.048

Lang, R., O'Reilly, M., Sigafoos, J., Machalicek, W., Rispoli, M., Lancioni, G. E., . . . Fragale, C. (2010). The effects of an abolishing operation intervention component on play skills, challenging behavior, and stereotypy. *Behavior Modification, 34,* 267–289. doi:10.1177/0145445510370713

Lischke, A., Gamer, M., Berger, C., Grossmann, A., Hauenstein, K., Heinrichs, M., . . . Domes, G. (2012). Oxytocin increases amygdala reactivity to threatening scenes in females. *Psychoneuroendocrinology, 37,* 1431–1438. doi:10.1016/j.psyneuen.2012.01.011

LoParo, D., & Waldman, I. D. (2015). The oxytocin receptor gene (OXTR) is associated with autism spectrum disorder: A meta-analysis. *Molecular Psychiatry, 20,* 640–646. doi:10.1038/mp.2014.77

Luu, T. M., Ment, L., Allan, W., Schneider, K., & Vohr, B. R. (2011). Executive and memory function in adolescents born very preterm. *Pediatrics, 127,* e639–e646. doi:10.1542/peds.2010-1421

Malaspina, D., Dracxler, R., Walsh-Messinger, J., Harlap, S., Goetz, R. R., Keefe, D., & Perrin, M. C. (2014). Telomere length, family history, and paternal age in schizophrenia. *Molecular Genetics & Genomic Medicine, 2,* 326–331. doi:10.1002/mgg3.71

Malaspina, D., Gilman, C., & Kranz, T. M. (2015). Paternal age and mental health of offspring. *Fertility and Sterility, 103,* 1392–1396. doi:10.1016/j.fertnstert.2015.04.015

Matthews, T. J., & Hamilton, B. E. (2014, May). First births to older women continue to rise. *National Center for Health Statistics Data Brief, 152,* 1–8. Retrieved from https://www.cdc.gov/nchs/data/databriefs/db152.pdf

McHale, S. M., Updegraff, K. A., & Whiteman, S. D. (2012). Sibling relationships and influences in childhood and adolescence. *Journal of Marriage and Family, 74,* 913–930. doi:10.1111/j.1741-3737.2012.01011.x

McQuaid, R. J., McInnis, O. A., Abizaid, A., & Anisman, H. (2014). Making room for oxytocin in understanding depression. *Neuroscience & Biobehavioral Reviews, 45,* 305–322. doi:10.1016/j.neubiorev.2014.07.005

Morris, J. K., Mutton, D. E., & Alberman, E. (2002). Revised estimates of the maternal age specific live birth prevalence of Down's syndrome. *Journal of Medical Screening, 9,* 2–6. doi:10.1136/jms.9.1.2

Naber, F. B., Bakermans-Kranenburg, M. J., Van Ijzendoorn, M. H., Swinkels, S. H., Buitelaar, J. K., Dietz, C., . . . Van Engeland, H. (2008). Play behavior and attachment in toddlers with autism. *Journal of Autism and Developmental Disorders, 38,* 857–866. doi:10.1007/s10803-007-0454-5

National Institute of Child Health and Human Development. (2017, January). *What can I do to promote a healthy pregnancy?* Retrieved from https://www.nichd.nih.gov/health/topics/preconceptioncare/conditioninfo/healthy-pregnancy

Nishimori, K., Takayanagi, Y., Yoshida, M., Kasahara, Y., Young, L. J., & Kawamata, M. (2008). New aspects of oxytocin receptor function revealed by knockout mice: Sociosexual behaviour and control of energy balance. *Progress in Brain Research, 170,* 79–90. doi:10.1016/S0079-6123(08)00408-1

Okabe, S., Kitano, K., Nagasawa, M., Mogi, K., & Kikusui, T. (2013). Testosterone inhibits facilitating effects of parenting experience on parental behavior and the oxytocin neural system in mice. *Physiology & Behavior, 118,* 159–164. doi:10.1016/j.physbeh.2013.05.017

Orsmond, G. I., & Seltzer, M. M. (2007). Siblings of individuals with autism spectrum disorders across the life course. *Mental Retardation and Developmental Disabilities Research Reviews, 13,* 313–320. doi:10.1002/mrdd.20171

Padilla-Walker, L. M., Harper, J. M., & Jensen, A. C. (2010). Self-regulation as a mediator between sibling relationship quality and early adolescents' positive and negative outcomes. *Journal of Family Psychology, 24,* 419–428. doi:10.1037/a0020387

Perrin, M. C., Brown, A. S., & Malaspina, D. (2007). Aberrant epigenetic regulation could explain the relationship of paternal age to schizophrenia. *Schizophrenia Bulletin, 33,* 1270–1273. doi:10.1093/schbul/sbm093

Ross, H. E., & Young, L. J. (2009). Oxytocin and the neural mechanisms regulating social cognition and affiliative behavior. *Frontiers in Neuroendocrinology, 30,* 534–547. doi:10.1016/j.yfrne.2009.05.004

Sanders, T., Liu, Y., Buchner, V., & Tchounwou, P. B. (2009). Neurotoxic effects and biomarkers of lead exposure: A review. *Reviews on Environmental Health, 24,* 15–45. doi:10.1515/REVEH.2009.24.1.15

Sandin, S., Schendel, D., Magnusson, P., Hultman, C., Surén, P., Susser, E., . . . Reichenberg, A. (2016). Autism risk associated with parental age and with increasing difference in age between the parents. *Molecular Psychiatry, 21,* 693–700. doi:10.1038/mp.2015.70

Shafer, D. P., Lehrman, E. K., Kautzman, A. G., Koyama, R., Mardinly, A. R., Yamasaki, R., . . . Stevens, B. (2012). Microglia sculpt postnatal neural circuits in an activity and complement-dependent manner. *Neuron, 74,* 691–705. doi:10.1016/j.neuron.2012.03.026

Sharma, R., Agarwal, A., Rohra, V. K., Assidi, M., Abu-Elmagd, M., & Turki, R. F. (2015). Effects of increased paternal age on sperm quality, reproductive outcome and associated epigenetic risks to offspring. *Reproductive Biology & Endocrinology, 13,* 35. doi:10.1186/s12958-015-0028-x

Tang, G., Gudsnuk, K., Kuo, S. H., Cotrina, M. L., Rosoklija, G., Sosunov, A., . . . Yue, Z. (2014). Loss of mTOR-dependent macroautophagy causes autistic-like synaptic pruning deficits. *Neuron, 83,* 1131–1143. doi:10.1016/j.neuron.2014.07.040

Van Kerkhof, L. W., Damsteegt, R., Trezza, V., Voorn, P., & Vanderschuren, L. J. (2013). Social play behavior in adolescent rats is mediated by functional activity in medial prefrontal cortex and striatum. *Neuropsychopharmacology, 38,* 1899–1909. doi:10.1038/npp.2013.83

Wickström, R. (2007). Effects of nicotine during pregnancy: Human and experimental evidence. *Current Neuropharmacology, 5,* 213–222. doi:10.2174/157015907781695955

Wong, C., Odom, S. L., Hume, K. A., Cox, A. W., Fettig, A., Kucharczyk, S., . . . Schultz, T. R. (2015). Evidence-based practices for children, youth, and young adults with autism spectrum disorder: A comprehensive review. *Journal of Autism and Developmental Disorders, 45,* 1951–1966. doi:10.1007/s10803-014-2351-z

Chapter 5

Problems of Childhood

Key Concepts

- Transdiagnostic approach
- Intellectual disability
- Verbal and crystallized intelligence
- Autism spectrum
- Ambiguous loss
- Attention deficits and hyperactivity
- Reactive attachment
- Separation anxiety
- Oppositional defiance
- Conduct problems
- Disruptive mood dysregulation

Aligned 2016 CACREP Standards

Standard 2.F.3.c. Theories of normal and abnormal personality development

Standard 2.F.3.e. Biological, neurological, and physiological factors that affect human development, functioning, and behavior

Standard 2.F.3.f. Systemic and environmental factors that affect human development, functioning, and behavior

Standard 2.F.7.e. Use of assessments for diagnostic and intervention planning purposes
Standard 2.F.7.l. Use of assessment results to diagnose developmental, behavioral, and mental disorders

• • •

One in 5 youth struggle with mental health challenges, according to the U.S. National Comorbidity Study (Merikangas et al., 2010). Several notable neurodevelopmental conditions emerge during childhood, including autism spectrum disorder and attention-deficit/hyperactivity disorder (ADHD). Children often present different symptoms than adults, and thus specialized knowledge is required for effective assessment and intervention.

In Chapter 4, we reviewed problems and abnormalities that can occur during neurophysiological and social development. This chapter expands on those insights to explore several neurodevelopmental disabilities and other mental health problems that can emerge during childhood, such as autism, attention deficits and hyperactivity, intellectual disability (ID), reactive attachment, oppositional defiance, conduct disorder (CD), separation anxiety, and disruptive mood dysregulation. We focus on these particular conditions because in our clinical experience counselors often work with these conditions. Although we reference the fifth edition of the *Diagnostic and Statistical Manual of Mental Disorders* (*DSM-5;* American Psychiatric Association [APA], 2013) to acknowledge the criteria of each disorder, we introduce a cross-cutting, transdiagnostic approach to assessment and intervention. Toward the end of the chapter, we use the case of Wayne to examine the application of the transdiagnostic model when selecting counseling approaches.

The Transdiagnostic Approach

One of the criticisms of the *DSM* nosology (i.e., classification of mental disorders) is the co-occurrence and comorbidity of mental health issues, which makes it challenging to categorize lists of symptoms in clinical practice (Nemeroff et al., 2013). In the absence of biomarkers for mental health conditions (e.g., lab tests), counselors must designate a category in which a child or adolescent's symptoms fit best. This can be complex, as many symptoms are cross-cutting. For example, rumination (the inability to shift thinking about a specific problem, paired with an inability to resolve the problem) can be a symptom of anxiety, autism, depression, obsessive-compulsive disorder, and even schizophrenia (McLaughlin & Nolen-Hoeksema, 2011). Although some mental health conditions are fairly well described, it is worth mentioning that the *DSM-5* intentionally widened the criteria for several mental health conditions, including neurodevelopmental issues such as autism (Nemeroff et al., 2013). This, in effect, has made mental disorder categories even less defined.

The transdiagnostic approach has been proposed as a solution to this conundrum because it focuses on symptom presentations rather than on formal mental disorder categories (McGorry & Nelson, 2016). There are several benefits to the transdiagnostic approach, such as facilitating earlier intervention rather than waiting for full criteria to manifest. This can be crucial for conditions such as those on the autism spectrum, which respond best to early intervention (McGorry & Nelson, 2016). The transdiagnostic approach also helps counselors to identify specific symptoms to focus on, which can be helpful because children and adolescents do not possess the same symptoms even within a diagnostic category. For example, some children may need more help concentrating on academic work, whereas others may need help with impulse control.

We mentioned in Chapter 1 that although diagnosis is largely unhelpful in guiding a counselor's approach with a child or adolescent, there are exceptions. Several of the symptom presentations covered in this section, such as autism and attention deficits and hyperactivity, require specific, sequential, and often repetitive approaches to skill building that are best addressed through a behavioral counseling approach. Identifying these conditions is therefore useful and important to treatment planning. In the sections that follow, we describe the characteristics and etiology (i.e., cause) of the mental health conditions listed previously.

ID

ID is a complex neurodevelopmental condition that tends to persist throughout a person's life. ID has three categories: mild, moderate, and severe (APA, 2013). Mild ID is by far the most common, accounting for 85% of ID (APA, 2013). The severity of ID is assessed through two main methods: IQ and level of functioning. IQ is assessed through intelligence tests such as the Wechsler Intelligence Scale for Children (Wechsler, 2014). The two main areas that are tested on IQ assessments are fluid and crystallized intelligence. Fluid intelligence pertains to a person's ability to respond in the moment and complete tasks without prior requisite knowledge (e.g., being able to complete maze-like puzzles). Crystallized intelligence is a person's ability to complete tasks using knowledge previously gained (e.g., being able to identify vocabulary synonyms or complete math problems). Many IQ tests measure verbal abilities and logic, mathematical, or spatial abilities and do not address the full spectrum of intellectual knowledge and skill (e.g., kinesthetic ability, music and rhythm, interpersonal and emotional ability; Gardner, 2006). For this reason, IQ testing has been criticized for selectively focusing on abilities that align with kindergarten–Grade 12 academic requirements (Gardner, 2006). IQ scores have an average of 100, with a standard deviation of 15. Consider a bell curve: Approximately 95% of people fall between −2 and +2 standard deviations from the mean or average, and only 5% of people fall below or above the mean. Thus, an IQ score of 70 or below (i.e., 2 standard deviations below the mean) is the threshold for mild ID. An IQ score of 55 or below is the threshold for moderate ID, and an IQ score of 40 or below is the threshold for severe ID. Figure 5.1 depicts the distribution of the IQ curve.

Characteristics

A child cannot be diagnosed with ID on the basis of IQ score alone. Thus, assessing one's level of adaptive functioning is crucial to making a diagnosis of ID (APA, 2013). Adaptive functioning has three main areas: conceptual, social, and practical (APA, 2013). Conceptual adaptive functioning is similar to intelligence as measured through IQ tests. It pertains to language abilities, reading, writing, mathematics ability, reasoning, and knowledge. Social adaptive functioning addresses the skills required to form and sustain relationships and friendships and includes empathy and verbal and nonverbal communication. Practical adaptive functioning pertains to a person's ability to live independently, such as managing money, maintaining personal care and hygiene, and completing activities of daily living. Counselors can assess adaptive functioning by asking the following types of questions: (a) To what extent can this person form and sustain meaningful relationships and friendships? (b) To what extent could this person live independently

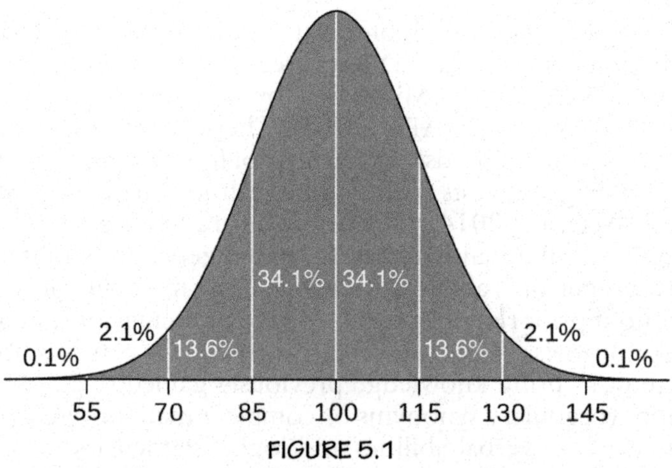

FIGURE 5.1

IQ Distribution

Note. From Dmcq, 2013. In Wikimedia Commons. Used under Creative Commons Attribution-Share Alike 3.0 unported license.

in adulthood, as evidenced by money management skills, personal care and hygiene, and completion of tasks of daily living? Note that these skills in adaptive functioning become more evident as a youth reaches adulthood. For example, an elementary-age child with or without ID would not be expected to possess independent living skills, whereas an 18-year-old adolescent would be expected to possess independent living skills.

Etiology

ID has a variety of etiologies and often develops during the natal or postnatal period. Many chromosomal issues (e.g., Down syndrome) and other neurodevelopmental issues such as autism can have a high co-occurrence with ID. Congenital issues described in Chapter 4, such as exposure to alcohol in utero and exposure to toxins such as lead, can also be associated with ID.

The Autism Spectrum

Autism is a complex neurodevelopmental disorder whose prevalence has increased dramatically over the past several decades (Zwaigenbaum et al., 2015). Children with autism have significant impairments that emerge during early childhood, typically before 5 years of age and often by 2 years of age (Zwaigenbaum et al., 2015).

Characteristics

Autism is characterized by deficits in social relationships and communication and by restricted and repetitive patterns of behavior (APA, 2013). In regard to impairments in social relationships and communication, children with autism experience difficulties with reciprocal interaction, difficulties understanding the thoughts and feelings of others, and impaired facial recognition and eye contact (APA, 2013). This can result in difficulties with pragmatic use of language; reduced sharing of emotions; limited social initiation; difficulties understanding humor and nonliteral speech, such as irony; and atypical speech (in terms of volume, intonation, rate, rhythm, prosody, or pitch). Children with autism can also have deficits in play behavior, especially symbolic and imaginative play, and may engage in repetitive and self-stimulatory behavior (Lang et al., 2010). We articulated in an earlier chapter that children with autism may need to develop play skills to later scaffold social skills. Early intervention for play skills is crucial, as play behavior can predict the quality of the child-caregiver relationship (Naber et al., 2008).

Another major characteristic of autism is restricted and repetitive patterns of behavior, such as repetitive verbalizations (e.g., paralanguage such as humming or squealing) and repetitive motor movements (e.g., hand flapping), ritualized behavior and rigid adherence to routines, difficulties with transitions between activities or changes to routine, limited and repetitive food preferences, and interests that fixate on a narrow and sometimes unusual range of topics (APA, 2013). Children may engage in echolalia (repeating the verbalizations of others verbatim), nonfunctional play with objects (e.g., flapping movements), and repetitive stereotypic movements (e.g., rocking). Children may also over- or underreact to sensory stimulation and may seek out or avoid sensory experiences. Behavioral problems can be common and can include self-injurious behavior, aggression, property destruction, and nonadherence to directions.

Autism can co-occur with a number of other conditions, especially intellectual deficits (60%–70%), seizure disorders (30%–50%), and sleep problems related to melatonin production (40%–86%; Maski, Jeste, & Spence, 2011; Polyak, Kubina, & Girirajan, 2015). Salazar and colleagues (2015) also found common co-occurrence with generalized anxiety (66%), phobias (52%), and ADHD (59%), with anxiety symptoms more pronounced in children with autism who have higher IQs. Mutations to oxytocin receptor genes have been proposed as a cause of increased social anxiety in children with autism, as oxytocin receptors are often located in the amygdala, and oxytocin reduces social anxiety (LoParo & Waldman, 2015).

Etiology

The exact etiology (i.e., cause) of autism is unclear, largely because autism is a complex condition that has several genetic and neurobiological correlates. In previous chapters, we reported several abnormalities associated with autism, including mutations to oxytocin receptor genes (LoParo & Waldman, 2015), reductions in synaptic pruning and increases in dendritic spine density (Tang et al., 2014), impairments to glia function, and higher than average numbers of degraded and older neurons (Tang et al., 2014). Parental age at conception also appears to be a risk factor (Sandin et al., 2016), perhaps because of the increased likelihood of DNA copy errors (Malaspina, Gilman, & Kranz, 2015).

The heritability of autism is not well understood. Although several genes have been connected with autism, it is considered a polygenic condition, in that multiple genes and gene sequences are implicated and no single gene is largely responsible (LoParo & Waldman, 2015). In addition, gene mutations largely occur spontaneously (known as *de novo mutations*) and are rarely inherited. Cell copy variants appear more common (LoParo & Waldman, 2015) in children with autism and seem to vary by individual. Genes associated with the development of gamma-aminobutyric acid, glutamate, serotonin, and the protein Reelin also seem to be implicated alongside oxytocin (LoParo & Waldman, 2015; Skaar et al., 2005).

Counselors who wish to conduct autism assessments should consider acquiring specialized training. A number of assessment tools exist. One of the most respected assessments is the Autism Diagnostic Observation Schedule (Gotham, Risi, Pickles, & Lord, 2007). This is an observational assessment of tasks that the child completes. Two raters score the child across a number of tasks and compare scores to ensure adequate consistency in ratings.

Impact on Family Functioning

Autism tends to be a lifetime diagnosis and persists throughout the life span (Blumberg et al., 2016). It appears that approximately 13% of children lose their diagnosis, largely because new information contradicts the diagnosis (rather than autism formally moving into remission; Blumberg et al., 2016). Because of its lifetime prevalence, parents often struggle to accept their child's diagnosis. Because of the child's lack of physical characteristics (sometimes referred to as having an *invisible disability*), parents can experience a phenomenon known as *ambiguous loss* (Cridland, Jones, Magee, & Caputi, 2014). During ambiguous loss, parents or guardians may see progress and improvement, which stirs up hope for their child's recovery from autism, only to reexperience loss again when their child does not sustain progress or regresses in some skills. Parents and guardians of children with autism face greater parenting stress, which includes more experiences of challenging child behavior, reduced satisfaction with the parent-child bond, and increased self-perception of negative parenting (Lai, Goh, Oei, & Sung, 2015). Parents and guardians of children with autism also engage in more avoidance coping, such as watching television, sleeping to avoid problems, and intentional forgetting (Lai et al., 2015). Parenting problems cannot be easily resolved, and thus active problem-solving can be ineffective at times. Siblings of children with autism also appear to be at heightened risk for social and behavioral problems (Orsmond & Seltzer, 2007).

Counselors can support families by providing a space for parents to process and work through their feelings of loss related to their child's disability (Cridland et al., 2014). Parents and guardians may need coaching on using active coping strategies, such as positive reappraisal. Referrals to caregiver support groups should also be considered, for parents and guardians can share resources with one another. Resource sharing can be very helpful for parents and guardians, who must navigate the sheer number of services that their child may require. Zablotsky and colleagues (2015) found that nearly all children with autism (98%) were currently receiving services, yet 30% of parents reported that their child's developmental needs were still not being met. Higher levels of social support and greater access to resources have been associated with reduced parental stress (Zaidman-Zait et al., 2017). See Reflection Question 5.1.

Reflection Question 5.1

Imagine that you are working with a parent of a child with autism and need to bring up the topic of ambiguous loss. Would you mention that autism is typically a lifetime diagnosis? Why or why not?

Attachment Problems

In Chapter 4, on the neurophysiological and social development of childhood, we reviewed the importance of attachment in the early childhood years. Attachment issues during early childhood can have profound and lasting impacts but can also be overcome with early intervention. The two attachment issues we explore in this section are reactive attachment and separation anxiety.

Reactive Attachment

Extreme neglect in early childhood has lasting impacts on child neural development. Living for more than 6 months in institutional settings such as overcrowded orphanages with little adult contact is especially iatrogenic (Sonuga-Barke et al., 2017). Without predictable and frequent interactions with a stable and nurturing caregiver, children are deprived of opportunities to learn basic emotional regulation and social learning. Instead, children turn inward, do not seek comfort when distressed or upset, and avoid emotional intimacy. The child may become unable to understand their own emotional experiences and struggle to understand the experiences of others. Such children may interact with others in their environment as objects more than people, with whom they have little emotional connection. Clinically speaking, we have found reactive attachment to be one of the most severe problems of childhood, because of the child's lack of emotional connection to the caregiver and often their willingness to harm caregivers without apparent concern to obtain desired objects.

Studies of maltreated children have found global reductions in gray matter, in particular in the orbitofrontal cortex and temporal lobe (De Brito et al., 2013), that impact emotional regulation and autobiographical memory. A larger amygdala volume has been found in children who have experienced institutional deprivation, which further suggests emotional regulation issues related to fear and threat in particular (Mehta et al., 2009).

One of the challenges of treating reactive attachment is that intervention can be complex and involves finding a consistent and emotionally stable attachment figure who can handle the challenging and often aggressive behavior of the child (Zeanah et al., 2016). Counselors should consider interventions that strengthen the relational bond between the caregiver and child and provide education on positive parenting when needed (Zeanah et al., 2016). Medications are not indicated for reactive attachment (Zeanah et al., 2016).

Separation Anxiety

Children with separation anxiety have difficulty being apart from major attachment figures (i.e., parents, guardians, caregivers). When separated, they experience high degrees of anxiety and fear, worrying that something terrible will happen to their major attachment figure, resulting in their losing the stability of this caregiver (APA, 2013). For example, children with separation anxiety may share fears that their major attachment figure will be killed in a car accident while they are at school and feel that they must go home immediately to make sure their parent is not in harm's way. Children with separation anxiety may struggle with attending school, and refusing to attend school can be common. Counselors can help children with separation anxiety restructure their worries cognitively. In-home therapy may be indicated when the child refuses to leave home for school and is at risk for entering the juvenile justice system on truancy charges. Systematic desensitization can be useful to help the child make slow but steady progress toward attending full days of school as required.

Attention Deficits and Hyperactivity

ADHD is among the most common problems of childhood, with approximately 8% of all children diagnosed with ADHD (Danielson et al., 2018).

Characteristics

Symptoms of ADHD include inattention and hyperactivity. Symptoms of inattention include lack of attention to detail and making careless mistakes, distractibility, difficulty listening during conversation, organizational problems, problems with task completion, missing deadlines, forgetfulness, and difficulties concentrating and putting forth sustained mental effort (APA, 2013). Hyperactivity includes having difficulties sitting still, acting as if driven by a motor, fidgeting, running or climbing when inappropriate, being unable to play quietly, talking more than is appropriate for the social setting and interrupting others, having low frustration tolerance, being impatient, and intruding on the boundaries of others (APA, 2013).

Etiology

ADHD has a number of neurological correlates, including reduced volume of the prefrontal cortex, insula, parietal lobe, and cerebellum (Hart, Radua, Mataix-Cols, & Rubia, 2012). These regions are associated with the hallmarks of ADHD, such as impaired executive functioning and impulse control, self-awareness and self-reflection, and motor control. Shaw, Gogtay, and Rapoport (2010) found that children with ADHD experience maturation delays in brain development trajectories. Children with ADHD have delays in peak cortical thickness during the onset of adolescence, which results in difficulties with working memory, inhibition, and impulse control. In a study of more than 1,700 14-year-olds with ADHD, Hoogman and colleagues (2017) found brain maturation delays in subcortical structures. Adolescents with ADHD had reduced volume of the nucleus accumbens, amygdala, hippocampus, and putamen compared to controls (Hoogman et al., 2017). This may explain why children with ADHD have difficulty with emotional identification and regulation in addition to working memory deficits. Amygdala volume has also been associated with hyperactivity (Frodl et al., 2010). As children with ADHD grow older, they eventually achieve peak cortical and subcortical thickness and then subsequently experience cortical thinning during the second major phase of synaptic pruning that occurs during adolescence. Thus, the frontal cortex and subcortex of adolescents with ADHD eventually mature, which may explain why only 37% of children with ADHD appear to retain the diagnosis throughout adulthood (Shaw et al., 2010).

Several congenital conditions, including premature birth, are risk factors for ADHD. Twin studies have found that ADHD is also highly inheritable (Thapar, Cooper, Eyre, & Langley, 2013). ADHD appears to have a heterogeneous genetic profile (i.e., different genetic sequences are involved with ADHD symptomatology) and has multiple genetic markers (Zayats et al., 2015). Researchers have identified genes involved with dopamine and brain-derived neurotrophic factor (Kebir, Tabbane, Sengupta, & Joober, 2009), though the gene *ENSG00000263745* appears to be the greatest predictor of ADHD (Zayats et al., 2015). DNA copy variants also appear to play a role, as with autism (Thapar et al., 2013).

Several notable social and cultural factors can contribute to an ADHD diagnosis. First, children who enter kindergarten at younger ages are at greater risk for an ADHD diagnosis (Layton, Barnett, Hicks, & Jena, 2018). Second, biological males have a 3 times greater incidence of ADHD compared to females and are 6 to 9 times more likely than females to receive treatment for ADHD (Bruchmüller, Margraf, & Schneider, 2012). There are neurophysiological and social reasons for this difference in incidence rate by biological sex. Males tend to have delayed frontal lobe maturation compared to their female counterparts, which may explain the difference in prevalence (Galván, 2017). It also appears that therapists overdiagnose ADHD in males. To explore the overdiagnosis of ADHD in males, Bruchmüller and colleagues (2012) sent case vignettes to 1,000 therapists. The case vignettes contained the same information, except the biological sex of the child was randomly assigned. Therapists in the study diagnosed males with ADHD at twice the rate of females (Bruchmüller et al., 2012), which suggests a bias toward ascribing an ADHD diagnosis to males.

Interventions

Assessments for ADHD often include parent, teacher, and child self-reports of symptoms. The Conners Rating Scale–Revised (Conners, Sitarenios, Parker, & Epstein, 1998) is a popular screening tool for ADHD. Some ADHD assessments are also computer-based continuous performance tests that measure a child's impulse control and attentional abilities (Wasserstein, 2005).

Impact on Family Functioning

Symptoms of ADHD can manifest differently at home and at school, in particular because the requirements of the academic setting are often quite different from those of the home setting (e.g., at school children are required to sit in their seats and pay attention for prolonged periods of time). Parents and guardians play an important role in establishing organizational habits at home.

Disruptive Behavior

Disruptive behavior during childhood is fairly common and somewhat typical for children who are learning to test social boundaries and rules (Kaminski & Claussen, 2017). Yet some children demonstrate disruptive behavior that causes clinically significant problems at school and in the home environment. Two such disruptive behavior problems are oppositional defiant disorder (ODD) and CD. Children who are oppositional or defiant can display an angry or irritable mood, may attempt to start and perpetuate power struggles with adults, and may demonstrate verbal and physical aggression at times (APA, 2013). Children with CD tend to display a willingness to harm or violate the rights of others, such as by stealing, threatening with a weapon, being cruel to animals, and callously disregarding the emotions of others. ODD and CD share symptoms with disruptive mood dysregulation, a childhood diagnosis that was added to the *DSM-5* (APA, 2013). Like ODD and CD, symptoms of disruptive mood dysregulation include emotional dysregulation, aggression, and damage to property. Children with disruptive mood dysregulation tend to have longer and more intense outbursts than is typical for their age, though they do not necessarily engage in power struggles like children with ODD or demonstrate the callous willingness to break rules and harm others that is characteristic of CD.

Children with CD can engage in impression management and mask their callous and rule-breaking tendencies until the opportune moment. We present the case of Tommie to further illustrate how symptoms of CD can manifest. Although Tommie is a younger child, CD symptoms can present similarly in adolescents. Here Michelle uses first-person narrative to describe the counseling process, see Case Vignette 5.1.

Case Vignette 5.1 Tommie

When Tommie, a 7-year-old African American male, entered the group home, he presented as quiet and reserved. Tommie kept to himself and attempted to stay out of regular group home mischief. At the group home, it was typical for the children to engage in behaviors such as teasing peers, stealing peers' personal items, ignoring basic rules, and resisting completing basic daily chores. Tommie demonstrated none of these behaviors at first and presented as an unlikely candidate to break the group home rules. He demonstrated little to no evidence of his previous CD diagnosis. His counselor at the group home had surprised the staff by suggesting that Tommie be closely supervised at all times, even if it appeared that he was being cooperative.

Roughly 2 months into his stay at the group home, his problematic behaviors became more apparent. The group home staff learned that Tommie hoarded food in his room under the bed and in his closet. When confronted, he spoke of never wanting to go hungry again. Despite having three scheduled meals and two scheduled snacks per day, Tommie did not trust that these meals would be available from day to day. His hoarding appeared to be a survival mechanism.

I worked as a house manager at the group home. In this role, I often advocated for Tommie to hang out (supervised) with some of the older male residents because he noted missing his older brother. Tommie had previously been raised in a dysfunctional environment and now had little to no contact with his biological family. Tommie presented as a young boy who was resilient and was slowly coming to terms with group home life.

Several months passed. One day, I was stunned to learn that Tommie had been making plans to break into the medicine room, which held all the residents' psychotropic medication. He had planned to steal Adderall or anything he thought he could misuse to get high and flee the group home. Tommie was successful in breaking into the medicine room but only gained access to Tylenol because all of the psychotropic medications were secured behind double-locked doors. Tommie ingested a large amount of Tylenol and was rushed to the emergency room to have his stomach pumped. He survived the incident and was ultimately moved to a more secure setting.

• • •

Michelle's work with Tommie highlights the difficulties of working with children with conduct problems. Tommie used his quiet demeanor to earn the support and trust of adult caregivers and therapists, which he would later manipulate. Because conduct problems are marked by disingenuous and callous manipulation of others, the most effective counseling approach is to draw attention to these patterns and help the child obtain the outcomes they want in the most adaptive manner (i.e., by strengthening relationships rather than harming others). For example, the early hoarding incident provided an opportunity to help Tommie process how he could get his needs met (i.e., be assured of food) without deceit.

Transdiagnostic Application: The Case of Wayne

Problems that emerge during childhood are often challenging to differentiate when attempting to make a diagnosis. We now introduce an in-depth case study (Case Vignette 5.2) to illustrate the use of the transdiagnostic model to identify cross-cutting symptoms and an appropriate counseling approach.

Wayne displays several concerning symptoms, some of which are posing a danger to himself and others. Wayne's physical aggression is his presenting issue and could be attributed to a number of childhood problems, including autism, reactive attachment, oppositional defiance, conduct problems, and disruptive mood dysregulation. Wayne also has symptoms of low frustration tolerance and task avoidance, which could be symptoms of ADHD in addition to autism and reactive attachment. An important symptom in this case is Wayne's lack of connection to others and his preference for playing alone for long periods. Such behavior is an unusual characteristic of ADHD, oppositional defiance, conduct problems, or disruptive mood dysregulation. Instead, autism and reactive attachment are commonly associated with this lack of connection to others and preference for solitary play. Wayne's proclivity for video games has the potential to be a restricted and repetitive pattern of behavior, which would suggest autism over reactive attachment. However, we may also wonder whether Wayne's early childhood history of being raised in an orphanage may have resulted in reactive attachment problems. Although Wayne's IQ score suggests the presence of mild ID, we would need to evaluate his adaptive functioning before making this diagnosis.

As the counselor, we could use the Autism Diagnostic Observation Schedule to assess whether Wayne meets criteria for autism. It is fairly unlikely that we could gather more historical information about the length of time Wayne lived in the orphanage and the quality of adult caregiver interaction during that period. Instead, it would be worth assessing the quality of Wayne's relationship with his current adoptive parents to ascertain whether attachment issues seem to be present.

Case Vignette 5.2 Wayne, Part 1

Wayne is an 8-year-old White male student receiving special education services at his elementary school. He was referred to your outpatient practice by his school counselor after several incidents of attacking teachers and other children in the classroom. Such aggression is not uncommon to the self-contained classroom at Maple Valley Elementary; however, Wayne's current behavior has become dangerous to the point that several instructional assistants have complained. During one incident, Wayne bit another child's ear, causing a partial tear. The school counselor tells you that the parents are "good people," though they rarely follow through with recommendations made by the school. School officials are feeling desperate, as they are not sure how long Wayne can be maintained in regular school if his behavior does not improve.

Wayne sits quietly during the intake interview, immersed in his portable video game. You notice that Wayne, who is wearing a tight-fitting T-shirt, is an obese child with several prominent stretchmarks on his lower belly. At 8 years of age, he already weighs more than 150 pounds and has a cholesterol level of 420. Wayne's current parents adopted him at 2 years of age from Ukraine. Wayne has three other adopted siblings. They are a fairly religious family and attend a Pentecostal church twice a week. When his parents first adopted Wayne, they noticed within the first few months that his behavior was dramatically different from that of their other adopted children. Having been raised in an orphanage, Wayne seems to have little to no connection with others and will spend days playing alone in his room if his parents do not intervene.

Wayne's IQ is apparently in the 55–65 range, and he struggles with academics at school. Having little frustration tolerance, Wayne will become aggressive when demands are placed on him. His parents believe that his most recent episode was caused by the teacher asking Wayne to complete his assigned math task instead of drawing pictures of video game characters. His parents claim that he is normally fairly calm, if aloof, at home. Wayne apparently has no chores and completes his homework at school before coming home ("Otherwise, he'd never do it"). They rarely take Wayne out into public because their son will begin destroying items in a store or restaurant if he does not get what he wants immediately. This is particularly true of video games.

(Continued)

Case Vignette 5.2 *(Continued)*

On the rare occasions when Wayne must attend a doctor's appointment, his parents have to stop at two different fast food restaurants to purchase chicken nuggets, soda, and ice cream. He only eats one of these meals, and the parents either discard the other meal or give it to Wayne's siblings. Attempts to curb this behavior have been unsuccessful; Wayne has unbuckled his seatbelt and grabbed the steering wheel when his parents "missed" a turn to a restaurant.

The parents complain several times that Wayne has received multiple behavioral services over the years, most of which have had minimal impact. Most of these interventions have used token economy systems. Apparently these work initially "but then he gets wise and isn't motivated by the rewards anymore." The most successful intervention was having a behavioral specialist at the school who provided one-on-one support to Wayne throughout the school day. This position was not funded for the current school year, as Wayne did so well at school last year.

• • •

The transdiagnostic model could be helpful in identifying targets of intervention. Regardless of diagnosis, Wayne displays several behavioral issues that are best addressed through a behavioral approach. See Reflection Question 5.2. For example, Wayne uses aggression to escape when demands are placed on him and to obtain tangibles. He would also benefit from developing frustration tolerance and starting to scaffold social skills so that he is engaged in more reciprocal play with others. His parents' avoidance of disciplinary measures in this case is certainly an area for intervention, and our direct work with Wayne would likely need to be paired with parent education. In the next chapter, we elaborate on counseling approaches that best address Wayne's presenting issues.

Conclusion

Working with children who experience neurodevelopmental issues can be challenging and often requires a different counseling approach

Reflection Question 5.2

How crucial do you think it is to differentiate autism from reactive attachment in the case of Wayne? How might a definitive diagnosis be helpful?

than traditional talk therapy. Because of the lifetime prevalence of some of these problems, counselors should use care before assigning diagnoses and should seek training in conducting reliable and validated assessments for these issues. The transdiagnostic approach can be helpful in identifying potential targets for intervention regardless of the formal diagnosis and planning counseling approaches accordingly.

Quiz Questions

1. The transdiagnostic approach seeks to
   a. Identify dimensional attributes of risk that may be shared by numerous disorders
   b. Adhere to the criteria established by the *DSM-5*
   c. Clarify whether problems are caused by nature or nurture
2. ADHD is characterized by
   a. Inattention, hyperactivity, and impulsivity
   b. Inactivity, anxiety, and restlessness
   c. Hyperfocus, agitation, and irritability
3. Callousness and cruelty are core characteristics of
   a. ODD
   b. CD
   c. Disruptive mood dysregulation

References

American Psychiatric Association. (2013). *Diagnostic and statistical manual of mental disorders* (5th ed.). Arlington, VA: Author.

Blumberg, S. J., Zablotsky, B., Avila, R. M., Colpe, L. J., Pringle, B. A., & Kogan, M. D. (2016). Diagnosis lost: Differences between children who had and who currently have an autism spectrum disorder diagnosis. *Autism, 20,* 783–795. doi:10.1177/1362361315607724

Bruchmüller, K., Margraf, J., & Schneider, S. (2012). Is ADHD diagnosed in accord with diagnostic criteria? Overdiagnosis and influence of client gender on diagnosis. *Journal of Consulting and Clinical Psychology, 80,* 128–138. doi:10.1037/a0026582

Conners, C. K., Sitarenios, G., Parker, J. D., & Epstein, J. N. (1998). Revision and restandardization of the Conners Teacher Rating Scale (CTRS-R): Factor structure, reliability, and criterion validity. *Journal of Abnormal Child Psychology, 26,* 279–291. doi:10.1023/A:1022606501530

Council for Accreditation of Counseling and Related Educational Programs. (2015). *2016 CACREP standards.* Alexandria, VA: Author.

Cridland, E. K., Jones, S. C., Magee, C. A., & Caputi, P. (2014). Family-focused autism spectrum disorder research: A review of the utility of family systems approaches. *Autism, 18,* 213–222. doi:10.1177/1362361312472261

Danielson, M. L., Bitsko, R. H., Ghandour, R. M., Holbrook, J. R., Kogan, M. D., & Blumberg, S. J. (2018). Prevalence of parent-reported ADHD diagnosis and associated treatment among US children and adolescents, 2016. *Journal of Clinical Child & Adolescent Psychology, 47,* 199–212. doi:10.1080/15374416.2017.1417860

De Brito, S. A., Viding, E., Sebastian, C. L., Kelly, P. A., Mechelli, A., Maris, H., & McCrory, E. J. (2013). Reduced orbitofrontal and temporal grey matter in a community sample of maltreated children. *Journal of Child Psychology and Psychiatry, 54,* 105–112. doi:10.1111/j.1469-7610.2012.02597.x

Frodl, T., Stauber, J., Schaaff, N., Koutsouleris, N., Scheuerecker, J., Ewers, M., . . . Möller, H. J. (2010). Amygdala reduction in patients with ADHD compared with major depression and healthy volunteers. *Acta Psychiatrica Scandinavica, 121,* 111–118. doi:10.1111/j.1600-0447.2009.01489.x

Galván, A. (2017). *The neuroscience of adolescence.* New York, NY: Cambridge University Press.

Gardner, H. (2006). *Multiple intelligences: New horizons in theory and practice.* New York, NY: Basic Books.

Gotham, K., Risi, S., Pickles, A., & Lord, C. (2007). The Autism Diagnostic Observation Schedule: Revised algorithms for improved diagnostic validity. *Journal of Autism and Developmental Disorders, 37,* 613–627. doi:10.1007/s10803-006-0280-1

Hart, H., Radua, J., Mataix-Cols, D., & Rubia, K. (2012). Meta-analysis of fMRI studies of timing in attention-deficit hyperactivity disorder (ADHD). *Neuroscience & Biobehavioral Reviews, 36,* 2248–2256. doi:10.1016/j.neubiorev.2012.08.003

Hoogman, M., Bralten, J., Hibar, D. P., Mennes, M., Zwiers, M. P., Schweren, L. S., . . . de Zeeuw, P. (2017). Subcortical brain volume differences in participants with attention deficit hyperactivity disorder in children and adults: A cross-sectional mega-analysis. *The Lancet Psychiatry, 4,* 310–319. doi:10.1016/S2215-0366(17)30049-4

Kaminski, J. W., & Claussen, A. H. (2017). Evidence base update for psychosocial treatments for disruptive behaviors in children. *Journal of Clinical Child & Adolescent Psychology, 46,* 477–499. doi:10.1080/15374416.2017.1310044

Kebir, O., Tabbane, K., Sengupta, S., & Joober, R. (2009). Candidate genes and neuropsychological phenotypes in children with ADHD: Review of association studies. *Journal of Psychiatry & Neuroscience, 34,* 88–101.

Lai, W. W., Goh, T. J., Oei, T. P., & Sung, M. (2015). Coping and well-being in parents of children with autism spectrum disorders (ASD). *Journal of Autism and Developmental Disorders, 45,* 2582–2593. doi:10.1007/s10803-015-2430-9

Lang, R., O'Reilly, M., Sigafoos, J., Machalicek, W., Rispoli, M., Lancioni, G. E., . . . Fragale, C. (2010). The effects of an abolishing operation intervention component on play skills, challenging behavior, and stereotypy. *Behavior Modification, 34,* 267–289. doi:10.1177/0145445510370713

Layton, T. J., Barnett, M. L., Hicks, T. R., & Jena, A. B. (2018). Attention deficit–hyperactivity disorder and month of school enrollment. *New England Journal of Medicine, 379,* 2122–2130. doi:10.1056/NEJMoa1806828

LoParo, D., & Waldman, I. D. (2015). The oxytocin receptor gene (OXTR) is associated with autism spectrum disorder: A meta-analysis. *Molecular Psychiatry, 20,* 640–646. doi:10.1038/mp.2014.77

Malaspina, D., Gilman, C., & Kranz, T. M. (2015). Paternal age and mental health of offspring. *Fertility and Sterility, 103,* 1392–1396. doi:10.1016/j.fertnstert.2015.04.015

Maski, K. P., Jeste, S. S., & Spence, S. J. (2011). Common neurological co-morbidities in autism spectrum disorders. *Current Opinion in Pediatrics, 23,* 609–615. doi:10.1097/MOP.0b013e32834c9282

McGorry, P., & Nelson, B. (2016). Why we need a transdiagnostic staging approach to emerging psychopathology, early diagnosis, and treatment. *JAMA Psychiatry, 73,* 191–192. doi:10.1001/jamapsychiatry.2015.2868

McLaughlin, K. A., & Nolen-Hoeksema, S. (2011). Rumination as a transdiagnostic factor in depression and anxiety. *Behaviour Research and Therapy, 49,* 186–193. doi:10.1016/j.brat.2010.12.006

Mehta, M. A., Golembo, N. I., Nosarti, C., Colvert, E., Mota, A., Williams, S. C., . . . Sonuga-Barke, E. J. (2009). Amygdala, hippocampal and corpus callosum size following severe early institutional deprivation: The English and Romanian Adoptees study pilot. *Journal of Child Psychology and Psychiatry, 50,* 943–951. doi:10.1111/j.1469-7610.2009.02084.x

Merikangas, K. R., He, J., Burnstein, M., Swanson, S. A., Avenevoli, S., Cui, L., . . . Swendensen, J. (2010). Lifetime prevalence of mental disorders in U.S. adolescents: Results from the National Comorbidity Study-Adolescent Supplement (NCS-A). *Journal of the American Academy of Child & Adolescent Psychiatry, 49,* 980–989. doi:10.1016/j.jaac.2010.05.017

Naber, F. B., Bakermans-Kranenburg, M. J., Van Ijzendoorn, M. H., Swinkels, S. H., Buitelaar, J. K., Dietz, C., . . . Van Engeland, H. (2008). Play behavior and attachment in toddlers with autism. *Journal of Autism and Developmental Disorders, 38,* 857–866. doi:10.1007/s10803-007-0454-5

Nemeroff, C. B., Weinberger, D., Rutter, M., MacMillan, H. L., Bryant, R. A., Wessely, S., . . . Malhi, G. S. (2013). *DSM-5:* A collection of psychiatrist views on the changes, controversies, and future directions. *BMC Medicine, 11,* 202. doi:10.1186/1741-7015-11-202

Orsmond, G. I., & Seltzer, M. M. (2007). Siblings of individuals with autism spectrum disorders across the life course. *Mental Retardation and Developmental Disabilities Research Reviews, 13,* 313–320. doi:10.1002/mrdd.20171

Polyak, A., Kubina, R. M., & Girirajan, S. (2015). Comorbidity of intellectual disability confounds ascertainment of autism: Implications for genetic diagnosis. *American Journal of Medical Genetics Part B: Neuropsychiatric Genetics, 168,* 600–608. doi:10.1002/ajmg.b.32338

Salazar, F., Baird, G., Chandler, S., Tseng, E., O'Sullivan, T., Howlin, P., . . . Simonoff, E. (2015). Co-occurring psychiatric disorders in preschool and elementary school-aged children with autism spectrum disorder. *Journal of Autism and Developmental Disorders, 45,* 2283–2294. doi:10.1007/s10803-015-2361-5

Sandin, S., Schendel, D., Magnusson, P., Hultman, C., Surén, P., Susser, E., . . . Reichenberg, A. (2016). Autism risk associated with parental age and with increasing difference in age between the parents. *Molecular Psychiatry, 21,* 693–700. doi:10.1038/mp.2015.70

Shaw, P., Gogtay, N., & Rapoport, J. (2010). Childhood psychiatric disorders as anomalies in neurodevelopmental trajectories. *Human Brain Mapping, 31,* 917–925. doi:10.1002/hbm.21028

Skaar, D. A., Shao, Y., Haines, J. L., Stenger, J. E., Jaworski, J., Martin, E. R., . . . Ashley-Koch, A. E. (2005). Analysis of the RELN gene as a genetic risk factor for autism. *Molecular Psychiatry, 10,* 563–571. doi:10.1038/sj.mp.4001614

Sonuga-Barke, E. J., Kennedy, M., Kumsta, R., Knights, N., Golm, D., Rutter, M., . . . Kreppner, J. (2017). Child-to-adult neurodevelopmental and mental health trajectories after early life deprivation: The young adult follow-up of the longitudinal English and Romanian Adoptees study. *The Lancet, 389,* 1539–1548. doi:10.1016/S0140-6736(17)30045-4

Tang, G., Gudsnuk, K., Kuo, S. H., Cotrina, M. L., Rosoklija, G., Sosunov, A., . . . Yue, Z. (2014). Loss of mTOR-dependent macroautophagy causes autistic-like synaptic pruning deficits. *Neuron, 83,* 1131–1143. doi:10.1016/j.neuron.2014.07.040

Thapar, A., Cooper, M., Eyre, O., & Langley, K. (2013). What have we learnt about the causes of ADHD? *Journal of Child Psychology and Psychiatry, 54,* 3–16. doi:10.1111/j.1469-7610.2012.02611.x

Wasserstein, J. (2005). Diagnostic issues for adolescents and adults with ADHD. *Journal of Clinical Psychology, 61,* 535–547. doi:10.1002/jclp.20118

Wechsler, D. (2014). *Wechsler Intelligence Scale for Children* (5th ed.). Bloomington, MN: Pearson.

Zablotsky, B., Pringle, B. A., Colpe, L. J., Kogan, M. D., Rice, C., & Blumberg, S. J. (2015). Service and treatment use among children diagnosed with autism spectrum disorders. *Journal of Developmental and Behavioral Pediatrics, 36,* 98–105. doi:10.1097/DBP.0000000000000127

Zaidman-Zait, A., Mirenda, P., Duku, E., Vaillancourt, T., Smith, I. M., Szatmari, P., . . . Zwaigenbaum, L. (2017). Impact of personal and social resources on parenting stress in mothers of children with autism spectrum disorder. *Autism, 21,* 155–166. doi:10.1177/1362361316633033

Zayats, T., Athanasiu, L., Sonderby, I., Djurovic, S., Westlye, L. T., Tamnes, C. K., . . . Haavik, J. (2015). Genome-wide analysis of attention deficit hyperactivity disorder in Norway. *PLoS ONE, 10,* e0122501. doi:10.1371/journal.pone.0122501

Zeanah, C. H., Chesher, T., Boris, N. W., Walter, H. J., Bukstein, O. G., Bellonci, C., . . . Hayek, M. (2016). Practice parameter for the assessment and treatment of children and adolescents with reactive attachment disorder and disinhibited social engagement disorder. *Journal of the American Academy of Child & Adolescent Psychiatry, 55,* 990–1003. doi:10.1016/j.jaac.2016.08.004

Zwaigenbaum, L., Bauman, M. L., Choueiri, R., Kasari, C., Carter, A., Granpeesheh, D., . . . Pierce, K. (2015). Early intervention for children with autism spectrum disorder under 3 years of age: Recommendations for practice and research. *Pediatrics, 136,* S60–S81. doi:10.1542/peds.2014-3667E

Chapter 6

Counseling Approaches I: Behavior Modification and Behavior Analysis

Key Concepts

- Operant conditioning
- Behavioral topography
- Function of behavior
- Positive and negative reinforcement and punishment
- Extinction, extinction burst, differential reinforcement, spontaneous recovery
- Reinforcement schedules
- Intermittent reinforcement and ratio strain
- Skills training
- Video modeling
- Token economy systems
- Applied behavior analysis
- Single-subject designs
- Specialty credentialing for behavior analysis

Aligned 2016 CACREP Standards

Standard 2.F.5.a. Theories and models of counseling
Standard 2.F.5.d. Ethical and culturally relevant strategies for establishing and maintaining in-person and technology-assisted relationships

Standard 2.F.5.f. Counselor characteristics and behaviors that influence the counseling process
Standard 2.F.5.i. Development of measurable outcomes for clients
Standard 2.F.5.j. Evidence-based counseling strategies and techniques for prevention and intervention
Standard 2.F.8.b. Identification of evidence-based counseling practices
Standard 2.F.8.d. Development of outcome measures for counseling programs
Standard 2.F.8.e. Evaluation of counseling interventions and programs
Standard 2.F.8.i. Analysis and use of data in counseling

• • •

Counselors can address problems that can emerge during childhood using foundational knowledge of neurophysiological and social development during this period. In previous chapters, we learned that young children do not have the cognitive development required for insight-oriented psychotherapy, have limited frustration tolerance, and process their experiences through play. We also learned that several problems of childhood are marked by skills deficits, in particular autism and attention-deficit/hyperactivity disorder. In this chapter, we describe behavioral approaches for helping young children develop skills and reduce problem behavior. We also consider behavioral approaches to parent education. We examine the neuroscientific basis for this approach. We integrate case studies to help you understand how the behavioral approach can be applied in practice.

Behavior therapy approaches are covered only briefly (if at all) in counseling theory courses during graduate-level counselor education, and thus we recommend that you consider exploring additional texts for a more in-depth understanding of the concepts in this chapter. This chapter was informed by *Applied Behavior Analysis* (2nd ed.) by Cooper, Heron, and Heward (2007) and the *Handbook of Applied Behavior Analysis* by Fisher, Piazza, and Roane (2013). Please note that the applied behavior analysis approach described in this chapter requires specialty training and certification to practice proficiently.

Behavioral Approaches With Children

In Chapter 5, we identified problems of childhood that cause fundamental deficits in the skills required for socioemotional learning. For example, children with autism and attention-deficit/hyperactivity disorder can have deficits in social skills such as reciprocal interaction, frustration tolerance, impulse control, and perspective taking. These skills are prerequisites to other therapeutic techniques and must be learned first. For example, children with deficits in object play skills (i.e., difficulties manipulating an object as it is meant to be used) and symbolic play (i.e., pretending, engaging in imaginative play, using everyday items in creative ways) are unlikely to benefit from play therapy approaches because they lack the skills to process their internal experiences through play behavior. Also, children who struggle with frustration tolerance and impulse control will struggle with reciprocal interaction (i.e., turn taking) in small-group counseling situations. In both scenarios, the children need to learn basic skills so that they can benefit from other modalities. For this reason, we first explore behavioral approaches for counseling children before later exploring play-based and creative counseling techniques, as we believe that skill development is essential to the outcome of subsequent counseling interventions. Furthermore, our review of parent education later in the chapter builds from basic principles of operant conditioning.

Articles are beginning to emerge in the literature regarding the confluence of behavioral approaches and behavioral neuroscience. In 2015, Schlinger wrote, "The physical basis of behavioral plasticity is neuroplasticity; that is, interactions between an organism's behavior and its environment cause changes in the structure of the brain" (p. 1). For example, researchers have found brain changes in functional magnetic resonance imaging scans following behavioral intervention, such as treatments for dyslexia (Temple et al., 2003). Although no formal neuroscience-informed approaches currently exist for behavioral intervention, experts such as Donahoe (2017) have argued that behavior analysis and neuroscience are "complimentary disciplines" (p. 301).

The Function of Behavior

Humans are social animals. In prior chapters, we noted that neurophysiological development is heavily influenced by the social environment in which children are raised. For example, during infancy, the quality of the nurturing relationship with one's caregiver influences which genes are expressed and which are silenced (Meaney & Szyf, 2005; Romens, McDonald, Svaren, & Pollak, 2015). The oxytocin-influenced bond of the caregiver-child relationship also helps the child to understand the emotional experiences of others, seek out comfort when distressed, seek nurturance and attention in appropriate ways, and learn other social skills through caregiver-child synchrony and subsequent emulation or mirroring. As the child develops, the actions of other people in the environment (caregivers, teachers, peers, etc.) can influence and shape their own response. Observing and assessing the behaviors of others in the child's environment is thus crucial to understanding a child's behavior.

One of the first tasks of the behavioral approach is to identify and understand a child's behavior. The counselor should first attempt to understand the specific aspects of the behavior the child is exhibiting, known as *behavioral topography* (Cooper et al., 2007; Fisher et al., 2013). For example, *tantrum* is a fairly nondescriptive term and could consist of physical aggression toward peers or screaming loudly with the head down and fingers covering the ears. These two behaviors are obviously quite different and may serve two entirely different purposes. Thus, describing the aspects of the behavior is an important first step in understanding why the child is behaving in this specific manner rather than displaying another behavior.

Once the counselor has adequately described the behavior, they must next seek to understand the function (i.e., purpose) of the behavior. There are four main functions of behavior (Cooper et al., 2007; Fisher et al., 2013): attention, escape, obtaining tangibles, and sensation related (either seeking sensation or avoiding sensations like pain). Children seek attention to gain the interest, attuned presence, and support of others in their environment. Children use escape behavior to avoid or ignore tasks that are not preferred. Behavior can be motivated by a desire to obtain objects of interest, such as mobile technology (e.g., an iPad), preferred foods (e.g., candy), or toys. Children may also seek sensation or act to reduce sensation (e.g., attenuate the sensation of pain).

Reinforcement and Punishment

We have established that the responses of others in the child's environment can shape the child's own responding. Skinner and Thorndike's principles of operant conditioning can help us to understand what factors are influencing a child's behavior (Cooper et al., 2007; Fisher et al., 2013). According to behavioral learning theory, all behaviors follow a three-step process. The person first experiences an antecedent (A) that influences their behavioral response (B). The consequences (C) of that behavior influence the likelihood of whether the person will continue to exhibit that same behavior in the future. For example, imagine a child hears an inappropriate joke at school and observes their peers laughing at the joke. The child may later share that joke with their caregiver in the hopes that the caregiver will laugh with the child. The antecedent to this behavior is seeing the caregiver and remembering the joke (A). The behavior is sharing the joke (B). If the caregiver laughs and engages with the child, the child is more likely to share the joke with the caregiver (C). If the caregiver does not laugh at the joke, ignores the child, or even chastises the child for telling an inappropriate joke, the child is less likely to share that joke in the future (C). In this example, the child learned a behavior from others in the environment (telling an inappropriate joke), which they then performed with others. Thus, the social environment influences how and why behaviors initially occur and whether they are sustained.

Operant conditioning involves reinforcement and punishment of a child's behavior by others in the environment through addition or subtraction. Reinforcement is likely to increase the frequency with which a behavior occurs in the future, whereas punishment is likely to reduce its frequency (Cooper et al., 2007; Fisher et al., 2013). Table 6.1 depicts the four types of reinforcement and punishment.

Positive reinforcement occurs when a child obtains a desired consequence immediately following the behavior. For example, imagine a scenario in which an adult wants a child to clean up some playdough after finishing playing. If the adult were to use positive reinforcement, they might start cleaning up the playdough themselves, invite the child to help, and provide positive feedback to the child for assisting. Negative reinforcement removes an undesired consequence following a child's behavior. In this scenario, the adult might warn the child that the playdough will become rock hard and unusable if it is not cleaned up. If the child responds by cleaning up the playdough, they avoid the undesired consequence of losing future playdough play and are thus negatively reinforced. The adult in this situation could also use punishment to influence the child's behavior. For example, the adult could give more chores to the child if the child does not clean up the playdough (positive punishment) or remove a preferred activity such as watching a television show later (negative punishment). Positive reinforcement is the most effective long-term method of shaping behavior because it builds relationships. Using punishment frequently can potentially cause ruptures in relationships, as children may come to resent adults for taking away preferred activities or items or giving them nonpreferred activities with the intent to control their behavior. Punishment is often alluring to the adult, however, because it tends to be fairly effective in the short term. Children will often respond quickly to the threat of losing a preferred activity or item or receiving an undesired consequence, and their speed of response is reinforcing to the adult. For example, spanking a child following a misdeed may result in an immediate response from the child (e.g., stopping the current behavior). However, spanking over time has been associated with a host of issues, including increased negativity in caregiver-child relationships and increased internalizing (e.g., anxiety) and externalizing (e.g., aggression) problems (Gershoff & Grogan-Kaylor, 2016).

TABLE 6.1

Reinforcement and Punishment

Behavior	**Adding**	**Subtracting**
Reinforcement (increase behavior)	Positive reinforcement Behavior → Obtaining a desired consequence	Negative reinforcement Behavior → Removing an undesired consequence
Punishment (decrease behavior)	Positive punishment Behavior → Obtaining an undesired consequence	Negative punishment Behavior → Removing a desired consequence

When using reinforcement, it is essential to understand the function of a child's behavior (Cooper et al., 2007; Fisher et al., 2013). A child's motivation can dictate whether something is reinforcing or punishing. For example, showering a child with attention can be aversive to a child who dislikes attention, and reprimanding a child can be reinforcing to a child who is seeking attention.

Extinction and Differential Reinforcement

In clinical settings, some child behaviors are so problematic that they need to be curtailed. Extreme aggression, for example, is typically untenable across settings (i.e., in school, at home, etc.). *Extinction* occurs when a child's problematic behavior is eventually attenuated, usually through changes in how others respond to the child's behavior (Cooper et al., 2007; Fisher et al., 2013). During the extinction process, the adults in the child's environment intentionally seek to withdraw reinforcement for the behavior. When this occurs, it is fairly typical for the child to increase the problem behavior at first in the hopes of eventually obtaining their intended outcome. This is called an *extinction burst* (Cooper et al., 2007; Fisher et al., 2013). For example, imagine an oldest child called Maya becomes physically aggressive when her caregiver is playing with her younger sibling. In response to this aggression, the caregiver shifts his attention to attend to Maya. To initiate extinction, the parent decides to keep playing with the younger child when Maya becomes aggressive rather than transition his attention. At first, Maya may increase the intensity of her aggression in an attempt to gain the caregiver's attention. If the caregiver shifts his attention at this point, he has taught Maya that increasing aggression will help her obtain her desired outcome. It is thus paramount that adults not revert to reinforcing problematic behavior during the extinction process. This often means that adults (caregivers, teachers) will need coaching to prepare for an increase in problem behavior before initiating the extinction process. For example, if Maya could potentially become aggressive to the other sibling, the caregiver should be aware of this before extinction is initiated and ensure that the younger child is shielded from attack. If a child might break or destroy items to gain the parent's attention, objects should be removed from the area before starting extinction procedures.

Eventually, through the extinction process, the child will realize that they can no longer gain the same outcome through the same behavior and will stop the behavior. In this example, Maya will gradually learn that she cannot gain her caregiver's attention with physical aggression. As a consequence, the child may eventually retreat from seeking the caregiver's attention or try other methods. In most cases, the function of a child's behavior is not necessarily negative; it can be beneficial to help the child find ways of obtaining their desired outcome without using problematic behavior. The process of teaching a child to use different methods to get the same outcome is called *differential reinforcement* (Cooper et al., 2007; Fisher et al., 2013). In the case of Maya, the caregiver could teach her to seek out and receive situationally appropriate attention without using problem behavior. For example, the caregiver could invite Maya into the play activity and give Maya positive feedback on their collaborative play with her sibling. This not only would provide the attention that Maya is seeking but also may facilitate sibling bonding. When it is not situationally appropriate for the caregiver to involve Maya in the activity, he could demonstrate other forms of attention, such as holding Maya's hand or stroking her back while playing with the younger sibling. A child could also be taught to develop frustration tolerance for short periods, such as waiting 2 minutes before receiving attention. Note here that the replacement behavior should serve the same function as the problem behavior. Giving a child a tangible (e.g., candy) would not satisfy their attentional needs, and we do not recommend giving children technology (iPads, etc.) when they have legitimate needs for caregiver attention.

On occasion, even after extinction, the child may have a spontaneous recovery of a problem behavior. See Reflection Question 6.1. In such instances, the adults in the environment need only to continue their extinction procedure (in the case above, providing differential reinforcement for attention) for the extinction process to be completed. Figure 6.1 illustrates the extinction process.

Skills Training

The principles of operant conditioning can help students to learn new skills in addition to extinguishing behavior. Learning new skills is often complex and requires that skills be broken down into their component

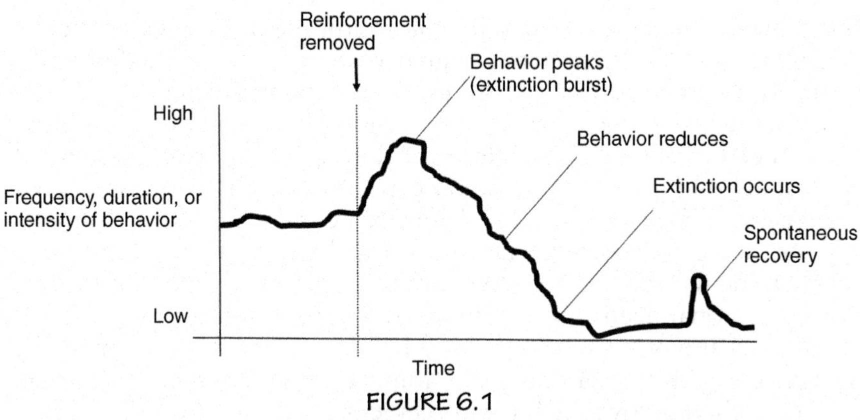

FIGURE 6.1

Extinction

Reflection Question 6.1

Identify a behavior problem that a child might struggle with. Develop a behavior intervention plan to extinguish the behavior that includes differential reinforcement.

parts (Cooper et al., 2007; Fisher et al., 2013). Each component can then be learned in a progressive sequence. Reinforcement can be used to help a child progress through each component. For example, to learn reciprocal interaction (i.e., turn taking), a child may need to master several components, such as (a) initiating interaction appropriately, (b) identifying a transitional moment in the conversation, (c) pausing or inviting input from the other person, (d) attending to the verbal communication of the other person, (e) waiting until the person has finished speaking before interjecting, and (f) responding directly to the verbal content of the other person. Technology can be facilitative to social skills development. For example, children with autism may benefit from watching a video recording of themselves or others completing this sequence, an intervention known as *video modeling* (Bellini & Akullian, 2007).

Reinforcement Schedules

When a child is learning play skills such as object play or symbolic play, the adult leading the intervention (parent, teacher, counselor, etc.) should consider the schedule by which they are providing reinforcement and clearly communicate this schedule to the child (Cooper et al., 2007; Fisher et al., 2013). For example, when teaching reciprocal interaction, the adult could provide reinforcement following each step of the six-part procedure. The adult could also provide reinforcement on a time system (e.g., every 2 minutes of attentive and engaged interaction in the skills training procedure). Reinforcement could also be provided on a ratio schedule (e.g., reinforcement received for the completion of two steps in the sequence) or an interval schedule (e.g., reinforcement for every 2 minutes of task engagement).

When learning new skills or reinforcing new behavior, children often need to start with smaller expectations for shorter amounts of time and build to larger and longer expectations as they become more proficient (Cooper et al., 2007; Fisher et al., 2013). For example, asking Maya to postpone her attentional needs for 10 minutes is likely to be too long at first. As Maya becomes more able to postpone her attentional needs for 2 minutes at a time, reinforcement (in this example, caregiver attention) should be provided after incrementally longer intervals (i.e., 4 minutes, 6 minutes, 8 minutes, etc.). Modifying the schedule by which reinforcement is provided is called *intermittent reinforcement* (Cooper et al., 2007; Fisher et al., 2013). As reinforcement becomes more challenging to achieve, it can actually increase the child's motivation to continue practicing the new behavior. Maya's motivation to wait for parental attention will increase if the length of time until reinforcement is extended. However, if her caregiver were to move to longer periods of time too quickly or have too great a jump in time until reinforcement (say, from 2 minutes to 10 minutes), Maya may experience difficulties adjusting to this new requirement. This adjustment problem is called *ratio strain* (Cooper et al., 2007; Fisher et al., 2013).

Token Economy Systems

Token economy systems are often used to help children understand that they are making progress toward receiving a reinforcer. In a token economy, the child receives stickers or tokens that they can eventually trade for the reinforcer (Cooper et al., 2007; Fisher et al., 2013). For example, a child engaging in reciprocal dialogue might receive a sticker for every 2 minutes of engagement in the procedure. After amassing five stickers, the child could elect to receive a preferred reward (e.g., time with mobile technology, a small prize, the ability to choose the story at story time). Because the reward should be motivating to the child, the token economy procedure should be individualized to each child.

A word of caution about token economy systems: We have worked in multiple settings that use token economies in a manner that is ineffective. The principles of operant conditioning that we described earlier are essential to the success of a token economy system. Each token economy system should (a) provide reinforcement on a predictable and achievable schedule; (b) clearly define the expected behavior for receiving reinforcement; (c) ensure that expected behaviors are based on a protocol for skills training and therefore are individualized to the procedure; (d) provide reinforcement that is motivating to the child; and (e) avoid removing tokens, stickers, or rewards later, because the system is designed for reinforcement rather than punishment. Thom once worked in a setting that did not adhere to any of these guidelines. The children had to complete an entire day of activities before receiving reinforcement (too long, behaviors were not well defined), children were only given the option of receiving a toy reinforcer at the end of the day (tokens were not individualized to the motivations of each child), and stickers and prizes were removed for undesired behavior such as aggression (punitive, not just reinforcing). Perhaps most important, the setting did not have a specific skills training plan on which to base the token economy system. Such token economy systems tend to reward compliance (i.e., following rules) rather than learning new skills. Children may develop a dislike of these token economy systems because they cannot see the apparent benefits of them (i.e., they do not feel they are learning new skills) and may perceive them as controlling.

In the case study of Mandy (see Case Vignetter 6.1), Thom provides a first-person account of the counseling process to explain how skills training can be used in counseling, using the earlier example of skill development for reciprocity (i.e., turn taking).

Case Vignette 6.1 Mandy

In private practice, I once worked with a 10-year-old Asian American cisgender female named Mandy. She was brought into counseling by her parents, who were concerned that Mandy seemed withdrawn socially. In the first few meetings, Mandy talked through the entire session without pause and without asking for my thoughts or input. Mandy's lack of reciprocity during dialogue was repeated in her relationships with peers. Mandy often reported that her peers typically ignored her when she started a conversation rather than seeking to join with her. Without intervention, Mandy would continue to struggle with forming relationships with peers. Reciprocal communication was thus an early target of intervention.

After Mandy agreed that learning reciprocal dialogue was an important counseling goal, I created and explained a skills training procedure for our sessions together. Each time Mandy paused her dialogue to invite input from me, she received a token. Each time she attended to my verbal communication, she received another token. On receiving six tokens, she was able to select a piece of preferred candy to take home with her. Often she shared this candy with her siblings. Her parents also approved of the procedure prior to its initiation.

The initial few weeks of the skills training procedure were challenging for Mandy. She would get lost in conversation and needed prompting to pause and ask for my input. When she did pause, her transitions were awkward. For example, Mandy would ask me about a topic unrelated to what she was discussing (e.g., "So what about you?") rather than invite my input into her dialogue. My feedback to her was thus crucial to her understanding of how reciprocal dialogue worked. Over time, Mandy's ability to invite me into her dialogue was much improved. As with all behavioral interventions, we eventually shifted the focus of our work to generalizing this skill to her peer relationships. As a result of our work, Mandy began to share stories of having deeper and more meaningful relationships with peers. After 2 years of therapy, Mandy was ready to stop counseling, having mastered her new skill of reciprocal interaction.

• • •

Applied Behavior Analysis

Perhaps the gold-standard intervention for autism is applied behavior analysis, which uses the behavioral principles described earlier to help children with autism learn a multitude of skills, including verbal behavior, play skills, and social skills in addition to academic knowledge and skills (Wong et al., 2015). Applied behavior analysis involves extensive and regular use of data collection to understand the function of behavior, antecedents to behavior, and consequences to behavior. Data are often collected via frequency counts (i.e., tallying) in addition to counting time length (e.g., time on task). Data are graphed to understand the response to an intervention and appraise the effectiveness of the current approach. For example, data can be compared among baseline, intervention, withdrawal of intervention, and return to intervention conditions. This is called an *A-B-A-B design* and is classified as a single-subject design because it measures the rate of change for a single person.

Applied behavior analysis is a specialized area of practice requiring additional coursework and experience beyond a master's degree. If you are interested in this intervention and would like more information, we recommend that you consider exploring organization websites, such as the website of the Association for Behavior Analysis International (https://www.abainternational.org/welcome.aspx). We also recommend that counselors who wish to specialize in behavioral approaches consider pursuing the Board Certified Behavior Analyst (BCBA) credential through the Behavior Analyst Certification Board. Note that the Behavior Analyst Certification Board recently changed its prerequisite requirements, so master's degrees in counseling may not necessarily meet prerequisite educational requirements for the BCBA post-master's course sequence. Counselors may need to complete a second master's degree, which is a significant barrier to counselors who wish to pursue BCBA certification.

Application to the Case of Wayne

To better understand how these behavioral principles can be comprehensively applied, we return to the case study of Wayne from the previous chapter to provide an in-depth example of applying positive reinforcement to extinguish problem behavior. Thom once worked with Wayne and uses first-person narrative to describe the counseling process (see Case Vignette 6.2).

In this case example, Wayne responded positively and made substantial progress because he understood the procedures by which he could earn his preferred activities and foods, and he understood that these procedures would help him acquire his desired objects or activities more easily and predictably. Children will often elect not to

Case Vignette 6.2 Wayne, Part 2

When I started working with Wayne, an 8-year-old Euro-American male, I noticed he exhibited multiple problematic behaviors, such as severe physical aggression toward his peers, teachers, and parents for the purpose of escaping academic work and obtaining tangibles (e.g., fast food, access to video games). Several of Wayne's behaviors had developed as a result of how others in his environment, in particular his parents, had responded to him. For example, his parents would purchase fast food from two restaurants, even though Wayne would not eat one of the meals, just to avoid his behavioral outbursts in the car. The parents were thus positively reinforcing Wayne's pursuit of tangibles by providing him with desired consequences (e.g., fast food) after Wayne became aggressive. They also negatively reinforced Wayne's escape behavior by withdrawing chore requirements following aggressive episodes. These parental behaviors taught Wayne that he was able to obtain desired objects and avoid nonpreferred tasks through physical aggression. At school, Wayne sought to use the same tactics, though they were less successful in this setting. As a result, Wayne preferred to remain at home rather than attend school because he had less control over the school environment. On the day he bit another child's ear, he had increasingly escalated his aggressive behavior to avoid academic work. His teacher and the teacher assistants had initially attempted to ignore the aggressive behavior rather than reinforce it, until Wayne escalated his behavior to the extent that a crisis ensued and his instructional staff could no longer push through the escape behavior because of safety concerns. School leaders reviewed the case subsequent to this incident and decided that Wayne's behaviors were too severe at this time for Wayne to remain at Maple Valley Elementary. Wayne was transferred to a more restrictive setting (i.e., a school designed for children with severe behavioral problems). I worked directly with Wayne in the specialized school environment.

As the counselor in this situation, I had several options for how best to address Wayne's behavior within the school context. One of Wayne's primary educational goals was to complete his assigned classwork. I collaborated with Wayne's teacher to create a behavior plan that used positive reinforcement to assist Wayne in task completion, pairing both escape and tangibles as reinforcers. Wayne was motivated by

(Continued)

Case Vignette 6.2 *(Continued)*

escape behavior, and so a reasonable behavior plan would grant Wayne enjoyable breaks from his academic work at designated time intervals. Wayne liked listening to music, and so his breaks usually involved listening to a preferred song using headphones. The length of these intervals was shorter at first and became longer as Wayne demonstrated successful response to the intervention. For example, Wayne could initially work for 5 minute intervals to receive a 5 minute break. As he made progress, he could work for 10 minute intervals (and so on) before receiving his 5 minute break. This approach was likely to be successful because (a) Wayne was better able to fulfill the function of his aggressive behavior (i.e., escape), (b) Wayne developed rapport with the staff because he was being reinforced rather than punished for his behavior, and (c) the length of time on task was fairly short at first and thus achievable for Wayne. Wayne responded well to this intervention and made rapid progress. By the end of the academic year, Wayne had mastered several new academic skills and displayed infrequent and fairly minor aggressive episodes at school.

Another major area of intervention was working with Wayne's parents to reduce his aggressive behavior at home. Wayne's parents attended several meetings at the school accompanied by Wayne's new in-home counselor to develop a behavior plan that they could implement at home. These meetings helped to ensure consistency in the implementation of the behavior plan between the school and home environments. Like at school, Wayne was motivated by task avoidance and obtaining tangibles at home. His parents disclosed that they had eventually granted Wayne access to screen time when he became aggressive after trying other methods. They understood that Wayne's aggression could now also serve the function of obtaining screen time. The parents also agreed that Wayne's fast food consumption needed to be curtailed for health reasons. I suggested that Wayne's preference for screen time could be a helpful motivational tool. The parents anticipated an initial extinction burst on restricting Wayne's screen time and fast food access, though they reported feeling ready to work through his initial increase in aggression with the in-home counselor's support.

Together we created a behavior plan that emphasized the use of positive reinforcement to learn new behaviors. To

(Continued)

Case Vignette 6.2 *(Continued)*

extinguish Wayne's aggressive behavior, we first identified differential reinforcement procedures. We created two different protocols, one for car rides and one for chore completion. The parents elected to give Wayne his choice of either screen time (30 minutes) or a preferred snack at home if he was able to complete a car ride without demonstrating aggression. The parents also granted Wayne screen time (30 minutes) if he completed daily chores. The ratio of chores to screen time was fairly low at first (i.e., relatively few chores were required to receive screen time) and increased gradually each week. The parents were also free to permit Wayne to watch television with them as a family so that Wayne did not associate them solely with withdrawing access to screen time. Providing reinforcement on a predetermined schedule without requiring task completion is known as *noncontingent reinforcement*. Because escape behavior was a motivation, the parents also granted breaks with preferred music when completing homework, using the same intervals as at school. Prior to initiating the intervention plan, the parents purchased an additional safety harness for the car that Wayne was unable to unbuckle while the car was in motion. The parents also removed valuable items from the house that Wayne could potentially destroy in response to these new expectations. Wayne responded surprisingly well to the behavior plan and even asked for the intervention plan to include his ability to earn other reinforcers for his behavior, such as playing video games on the computer with his father (they enjoyed playing a specific game together). Although Wayne still asked frequently for fast food during car rides, he seemed satisfied with receiving a healthier preferred snack at home.

• • •

use physical aggression if an easier option is available for achieving their desired outcome. Thom also identified the topography (physical aggression) and the function of Wayne's behavior (escape and obtaining tangibles) and used this information to inform intervention planning. Note that previous token economy systems had not worked with Wayne, and the intervention plan did not use a token economy system. Aside from fast food (which was not a feasible reinforcer), Wayne was motivated by screen time. Placing screen time on a token economy system was likely to be unsuccessful, because Wayne would need more immediate access to this reinforcer following task completion. In our experience, token economies work best for obtaining larger reinforcers and are also quite difficult to maintain (i.e., the parent has to remember to give the child a token or sticker at regular intervals). See Reflection Question 6.2. Because of this, we do not recommend that token economies be the automatic go-to intervention when planning behavior modification.

Parent Education

When working with children from a behavioral approach, we have found it crucial to include caregivers in intervention planning. Some caregivers can have an important role in sustaining problem behaviors (as seen in the case of Wayne), and modifying their response to the child's behavior is central to the change process and the outcomes of counseling. Other caregivers have a more peripheral role in a child's problem behavior (e.g., the child's behavior may occur at school only) but may still have a role in reinforcing new skills in the home environment. We have observed that when caregivers do not adhere to a behavior intervention plan at home, the child's ability to make sustained and generalized changes is limited significantly. When the child's problem behavior is occurring at school, the counselor should attempt to make contact with the child's teacher and include them in intervention planning.

Caregivers have important roles throughout the intervention process, and education can be helpful at different intervals in treatment. In the case of Wayne, the caregivers being aware of and planning for his anticipated extinction burst was a crucial aspect of the intervention. For the intervention to be successful, the counselor needed to first educate the parents on the concepts of extinction and extinction bursts and then problem-solve how to manage anticipated spikes in problem behavior. After Wayne's parents initiated the extinction protocol, they should have consulted with the counselor to troubleshoot and process events that occurred in response to the intervention. The counselor (if an in-home therapist) should have observed these interactions. Principles of positive reinforcement remain important during parent education. Caregivers should be able to understand and identify the exact behaviors they are expected to manifest and should receive positive reinforcement from the counselor for following the protocol and making gains in changing their response to

Reflection Question 6.2

The behavioral approach was highly successful with Wayne. Why might it have been a good fit for Wayne? What benefits does this behavioral intervention have over other approaches?

the child. Remember, change is a challenging process for everyone, regardless of age!

When providing parent education about the behavioral approach, we recommend providing examples to explain behavioral terminology and using graphic figures as needed. Parents may be confused by concepts such as reinforcement and punishment, and examples can help to clarify these terms. In addition, we recommend that counselors write the behavior plan in a manner that is understandable to the parent and thus more easily followed.

Conclusion

Child neural development is heavily dependent on environmental influences and events, such as attachment to parents and guardians. Behavioral approaches are helpful for reducing problem behavior and assisting children to develop new skills, because these approaches have the potential to change environmental influences that shape a child's behavior (e.g., how others respond to the child). Counselors who use behavioral approaches should become familiar with and competent in the fundamental underlying principles of operant conditioning, such as topography, the function of behavior, positive reinforcement, extinction and differential reinforcement, reinforcement schedules, and intermittent reinforcement. Without an understanding of these principles, counselors are likely to misapply this approach and experience less success with their child clients. Counselors should also consider how to educate caregivers in this approach so that caregivers can also adhere to intervention protocols.

Quiz Questions

1. A parent asks their child to take a time out in the bedroom after the child becomes physically aggressive. The child experiences this as aversive, as they want to continue playing a game in the living room. This is an example of
   a. Negative reinforcement
   b. Positive punishment
   c. Negative punishment
2. A parent asks their child to take a time out in the bedroom after the child becomes physically aggressive. The child experiences this as rewarding, as they want to avoid homework. This is an example of
   a. Negative reinforcement
   b. Positive punishment
   c. Negative punishment

3. Token economy systems are frequently unsuccessful because
   a. Children are generally unable to understand the abstract value of a token
   b. The system does not follow the principles of operant conditioning
   c. Adults are generally unwilling to give rewards for desired behavior

References

Bellini, S., & Akullian, J. (2007). A meta-analysis of video modeling and video self-modeling interventions for children and adolescents with autism spectrum disorders. *Exceptional Children, 73,* 264–287. doi:10.1177/001440290707300301

Cooper, J. O., Heron, T. E., & Heward, W. L. (2007). *Applied behavior analysis* (2nd ed.). New York, NY: Pearson.

Council for Accreditation of Counseling and Related Educational Programs. (2015). *2016 CACREP standards.* Alexandria, VA: Author.

Donahoe, J. W. (2017). Behavior analysis and neuroscience: Complimentary disciplines. *Journal of Experimental Analysis of Behavior, 107,* 301–320. doi:10.1002/jeab.251

Fisher, W. W., Piazza, C. C., & Roane, H. S. (2013). *Handbook of applied behavior analysis.* New York, NY: Guilford Press.

Gershoff, E. T., & Grogan-Kaylor, A. (2016). Spanking and child outcomes: Old controversies and new meta-analyses. *Journal of Family Psychology, 30,* 453–469. doi:10.1037/fam0000191

Meaney, M. J., & Szyf, M. (2005). Environmental programming of stress responses through DNA methylation: Life at the interface between a dynamic environment and fixed genome. *Dialogues in Clinical Neurosciences, 7,* 103–123.

Romens, S. E., McDonald, J., Svaren, J., & Pollak, S. D. (2015). Associations between early life stress and gene methylation in children. *Child Development, 86,* 303–309. doi:10.1111/cdev.12270

Schlinger, H. D. (2015). Behavior analysis and behavioral neuroscience. *Frontiers in Human Neuroscience, 9,* 1–4. doi:10.3389/fnhum.2015.00210

Temple, E., Deutsch, G. K., Poldrack, R. A., Miller, S. L., Tallal, P., Merzenich, M. M., & Gabrieli, J. D. E. (2003). Neural deficits in children with dyslexia ameliorated by behavioral remediation: Evidence from functional MRI. *Proceedings of the National Academy of Sciences, USA, 100,* 2860–2865. doi:10.1073/pnas.0030098100

Wong, C., Odom, S. L., Hume, K. A., Cox, A. W., Fettig, A., Kucharczyk, S., . . . Schultz, T. R. (2015). Evidence-based practices for children, youth, and young adults with autism spectrum disorder: A comprehensive review. *Journal of Autism and Developmental Disorders, 45,* 1951–1966. doi:10.1007/s10803-014-2351-z

Chapter 7

Counseling Approaches II: Play Therapy and the Creative Arts

Key Concepts

- Child-centered play therapy
- Four basic messages
- Playroom specifications
- Toy categories (real-life, aggressive, creative expression)
- Limit setting and the ACT model
- Therapist presence
- Verbal tracking
- Interpretation
- Creative counseling approaches
- Specialty credentialing for play therapy

Aligned 2016 CACREP Standards

Standard 2.F.5.a. Theories and models of counseling

Standard 2.F.5.d. Ethical and culturally relevant strategies for establishing and maintaining in-person and technology-assisted relationships

Standard 2.F.5.f. Counselor characteristics and behaviors that influence the counseling process

Standard 2.F.5.j. Evidence-based counseling strategies and techniques for prevention and intervention

Standard 2.F.8.b. Identification of evidence-based counseling practices

• • •

In Chapter 4, on neurophysiological and social development during childhood, we reviewed the neuroscientific and empirical support for the importance of child engagement in play behavior. To summarize, play is associated with enhanced synaptic connections from brain-derived neurotrophic factor transcription in the amygdala and dorsolateral prefrontal cortex (Gordon, Burke, Akil, Watson, & Panksepp, 2003) and with activation in the prefrontal cortex and striatum (Van Kerkhof, Damsteegt, Trezza, Voorn, & Vanderschuren, 2013). These impacts on brain function are associated with enhanced regulatory capacity over directed attention, motivation, and emotional processing (Gordon et al., 2003; Van Kerkhof et al., 2013). Children often use play to process their emotional experiences, and unstructured and self-directed play that facilitates creativity and mental processing is most helpful in this regard (Ginsberg & Committee on Communications, 2007). Observing a child's play behavior thus gives adults and caregivers an insight into the child's inner world (Ginsberg & Committee on Communications, 2007). Interacting with a child during play is also a vehicle for adults to demonstrate an attentive presence and caring about what is important to the child. Play therapy and other creative approaches thus have a strong neuroscientific basis for helping children process their emotional experiences and enhancing children's regulatory capacity. They can also impact the counseling process by facilitating the development of initial rapport, deepening existing relationships, and helping the counselor understand the inner world of the child.

Play therapy and creative approaches are particularly important with children because of their stage of neural development. Children have not fully developed structures of the prefrontal cortex associated with emotional regulation and self-awareness. They are thus less able to put words to their experience and engage in self-appraisal tasks associated with insight-oriented approaches, such as appraising thoughts in cognitive behavior therapy (T. A. Field, Beeson, & Jones, 2015). Play-based and creative approaches are developmentally appropriate approaches for work with children because they do not require highly developed verbal skills. The neural mechanisms of play therapy seem similar to those of talk therapies (e.g., activation of the prefrontal cortex to regulate emotions).

In this chapter, we describe Landreth's (2012) child-centered play therapy (CCPT) approach in depth to promote a deeper understanding of how to apply play therapy with children. We recommend that you consider reading Landreth's seminal text *Play Therapy: The Art of the Relationship* (3rd ed.) for more information about CCPT, in addition to a text by Ray (2011) that contains a treatment manual in the appendix. Although we primarily cover CCPT in this chapter, we should mention that play therapy has a number of theoretical models (Crenshaw & Stewart, 2016; Kottman, 2014). If you want to explore other theoretical approaches to play therapy in addition to CCPT, we recommend two texts that comprehensively cover different play therapy theories: *Play Therapy: A Comprehensive Guide to Theory and Practice* by Crenshaw and Stewart (2016) and *Play Therapy: Basics and Beyond* (2nd ed.) by Kottman (2014).

Neuroscience has not yet been comprehensively integrated into existing play therapy and creative arts approaches, and formalized neuroscience-informed approaches to play therapy and the creative arts do not exist at the time of this writing. To help you apply neuroscience to play therapy, we include an abridged and modified version of a case vignette that was published in an article on the application of neuroscience to play therapy by Stewart, Field, and Echterling (2016). We recommend that you consider reading this article for more information about how to integrate neuroscience into play therapy practice.

CCPT

CCPT has its roots in person-centered therapy (Landreth, 2012). One of Carl Rogers's students, Virginia Axline, applied Rogerian principles to her work with children. As with person-centered therapy, the goal of CCPT is to provide the core conditions of genuineness, accurate empathic understanding, and unconditional positive regard to grant children the space to process their emotions and experiences through self-direction (Axline, 1947). Thus, CCPT is a way of being rather than specific interventions per se (Sweeney & Landreth, 2009). The counselor's role is to deliver four basic messages through their presence and actions: *I am here, I hear you, I understand, I care* (Sweeney & Landreth, 2009). CCPT is believed to empower children through the counselor's belief in their abilities to process their own experiences (Landreth, 2012). Landreth (2012) created 10 basic tenets for CCPT that include respect for the child (e.g., children think and act differently from adults and are not mini-adults, children are capable of complex emotions and thoughts, children are unique and resilient), a belief in the child's self-directed capabilities, and the importance of counselor knowledge of developmental trajectories (e.g., child development cannot be sped up by adults).

Playroom Specifications

CCPT should take place in a sufficiently prepared playroom. The playroom should be of sufficient size that the child can move freely without becoming overwhelmed by space (Ray, 2011). Landreth (2012) suggested that the optimal size of a playroom is typically 12 × 15 feet. The playroom should ideally have access to a sink for cleaning up paints and other things, have uncarpeted floors, and have a two-way mirror for observation (e.g., parent observation; Ray, 2011).

Object and Toy Categories

During CCPT, the counselor sets up the playroom with different types of objects and toys for the child to explore. The types of objects typically found in a playroom can include figurines, masks, puppets, a paint easel, dress-up clothes, a dollhouse, a toy kitchen, medical toys, musical instruments, playdough, sand trays, animal family figurines, and so on. These objects should represent the three broad categories of real-life toys (e.g., toy kitchen, medical toys), aggressive toys (e.g., toy swords, superhero figures), and creative expression (e.g., puppets, playdough, musical instruments; Landreth, 2012). Objects in the playroom should be selected on the basis of three principles: The object should serve a therapeutic purpose, enable the child to express themselves, and help the counselor build a relationship with the child (Ray, 2011). Common play objects such as computer games, puzzles, and books may not meet these criteria (Ray, 2011). The placement of items in the room should make logical sense to the child, with similar toys grouped together (Ray, 2011). Toys should also be stored in the same place so that the child becomes familiar with where the objects in the room are located across sessions. This predictability is important to reduce the chaos that children often experience outside of the playroom (Ray, 2011). See Reflection Question 7.1.

Limit Setting and the ACT Model

Once the child enters the playroom, they should be oriented to a few basic limits for emotional and physical safety, such as no physical aggression toward others (e.g., toward the therapist) and staying in the playroom until the end of the session except in case of an injury or desperately needing the bathroom (Ray, 2011). Providing too many limits can stunt creativity, so the counselor must be thoughtful when selecting rules to strike a balance (see Reflection Question 7.2). Landreth (2012) proposed that if a child breaks or challenges a limit, such as by destroying toys or attacking the counselor, the counselor should respond using the ACT model (Acknowledge the

Reflection Question 7.1

Imagine you are working in a setting that does not have a dedicated playroom, yet you want to use play therapy with your clients. How could you use the principles listed here to adequately set up a room for play therapy?

Reflection Question 7.2

Imagine you are setting up a play therapy practice. Which three or four rules would you select to emphasize with all children who will receive play therapy? Why would you choose these rules over others?

wants and feelings of the child, Communicate the limit, Target reasonable alternatives). In rare cases when the child does not respond to limit setting, the play therapy session should be concluded early.

Therapeutic Presence

During the play therapy session, the task of the counselor is to demonstrate a grounding presence through an open posture and calm tone of voice while also avoiding an overly animated display of affect (Ray, 2011). During the session, the counselor uses concise and succinct reflections of content, feeling, and meaning to verbally track the behavior of the child (Ray, 2011). Comments should facilitate creativity and assist with the development of self-esteem (e.g., "You did it!" and "You made that look just like you wanted"). Verbal communication by the counselor should demonstrate attentive observation and use interpretation sparingly. Providing too much interpretation in CCPT is believed to restrict the child's own self-direction. Interpretations are reserved for important connections that help the child understand the context of their behavior with the outside world (e.g., "The daddy bear is angry and attacks the other bears"). Most verbal tracking is therefore observational in nature, and counselors should be careful to avoid adding unnecessary interpretations. For example, when making an observation about a child's decision to select a certain toy, the comment "You have selected that red car" is preferable to an interpretive statement such as "I see you went for the fastest car."

Application to the Case of Michael

To show how the CCPT model can be applied with children, we present the following Case Vignette 7.1 of Michael. This abridged and modified version of a case from an article by Stewart et al. (2016) provides an example of how to apply neuroscience in play therapy practice. Thom uses first-person narrative to describe the counseling process.

In working with Michael, Thom became aware of his need to process his thoughts and feelings regarding his transition between households every 2 weeks. By providing the core conditions, Michael was able to play out his internal thoughts and feelings. On learning about Michael's adjustment difficulties and the neuroscientific reasons

Case Vignette 7.1 Michael

In my private practice, I worked with a 6-year-old African American male named Michael. His parents brought him to counseling at the suggestion of his school counselor. Michael had been disruptive in the classroom at school and was having difficulty sitting still and following directions. He also tended to shut down quickly on making errors in his work. His teacher and parents both completed a hyperactivity screening inventory, and the results did not suggest the presence of attention-deficit/hyperactivity disorder.

At home, Michael could become defiant, aggressive, and destructive at times. His parents were unsure of the exact antecedent. Michael's parents had divorced a few years ago, and he had been living with his mother and father since then, alternating between households every week. The day of the transition between households was the most difficult day of the week for Michael.

During the first session of play therapy, Michael selected a dollhouse and played through daily routines with African American figurines. Within a few sessions, Michael began playing out more destructive themes in his play with the dollhouse. Michael moved the dollhouse between different stations within the room. During transitions, Michael would aggressively attack the dollhouse so that it collapsed before moving all of the pieces to another part of the room. He would also throw the figures around the room during these transitions.

After five sessions, the room in which I conducted therapy had been reassigned to a full-time therapist and I was asked by office staff to move to another room in the building. Michael's first session in the new room was (somewhat predictably) a challenging one, as he refused to follow the limits of the playroom and attempted to throw larger objects around the room. I used the Landreth ACT model to set limits, which helped Michael to eventually temper his aggression that day.

This event helped me understand that Michael was processing his thoughts and feelings about transitioning between households in his play. The change in households caused him internal anxiety and anger, which he was unable to fully express through words. During the 10th session, I invited the parents into the session to observe Michael's play and explained to them afterward what I thought was occurring. The parents were relieved to learn that Michael's

(Continued)

Case Vignette 7.1 *(Continued)*

behavior made sense. Both parents committed themselves to implementing a plan that would reduce Michael's frustration by informing him about transitions ahead of time, even playing them out with him, and also attempting to increase consistency in expectations and limits between households. They also agreed to be more nurturing and understanding of Michael if he demonstrated problem behaviors during transitions between households.

Michael's parents were impressed by the effectiveness of play therapy and wanted to understand how it was helping Michael. I provided a neuroscientific explanation for why play therapy was more helpful for children than insight-oriented talk therapy approaches. In terms the parents could understand, I described the ongoing development of the prefrontal cortex and children's inability to put words to their experiences. I also described the use of play to activate the prefrontal cortex and striatum to regulate emotions through expressing and communicating emotional experiences. The parents reported that this explanation made intuitive sense to them.

Over time, Michael formed a strong bond with me and looked forward to his play therapy sessions. As I had expected, Michael's 18th and final session was a challenge for him. I prepared Michael for the transition ahead of time, giving him a countdown calendar for three consecutive weeks. In the final session, Michael had difficulty remaining on task and moved frequently from station to station around the room. He rebuffed my suggestion to create a book of the drawings that he had created during therapy as a closing activity. As the session drew to an end, Michael paced the room and eventually was able to express "Why can't I keep coming?" I reflected that Michael wanted to keep coming and found this change to be stressful and difficult. I also reinforced his ability to communicate his wants and needs. I then explained that we had achieved our goals for therapy, as his teacher and parents felt he was better able to cope with change at school and home. Michael accepted this explanation, gave me a final high five, and left the room with his mother.

• • •

for why he was not able to communicate these difficulties directly, Michael's parents helped him adjust better to transitioning between households. Michael's attention and concentration at school improved, perhaps as a result of feeling less angst about transitions at home. This case illustrates the importance of closely attending to and observing a child's behavior and using several data points (e.g., play involving the dollhouse, the child's reaction to moving to a different therapy room) to make an interpretation.

Play Therapy Outcomes

Meta-analyses have found CCPT to be an effective intervention, in particular for (a) children younger than 7 years of age; (b) children from African American, Latinx, and Asian or Asian American ethnic backgrounds; and (c) children struggling with self-efficacy and caregiver-child relationship stress (Lin & Bratton, 2014). Play therapy seems most effective with full parental involvement (Lin & Bratton, 2014), and we recommend that counselors equip their playrooms with two-way mirrors to facilitate parental involvement.

We encourage counselors who have an interest in becoming proficient in play therapy to visit the website of the Association for Play Therapy (https://www.a4pt.org/) and consider pursuing the Registered Play Therapist credential. Many states also have branches of the Association for Play Therapy. Attending a state branch event would provide the opportunity to meet other counselors who are practicing play therapy.

The Creative Arts in Counseling

In addition to play therapy, we have often used other creative approaches to help children process their thoughts and feelings. Like play therapy, creative arts approaches are helpful for children whose prefrontal cortex is under development and thus whose verbal capacity for insight-oriented talk therapy is limited. A multitude of activities and exercises use the creative arts in counseling. In this section, we present several examples of creative approaches that are useful for both individual and group counseling modalities. For more examples, we recommend the excellent comprehensive guide to the use of creative arts in counseling by Gladding (2016). Although we do not cover art therapy, dance therapy, and music therapy in this chapter, it is worth mentioning that these creative art disciplines have specialized training and credentialing.

Therapeutic Letters

Unresolved issues in relationships can cause us great internal stress, at times inducing anxiety and depression. In inpatient and residential settings, we often worked with children who were struggling with aspects of their relationships with former or current caregivers. For example, children may experience parental absenteeism, loss and grief, abuse and neglect, domestic violence, and foster care placements, among other stressors. In many of these situations, children are unable to talk through their feelings with the person toward whom they have unresolved feelings. They may be unable to contact the person because the caregiver has disappeared, there is a court order, or so on. They may also feel that the person in question would be unable to hear their perspective or fear (often justifiably) that the person would not respond in a productive manner. In such scenarios, we have used therapeutic letter writing as a means of helping children to express their thoughts and feelings.

In most cases, children need very little direction to complete a therapeutic letter. This letter is typically not sent, which enables children to express themselves without fear of retaliation. This activity often generates strong emotional responses from the child, and for this reason it can be useful for the child to write the letter during a counseling session, so that the child can process their feelings afterward. Many children can anticipate that writing a therapeutic letter will be activating and may hesitate to complete the task. We recommend that counselors fully explore a child's readiness to write a letter prior to assigning it as a therapeutic task.

Another useful approach for addressing unresolved issues in counseling is to ask the child to give voice to their thoughts and feelings by imagining the person toward whom they have unresolved issues and talking aloud to that person as if the person were in the room. The child can then imagine the person's response and give voice to it. This back-and-forth inner dialogue can be repeated until the child has fully processed their thoughts and feelings. This intervention is a modification of the empty chair technique from gestalt therapy (N. P. Field & Horowitz, 1998). In our experience, children often balk at the counselor's direction to talk directly to a chair. However, they may be willing to talk aloud to an imaginary figure in the room, which serves the same purpose. Like therapeutic letter writing, this intervention is likely to generate significant affect for the child, and the child should be informed about the activating nature of the exercise before its initiation.

To show the value of therapeutic letter writing as a creative arts intervention with children, we present Case Vignette 7.2 of Denise. Michelle uses first-person narrative to describe the counseling process.

In working with Denise, Michelle realized just how much Denise had survived. Reading her words from a piece of paper seemed to hurt Denise a bit less than engaging in general talk therapy about all of the trauma she had experienced. Michelle was able to support Denise while providing her with a creative way to share her story. Denise's case illustrates that finding other ways to allow children to express themselves, tell their story, and be heard is important to their healing. The letter also provided documented evidence from the survivor that Denise felt comfortable sharing with her court advocate.

Case Vignette 7.2 Denise

As an intensive in-home therapist, I had the opportunity to work with a 10-year-old Euro-American female named Denise. Denise entered therapeutic foster care because she was having a difficult time in a foster home and needed more intensive services. She had been in the foster home for approximately 2 months and all had seemed to be going well until the foster parent noticed that Denise was touching her dolls inappropriately during daily play. This information was reported to Denise's outpatient therapist, who believed that Denise should be removed from the setting to avoid contagion behaviors in other children. Denise was not able to reside with her biological parents because of inappropriate sexual behaviors. Her biological parents were under investigation by Child Protective Services.

Denise appeared to be a typical 10-year-old girl. She enjoyed school and was an average student academically. She talked about her friends and enjoyed playing dress up and riding her bike. We worked together for almost 18 months. From time to time, I asked her what she missed about her biological family. During one session, she mentioned that she really liked her new therapeutic foster home because she was the only child there and liked having all of the attention to herself. When she was in her biological home, she had to share everything with her younger twin brothers, whom she recalled would often take and break her stuff.

A few minutes into the conversation, Denise began to shut down. She was not able to make eye contact, struggled to engage in the activity, and started wiping away her tears. I asked Denise, "If your tears could speak, what would they tell me?" She hunched her shoulders and said, "I can't talk about it right now." We returned to the topic later that evening (I typically met with children for 3 to 4 hours at a time while providing intensive in-home therapy).

After playing a game and getting her homework done, I said, "If you would ever like to write your family or draw a picture for them, then let me know." Denise asked, "Like a real letter?" I affirmed this and further clarified that she could also write them a letter that would never be shared with them, if she wished. Denise seemed excited to write a note to her brothers, whom she acknowledged she missed dearly.

(Continued)

Case Vignette 7.2 *(Continued)*

Denise wrote parts of this letter over a period of weeks. She only worked on it when we were together, so it took a bit of time to finish the letter. The letter was written completely by her and addressed to her younger twin brothers. Once she wrote her thoughts down, Denise read them aloud to me and we would talk about them while playing a game or during the long ride back to her therapeutic foster home. In the letter, Denise made several disclosures about sexual acts that her parents had forced her to perform with her siblings and had also forced to watch her parents perform. Writing the letter gave her the words to describe her experience and process her feelings.

• • •

Denise's parents lost their parental rights and she continued to thrive in foster care, where she received the therapeutic support she needed.

Exploring Current Relationships

Children often benefit from processing their relationships with others. We have used several activities to facilitate children's exploration of their current relationships. One of the activities we have used is called *relationship rings.* In this activity, we ask the child to draw concentric circles on a piece of paper and to identify relationships that are more central to their life, relationships that are important though not central, and relationships that are more peripheral.

After the child has categorized these relationships, we ask questions that help the child further examine these relationships, such as (a) Have any relationships changed in their position on your chart during the past year? How do you feel about those changes? (b) Are there any relationships whose position you want to change on the chart? Help me understand your reasons for wanting to change the position of these relationships. (c) What could you do to change the position of these relationships? What would you need to make those changes yourself?

We have also used the creative arts in group counseling with children to help children develop self-perception. In an activity called *self-esteem flowers,* children cut out petal shapes from a paper template, one petal for each person in the group. They then write a positive attribute on each petal and a person's name on the other side of the petal. After all petals have been completed, the children distribute them to the other group members so that each group member has petals with only their name on the back. The group member then creates a collage of a flower with the petals. At the end of the activity, each group member shares their petals and responds to prompts such as (a) Which adjective or attribute was most surprising to you, and why? (b) Which adjective or attribute was least surprising to you, and why? (c) Was there an adjective or attribute that you wanted to receive but did not? Why might this have been missed? This exercise is often useful for helping children to develop a better sense of how others perceive them and how they impact their own environment.

Conclusion

Play therapy and the creative arts are developmentally appropriate approaches for working with children who do not yet have the capacity for insight-oriented talk therapies because their verbal and linguistic skills are still developing. Play therapy activates the prefrontal cortex and assists with emotional processing and regulation. CCPT is one form of play therapy that appears to be effective for young children with low self-efficacy and caregiver-child relationship stress. Children from ethnic minority backgrounds in particular seem to benefit. Parental involvement is important to the success of CCPT, and the ideal playroom contains two-way mirrors that facilitate parent observation and subsequent parent education. In the case of Michael, the parents' response to the counselor's interpretation of Michael's play behavior (difficulty with transitions) was crucial to the overall success of the intervention.

The creative arts offer another avenue of emotional expression and processing for children. In the examples we presented in this chapter, the counselor's processing of the exercise afterward is a vital part of the intervention's overall effectiveness. We therefore recommend that counselors develop processing questions when providing creative arts interventions. It is worth mentioning that although some adolescents benefit from play-based and creative arts approaches, many adolescents may find such approaches to be inadequate for addressing their issues (e.g., current dating relationships). Adolescents may have developed the verbal and mental capacity for insight-oriented talk therapies and may prefer these interventions over play-based and creative arts approaches. We therefore recommend that counselors carefully discern the needs of their adolescent client before using play therapy and creative arts techniques.

Quiz Questions

1. A child repeatedly asks the counselor, "What am I meant to do with these toys?" In CCPT, the counselor should respond by saying
   a. "Whatever you want to do."
   b. "You are curious about what to use these toys for."
   c. "I selected these toys so that young people like yourself could have fun and explore. The only rules in the playroom are to keep toys in the playroom, use gentle hands, and stop when it's time."

2. When a child tests the limits of the playroom, counselors using the CCPT model should
   a. Ask the child to stop, Contain the child's emotions, Transition to another activity
   b. Anticipate the consequences, Collaboratively problem solve, Teach different skills
   c. Acknowledge the feelings of the child, Communicate the limit, Target reasonable alternatives
3. You are working with a child who is processing the loss of their mother's boyfriend, whom the child considered their stepfather. The boyfriend abruptly moved out of the country without notice. Which creative intervention is likely to be most effective?
   a. A therapeutic letter
   b. Relationship rings
   c. Self-esteem flowers

References

Axline, V. (1947). *Play therapy.* New York, NY: Ballantine Books.

Council for Accreditation of Counseling and Related Educational Programs. (2015). *2016 CACREP standards.* Alexandria, VA: Author.

Crenshaw, D. A., & Stewart, A. L. (2016). *Play therapy: A comprehensive guide to theory and practice.* New York, NY: Guilford Press.

Field, N. P., & Horowitz, M. J. (1998). Applying an empty-chair monologue paradigm to examine unresolved grief. *Psychiatry, 61,* 279–287. doi:10.1080/00332747.1998.11024840

Field, T. A., Beeson, E. T., & Jones, L. K. (2015). The new ABCs: A practitioner's guide to neuroscience-informed cognitive-behavioral therapy. *Journal of Mental Health Counseling, 37,* 206–220. doi:10.17744/mehc.37.3.02

Ginsberg, K. R., & Committee on Communications, Committee on Psychological Aspects of Child and Family Health. (2007). The importance of play in promoting healthy child development and maintaining strong parent–child bonds. *Pediatrics, 119,* 182–191. doi:10.1542/peds.2006-2697

Gladding, S. T. (2016). *The creative arts in counseling* (5th ed.). Alexandria, VA: American Counseling Association.

Gordon, N. S., Burke, S., Akil, H., Watson, S. J., & Panksepp, J. (2003). Socially-induced brain "fertilization": Play promotes brain derived neurotrophic factor transcription in the amygdala and dorsolateral frontal cortex in juvenile rats. *Neuroscience Letters, 341,* 17–20. doi:10.1016/S0304-3940(03)00158-7

Kottman, T. (2014). *Play therapy: Basics and beyond* (2nd ed.). Alexandria, VA: American Counseling Association.

Landreth, G. L. (2012). *Play therapy: The art of the relationship* (3rd ed.). New York, NY: Routledge.

Lin, Y. W., & Bratton, S. C. (2014). A meta-analytic review of child-centered play therapy approaches. *Journal of Counseling & Development, 93,* 45–58. doi:10.1002/j.1556-6676.2015.00180.x

Ray, D. (2011). *Advanced play therapy: Essential conditions, knowledge, and skills for child practice.* New York, NY: Routledge.

Stewart, A. L., Field, T. A., & Echterling, L. G. (2016). Neuroscience and the magic of play therapy. *International Journal of Play Therapy, 25,* 4–13. doi:10.1037/pla0000016

Sweeney, D. S., & Landreth, G. L. (2009). Child-centered play therapy. In K. J. O'Connor & L. D. Braverman (Eds.), *Play therapy theory and practice: Comparing theories and techniques* (pp. 123–162). Hoboken, NJ: Wiley.

Van Kerkhof, L. W., Damsteegt, R., Trezza, V., Voorn, P., & Vanderschuren, L. J. (2013). Social play behavior in adolescent rats is mediated by functional activity in medial prefrontal cortex and striatum. *Neuropsychopharmacology, 38,* 1899–1909. doi:10.1038/npp.2013.83

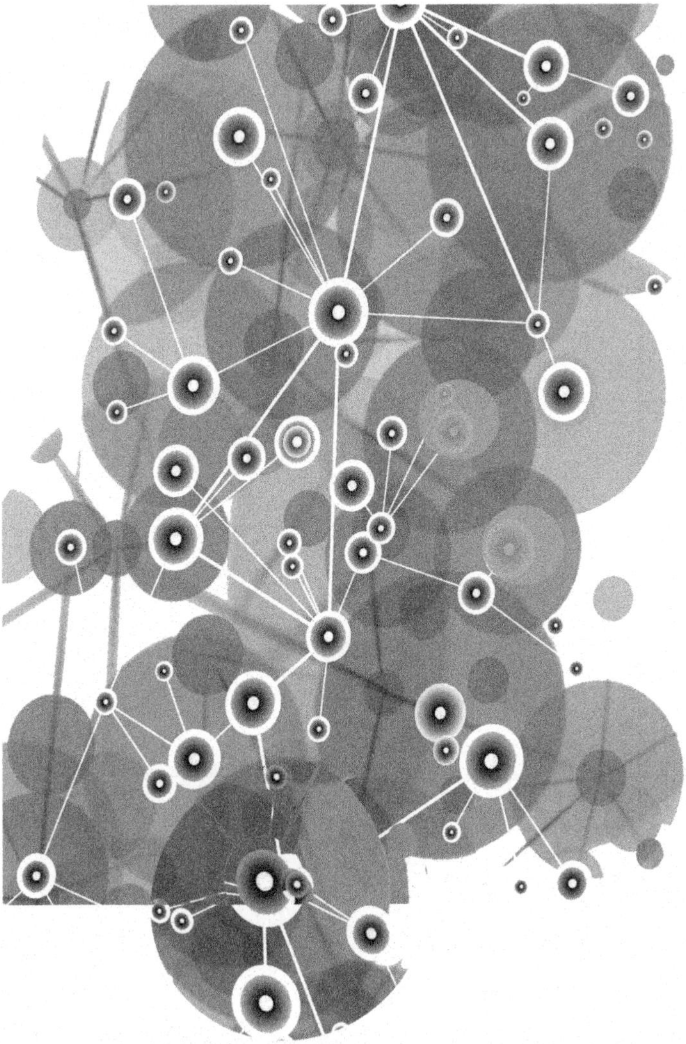

Section III

Adolescence

Chapter 8

Neurophysiological and Social Development During Adolescence

Key Concepts

- Synaptic density and cortical thinning
- Imbalance model of adolescent brain development
- Genetic life-span calendar
- Sex hormones (estrogen and estradiol, progesterone, testosterone)
- Thelarche, menarche, adrenarche
- Cortisol trajectories
- Rejection sensitivity
- Mentalization and theory of mind
- Metacognition
- Gender and sexual identity development
- Ethnic and racial identity development

Aligned 2016 CACREP Standards

Standard 2.F.3.b. Theories of learning
Standard 2.F.3.c. Theories of normal and abnormal personality development
Standard 2.F.3.e. Biological, neurological, and physiological factors that affect human development, functioning, and behavior
Standard 2.F.3.f. Systemic and environmental factors that affect human development, functioning, and behavior

• • •

In this chapter, we examine neurophysiological and social development that extends from childhood into adolescence. Some of the developmental issues explored in this chapter, such as the development of sex characteristics and gender and sexual identity, have their beginnings in early childhood but become more prominent during adolescence. In this chapter, we review the second major stage of synaptic pruning and cortisol trajectories during childhood and adolescence. We also explore the different speed of neural growth in the limbic versus prefrontal cortex, the development of the dopaminergic system, and improved mentalization and metacognitive capacities during adolescence. When writing this chapter we adhered to our definition of *adolescence* in the preface as encompassing the period from 12 to 18 years of age, recognizing that the range for pubertal onset is from 9 to 16 years (Galván, 2017).

In writing this chapter, we were informed by the following texts: *Developmental Cognitive Neuroscience: An Introduction* (4th ed.) by Johnson and de Haan (2015) and *The Neuroscience of Adolescence* by Galván (2017). We recommend these texts as additional resources if you would like more information about adolescence.

Neural Development During Adolescence

As we learned in Chapter 4, the prefrontal cortex is the last major brain region to fully myelinate during childhood (Galván, 2017). This trend of extended prefrontal cortex development continues into adolescence and even emerging adulthood. As the cerebrum becomes fully myelinated, and more gray matter transforms into white matter, the speed of neurotransmission increases. The cerebrum also becomes more efficient as synapses are pruned during the second major phase of synaptic pruning, which occurs during mid to late adolescence (Spear, 2013).

Biological sex plays a role during adolescent brain maturation. Adolescents whose biological sex is female reach peak cerebral volume at 10.5 years compared to 14.5 years for males (Galván, 2017). This difference, alongside other neurophysiological developments such as pubertal onset (which is also earlier for females), may explain why females are higher academic achievers than males on average during adolescence (Galván, 2017).

Subcortical Versus Cortical Development

The limbic system and striatum develop at a faster speed than the prefrontal cortex during adolescence (Casey, Jones, & Hare, 2008; Tyborowska, Volman, Smeekens, Toni, & Roelofs, 2016). Compared to adults, adolescents experience greater extremes of emotion associated with amygdala activity (Tyborowska et al., 2016), such as euphoria and depression in response to life events such as interactions with peers (Weinstein & Mermelstein, 2007). The adolescent brain also seems to be more responsive to novel changes in the environment, as new neurons are produced at a rate 4 to 5 times greater than adult neurogenesis (He & Crews, 2007). The striatum is associated with motivation and conditioning learning related to rewards, and its faster development than that of the prefrontal cortex explains why adolescents seek out novel and high-sensation (i.e., thrill) experiences in certain social contexts, even if they are potentially threatening (Baker, Bisby, & Richardson, 2016). This pull toward novel and risky experiences can be understood when one examines the development of the striatum structure of the nucleus accumbens relative to the prefrontal cortex (and especially the orbitofrontal area; Galván et al., 2006). The nucleus accumbens has a major role in the dopaminergic system, with production increasing two- to sevenfold during adolescence (Galván et al., 2006). This results in stronger motivational drives, especially toward reward seeking and risk taking (Galván, 2017; Galván et al., 2006). This development of the dopaminergic system is believed to be an underlying mechanism for why substance use increases markedly during adolescence (Galván, 2017). Most drug addictions begin during adolescence (Arain et al., 2013).

The faster speed of subcortical (i.e., limbic system) than cortical (i.e., prefrontal cortex) development helps us understand why adolescents experience deep and intense emotions without the circuitry yet to fully process and regulate their emotions. It also helps us understand why adolescence is marked by risk taking and experimentation. Adolescents are more likely than adults to place greater weight on the potential benefits of an action than the potential negative consequences (Arain et al., 2013). Most risk taking is healthy, as it enables adolescents to form new relationships and be exposed to new experiences (Spear, 2013). But risk taking can also result in dangerous consequences for health at times, such as driving without a seatbelt, engaging in unprotected sex, and so forth.

The faster pace of neural development for the limbic region versus the prefrontal cortex has been called the *imbalance model of adolescent brain development* (Casey, Jones, et al., 2008). As depicted in Figure 8.1, the prefrontal cortex continues to develop until a person is in their 20s (Arain et al., 2013; Casey, Getz, & Galvan, 2008). As the adolescent matures during puberty, stronger connections are forged between subcortical structures such as the amygdala and cortical structures such as regions of the prefrontal cortex, resulting in improved abilities to regulate emotions and control impulses (Guyer, Silk, & Nelson, 2016; Tyborowska et al., 2016).

The hyperemotionality of adolescence has also been associated with an increased risk of psychopathology and developing mental health conditions, in particular anxiety, bipolar disorder, depression,

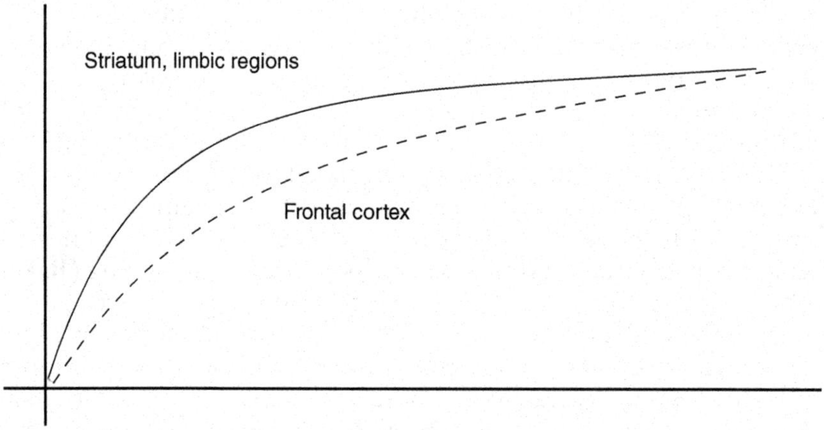

FIGURE 8.1

The Imbalance Model of Adolescent Brain Development

Note. Adapted from articles by Casey, Getz, et al. (2008), Casey and Jones (2010), and Casey (2015).

and substance use disorders (Guyer et al., 2016). The age of onset for many mental health conditions is during adolescence (Guyer et al., 2016). It is believed that the second major period of synaptic pruning, alongside development and activation of the striatum and amygdala, may contribute to this vulnerability to developing mental health conditions (Baker et al., 2016).

Counseling Approaches With Adolescents

When working with adolescents, counselors should understand why it can be a challenge for adolescents to prioritize long-term over short-term benefits and moderate their impulses toward sensation seeking and risk taking. In counseling sessions, we have found it useful to validate and support adolescents' intent to make independent decisions while also introducing questions that help them consider what they want to achieve in the long term. In the case study of Luciana (see Case Vignette 8.1), we show how to engage an adolescent in longer term planning in a manner that is nonjudgmental and supportive. Michelle uses first-person narrative to describe the counseling process.

This case study illustrates a few key counseling skills. First, validating the adolescent's thoughts and feelings is an important first step. If Michelle had not demonstrated understanding and validation before attempting to problem-solve or give advice, Luciana may have felt invalidated and could have developed a strong negative reaction toward Michelle. Second, clarifying the adolescent's ultimate long-term objective when making decisions can help to provide direction during their innate attempts at problem-solving. Third, the counselor should

Case Vignette 8.1 Luciana

Luciana was a 15-year-old cisgender Latinx female who was tearful when retelling events of the past week. For the past 3 months, she had been dating Rose, a 17-year-old female who attended the same high school. A few days ago, Luciana had found out through a friend that Rose had recently had sex at a party with one of her male friends, Daniel. Luciana felt devastated. She had inclinations to shame Daniel by sharing rumors about him at school. She had also thought about slashing the tires of Daniel's car. During the session, I validated Luciana's feelings ("You are understandably deeply hurt and angry") and described her thought process without judgment ("You are weighing your options about how to respond"). I also asked an important question about what Luciana wanted to accomplish by her actions ("I'm wondering what you most want out of this situation—is it to exact revenge on Daniel and Rose? Or something else?"). Luciana was surprised by this question and admitted that she wanted to distance herself from Daniel but keep her relationship with Rose intact. She also wanted to verbalize her feelings to Rose about what had occurred and make it clear that their relationship must be monogamous or she would leave. Luciana was not sure how to have this conversation with Rose and asked for my help.

• • •

wait for the adolescent to request advice or direction before providing it. Adolescents need less direction and guidance than children, and thus counselors should attempt to facilitate adolescent autonomy and empowerment to the extent possible.

Social Relationships During Adolescence

Nelson, Jarcho, and Guyer (2016) contended that neurophysiological changes during adolescence occur in the context of burgeoning social relationships and affiliations. During adolescence, youth transition in their social behavior from engaging in peer-focused play behavior with their parents or guardians as their base to fully joining with their peer group (Nelson et al., 2016). The peer group social environment provides opportunities for novel and sensation-seeking experiences (e.g., first sexual experiences). Several changes occur in the brain during adolescence that assist young people to form deeper emotional bonds with peers.

Facial Recognition

Facial recognition continues to develop during early adolescence (Galván, 2017). Recognizing and understanding facial expressions has a prominent role in appraising the emotional states of others. The *fusiform face area* (FFA) of the fusiform gyrus has been strongly associated with facial recognition (Galván, 2017). FFA activation is crucial to social relationships. Young adolescents (11–14 years old) have similar FFA activation to adults when presented with images of faces (Scherf, Luna, Avidan, & Behrmann, 2011). This activation is almost absent in younger children (5–8 years old). FFA activation is impaired in children with autism (Nomi & Uddin, 2015), who also have difficulties sustaining eye contact and eye gaze (Pelphrey, Shultz, Hudac, & Vander Wyk, 2011). This causes impairments in recognizing and understanding the emotions of others (Galván, 2017).

Mentalization and Theory of Mind

Improvements in perspective-taking abilities help adolescents to form deep empathic bonds with their peers. The ability of an adolescent to form an empathic understanding of a peer's thoughts and feelings is known as *mentalization* or *theory of mind* (Guyer et al., 2016). Perspective taking assists adolescents in anticipating and understanding the goals and behaviors of others and responding accordingly. Fully joining with peers requires this ability to forge a deeply emotional and empathic connection. For example, an adolescent might intentionally seek to reach out to a member of their peer group whom they realize is upset from being excluded socially. Mentalization capacities are facilitated by brain development during adolescence. The ability to understand another's perspective is associated with maturation of the prefrontal cortex, in particular the dorsolateral and medial regions (van den Bos, van Dijk, Westenberg, Rombouts, & Crone, 2011). In addition, enhanced connectivity between the amygdala and prefrontal cortex grants adolescents the ability to gain emotional insight into their own experiences as well as the experiences of others.

Metacognition

In addition to facilitating mentalization, prefrontal brain development enables adolescents to appraise their own thoughts, known as *thinking about thinking* or *metacognition* (Guyer et al., 2016). This ability assists with self-referential and self-reflective thinking, which is a precursor to enhanced self-awareness. Adolescents with metacognitive capacities can appraise whether their thinking and behavioral response is accurate and fair in a given situation (Gross & Jazaieri, 2014; McRae et al., 2012). Such self-reflection grants adolescents the ability to benefit from insight-oriented counseling approaches such as cognitive behavior therapy, among others. Learning to manage enhanced emotions and moods is an important task of adolescent development (Gross & Jazaieri, 2014).

Self-reflective abilities also support identity development, which is a crucial task during adolescence (Meeus, 2011). The reciprocal interaction between person and environment is crucial to identity development. As adolescents develop prefrontal functions and amygdala-prefrontal circuitry associated with higher order cognitive capacities such as mentalization and metacognition, they forge deeper relationships with their peers. These peer relationships then exert a substantial influence on the adolescents' development of identity, values, and behavior (Cheung, Chudek, & Heine, 2011).

Rejection Sensitivity

Alongside development of the limbic system (especially the amygdala), developments in the anterior cingulate cortex during adolescence have been associated with heightened sensitivity to social ostracism and rejection (Collins, Welsh, & Furman, 2009). *Rejection sensitivity* has been associated with increased activation of the amygdala during adolescence, along with other subcortical structures, including the anterior cingulate cortex, insula, and striatum (Sebastian, Viding, Williams, & Blakemore, 2010; Silk et al., 2013). Longitudinal studies have found that heightened rejection sensitivity during adolescence is associated with the severity of depression symptoms (Masten et al., 2011) and is thus an important target of intervention.

Pubertal Development

Puberty is a transitional stage that results in a young person developing adult physical characteristics and becoming capable of sexual reproduction (Colvin & Abdullatif, 2013). The onset of puberty is on average 10 to 11 years of age for children with female biological sex characteristics and 11 to 12 years of age for children with male biological sex characteristics (Shumer, Nokoff, & Spack, 2016). Galván (2017) estimated that the range for pubertal onset is from 9 to 16 years. Some children develop secondary sex characteristics early, such as in third or fourth grade of elementary school. Other adolescents develop secondary sex characteristics later, such as in middle school or even high school. Pubertal onset varies by ethnic background, with African American and Latinx youth starting puberty slightly earlier than Euro-American youth (Colvin & Abdullatif, 2013). Tyborowska and colleagues (2016) found that an adolescent's pubescent stage had a strong relationship with their stage of brain development. In their study, prefrontal development was associated with the stage of gonadal hormone (i.e., testosterone) secretion rather than with age in years.

Secondary Sex Characteristics

During puberty, adolescents develop secondary sex characteristics, which results in the growth and maturation of their genitals, breasts, muscles and skeleton, and facial and body hair (Galván, 2017). Pubertal development is initiated by activation of the hypothalamic-pituitary-gonadal axis. During adolescent maturation, the hypothalamus projects gonadotropin-releasing hormone to the pituitary gland, which in turn secretes luteinizing hormone and follicle-stimulating hormone. Luteinizing hormone facilitates the production of sex hormones (i.e., ovaries and testes) in the gonads. Estrogen is developed in the ovaries. There are three estrogens: estrone, estradiol, and estriol.

Luteinizing hormone also facilitates the development of androgens, such as testosterone in the testes. Estrogen and testosterone are sex hormones. Both females and males develop and secrete androgens and estrogens, with children of female biological sex typically secreting larger amounts of estrogens and children of male biological sex typically secreting larger amounts of androgens (Galván, 2017). Follicle-stimulating hormone supports the development of ovarian follicles that will contain egg cells known as *oocytes*. Follicle-stimulating hormone also facilitates the enlargement of the testicles.

At approximately 6 to 8 years of age, the early pubertal period is initiated when the adrenal glands produce and secrete adrenal androgens such as dehydroepiandrosterone (Galván, 2017). These androgens assist with the development of pubic hair, body odor, and skin oil that can result in acne. This secretion of adrenal androgens is known as *adrenarche*.

Estrogen and progesterone production during adolescence results in *thelarche*, or secondary breast development (Galván, 2017). Estrogen facilitates the development of adipose breast tissue that begins with breast budding. Progesterone initiates development of the mammary glands. Breast development is typically completed within 4 to 5 years. Estrogen production and the development of ovarian follicles contribute to the onset of *menarche*, or the first occurrence of menstruation. Menstruation and menses typically begin approximately 2 years after the start of breast budding.

Testosterone production supports the enlargement of the phallus and testes; thinning of the scrotal skin; enlargement of the larynx and a deeper vocal tone; and musculoskeletal changes such as an increase in muscle mass, a widening of the shoulders, and increases in height. The development of facial hair in children with male biological sex characteristics begins later than genital development.

Metabolism seems to be related to pubertal onset, with energy and fuel stores essential to the production and excretion of gonadotropin-releasing hormone (Sanchez-Garrido & Tena-Sempere, 2013). Obesity has been associated with earlier onset of puberty, as has the adipose (i.e., fatty tissue) hormone leptin (Sanchez-Garrido & Tena-Sempere,

2013). Leptin is associated with hunger inhibition and satiation. Leptin levels climb just prior to the onset of puberty (Galván, 2017). Children with decreased leptin production and secretion do not begin puberty until synthetic leptin has been introduced (Sanchez-Garrido & Tena-Sempere, 2013). Presumably because of depleted energy stores, anorexia nervosa has also been associated with delays in pubertal onset (Katz & Vollenhoven, 2000).

Hormonal Changes and Cycles

The increased production and secretion of gonadal hormones during adolescence has a marked impact on emotions and moods (Guyer et al., 2016). During the female reproductive cycle, the secretion of gonadal hormones varies substantially. Estrogen levels begin to rise before ovulation, then decrease after ovulation and fall significantly just before menstruation (Sacher, Okon-Singer, & Villringer, 2013). Progesterone secretion rises after ovulation and also falls rapidly just before menstruation (Sacher et al., 2013). These changes in the excretion of estrogen and progesterone during ovulation and menstruation have been linked to changes in acetylcholine, dopamine, norepinephrine, oxytocin, and serotonin activity (Sacher et al., 2013). Falling estradiol (a type of estrogen) and progesterone levels are linked to depressive symptomatology, whereas higher estradiol and progesterone levels enhance serotonin secretion and have antidepressant-like effects in both females and males (Benmansour, Weaver, Barton, Adeniji, & Frazer, 2012; Lanzenberger et al., 2011). Low estradiol and progesterone have been associated with increased suicide attempts in women (Baca-Garcia et al., 2010). Testosterone does not appear to influence serotonergic functioning (Montoya, Terburg, Bos, & van Honk, 2012).

Estrogen, progesterone, and testosterone appear to have different impacts on amygdala coupling with prefrontal regions (van Wingen, Ossewaarde, Bäckström, Hermans, & Fernández, 2011). All three gonadal hormones appear to stimulate activation of the amygdala, which is associated with emotional and fear-based responses. However, estrogen and progesterone increase amygdala projections to the medial prefrontal cortex, whereas testosterone reduces amygdala projections to the orbitofrontal cortex (van Wingen et al., 2011). Activation of the medial prefrontal cortex is associated with higher order rational processing of emotions and can result in internalizing problems (Balzer, Duke, Hawke, & Steinbeck, 2015), such as rumination about negative emotions (van Wingen et al., 2011). Reduced activation of the orbitofrontal cortex predisposes a person to becoming behaviorally inhibited and engaging in more impulsive and aggressive behaviors (van Wingen et al., 2011). In summary, the differing effects of these gonadal hormones (estrogen and estradiol, progesterone, testosterone) might partially explain differences in the prevalence of internalizing (anxiety, depression) and externalizing (aggression, impulse control issues, substance use) problems by biological sex (Soares & Zitek, 2008).

Cortisol Trajectories

Differences in cortisol secretion during adolescence, known as *cortisol trajectories,* may also help to explain the increased incidence of anxiety and depression during early adolescence. A longitudinal study by Shirtcliff and colleagues (2012) followed children from third through ninth grade. The authors found that cortisol production initially decreases between ages 9 and 11 and then increases again during early adolescence. By 15 years of age, adolescents have lower morning cortisol than at 9 years of age but higher evening cortisol. Note that cortisol is higher among children whose biological sex is female and declines less during the day compared to children whose biological sex is male (Shirtcliff et al., 2012). Shirtcliff and colleagues proposed that this increase in daily circulating cortisol during early adolescence may explain increases in anxiety and depression, especially in females.

Chronic Stress and Maturation

Chronic stress impacts the speed of sexual maturation. Adolescents who experience chronic stress during childhood have increased basal (i.e., baseline) cortisol production, which accelerates adrenarche (Belsky, Ruttle, Boyce, Armstrong, & Essex, 2015). Noll and colleagues (2017) found that sexual abuse was associated with accelerated breast development (8 months earlier than controls) and pubic hair development (12 months earlier than controls) in adolescents with female biological sex. These findings were observed after confounding variables, such as ethnicity and obesity, were controlled for. Accelerated sexual maturation has been associated with physical and mental health problems (Belsky et al., 2015). Negriff, Saxbe, and Trickett (2015) found in a longitudinal study that early pubertal change predicted delinquency in males and substance use in females.

Addressing Pubescent Development During Counseling

Counselors working with adolescents who are experiencing hormone fluctuations can use this information to normalize experiences with emotions and mood changes and support the adolescents' management of such symptoms. Adolescents might be confused about these changes or privately worry that they are developing at a different rate than their peers. Understanding the basics of gonadal hormones and secondary sex characteristics can help adolescents quell these anxieties. See Reflection Question 8.1.

Reflection Question 8.1

Under what circumstances might you bring the topic of secondary sex characteristics into conversation with an adolescent client? What information would you include?

Identity Development

Adolescence is a period marked by exploration of one's own identity (Cheung et al., 2011). Although identity development has important beginnings in childhood, adolescence tends to be the time when identity becomes a more crucial focal point of a child's developmental experience. During this time, many adolescents seek to separate from their parents and families of origin to forge their own independent identities and accordingly begin to look to peer groups for social affiliation. We now explore the development of gender, sexual, and ethnic identity.

Gender Identity

Children are "born into a gendered world" (Shumer et al., 2016, p. 82) in which dress, games, and styles of play are influenced by assigned gender and gender labels. A child's ability to distinguish faces by gender begins early, at approximately 6 months of age (Quinn, Yahr, Kuhn, Slater, & Pascalis, 2002). By 2 years of age, children begin to ascribe gender labels to themselves and others (Shumer et al., 2016; Stennes, Burch, Sen, & Bauer, 2005). Children may identify as having a gender that is not in alignment with their biological sex, with gender-nonconforming behaviors developing as early as 3 years of age (Shumer et al., 2016).

By and large, young children tend to prefer clothing, toys, and objects that correspond to their identified gender (Fast & Olson, 2018). This is also true of socially transitioned children who identify as transgender. Olson, Key, and Eaton (2015) examined gender recognition in 5- to 11-year-old children who identified as transgender and cisgender. The researchers found that transgender children had a strong implicit preference for their expressed gender, similar to cisgender children.

Gender identity development is complex and involves genetic, hormonal, and environmental factors (Shumer et al., 2016). No single gene has been identified as causative for transgender identity development, though twin studies suggest some degree of genetic influence. Heylens and colleagues (2012) found that *gender dysphoria*, defined as a person's dissatisfaction with their biological sex, was concordant in approximately 40% of monozygotic (i.e., identical) twin pairs. Although one might imagine that prenatal hormone release might be related to gender identity, studies on the influence of sex hormone release during pregnancy on gender identity development have not yielded any significant relationship as yet (Shumer et al., 2016).

Sexual/Affective Identity

Romantic attraction also begins to develop during the childhood period. Although the age by which children start to develop romantic interests can vary, feeling romantic attraction is fairly common by middle school age. More than half of middle schoolers report having a current romantic crush (Bowker, Spencer, Thomas, & Gyoerkoe, 2012). During childhood, children become aware of their sexual/affective orientation and may begin to identify as lesbian, gay, bisexual, transgender, nonbinary, queer, questioning, intersex, and/or asexual (LGBTQQIA). Calzo, Antonucci, Mays, and Cochran (2011) examined the retrospective recall of sexual identity development during childhood among more than 1,000 gay, lesbian, and bisexual adults. Of those in the study, 22% reported coming out before adolescence. Research has found several indications of genetic influences on sexual identity development, such as a higher concordance of gay or lesbian children of gay or lesbian parents and higher concordance rates among monozygotic (i.e., identical) versus dizygotic (i.e., fraternal) twins (Shumer et al., 2016). In a large study of nearly 500,000 people, Ganna et al. (2019) found that genetics explained between 8% and 25% of same-sex sexual behavior. Sanders et al. (2015) conducted another large study of more than 400 pairs of gay brothers and found that the *Xq28* region of the genetic sequence seemed to play a role in sexual orientation development for males. Subsequent studies have also observed other chromosomal correlates with gay and lesbian sexual orientation, such as the *SLITRK6* gene on chromosome 13 and the thyroid-stimulating hormone receptor (*TSHR*) on chromosome 14 (Sanders et al., 2017). *SLITRK6* on chromosome 13 and *TSHR* on chromosome 14 are particularly intriguing, because they are associated with hypothalamic function. Sanders and colleagues (2017) argued that the thyroid functions differently in people who identify as gay and lesbian.

Children who identify as LGBTQQIA experience far greater incidences of stigma, bullying, and harassment (Reisner et al., 2015). Consequently, mental health problems such as anxiety, depression, self-injurious behavior, and suicidal ideation and suicide attempts are 2 to 3 times more common in children who identify as transgender compared to children who identify as cisgender (Reisner et al., 2015). By adulthood, 41% of transgender adults will have attempted suicide, a staggering number (Shumer et al., 2016).

First Sexual Experiences

Peer group socialization diminishes somewhat after romantic relationships begin to form (Collins et al., 2009). Romantic relationships are common during later adolescence. The majority (70%) of 17-year-olds report that they have been in a romantic relationship in the past year (Collins et al., 2009). As adolescents reach reproductive capability, they begin to experience sexual interest. By age 14, nearly 90% of males and 20% of females have masturbated (Fortenberry, 2013). The average age of first sexual intercourse is 17 years for both males and females (National Center for Health Statistics, 2017).

The Role of Oxytocin

Oxytocin has an important role in the development of sexual relationships. During puberty, gonadal hormones assist with the proliferation of oxytocin receptors in the amygdala and nucleus accumbens in the limbic system (Albert, Chein, & Steinberg, 2013; Spear, 2009). Enhanced oxytocin activity in the limbic system is associated with improved emotional bonding, which is important to romantic relationships that are formed during adolescence. Oxytocin is secreted before, during, and after sexual activity and promotes partner bonding and affiliation (Gonzaga, Turner, Keltner, Campos, & Altemus, 2006). Oxytocin levels are higher among new lovers than single people and remain high for at least the first 6 months of a sexual relationship (Schneiderman, Zagoory-Sharon, Leckman, & Feldman, 2012). Females have greater oxytocin release during sexual activity than males, with the intensity of the orgasm related to oxytocin release (Carmichael, Warburton, Dixen, & Davidson, 1994; Gonzaga et al., 2006). Adolescents may feel closely bonded with their sexual partners, especially females, even if the relationship is still in an early stage of development. This superficially close bond can give rise to topics that are frequently discussed in counseling sessions, such as intense relationships, fair expectations of partners, and fears of rejection (see Reflection Question 8.2). Hurlemann and Scheele (2016) proposed that the disrupted oxytocin signaling that occurs following the loss of affection bonds (e.g., the breakup of a sexual relationship) can elevate the risk of stress-related adjustment problems.

Ethnic and Racial Identity Development

Ethnic and racial identity develops throughout childhood (Pahl & Way, 2006). The general phases of ethnic and racial identity development have been differentiated by early, middle, and late childhood (Umaña-Taylor

Reflection Question 8.2

Recall the case of Luciana that was described earlier in this chapter.

During her third session, Luciana worries that she feels more closely bonded to Rose than Rose does to her. Luciana also worries that she is not attractive enough to Rose. Luciana tried to keep Rose's interest by sending her nude photos through text messages on her cell phone. How might you help Luciana process her rejection sensitivity?

et al., 2014). Early childhood is marked by differentiation of self and other alongside ethnic labeling and knowledge (Umaña-Taylor et al., 2014). Early adolescence has been associated with an awareness of bias and social hierarchy and in-group/out-group dynamics (Umaña-Taylor et al., 2014). Late childhood (i.e., adolescence) has been connected with self-identification with ethnic practices and values, exploration of self-identity and collective self-verification, understanding of one's common fate or destiny with others in one's ethnic group, and internalization or self-denial of cultural identity (Umaña-Taylor et al., 2014). Perceived and actual discrimination by peers may moderate the speed of ethnic identity development (Pahl & Way, 2006).

We encourage counselors to ask their adolescent clients about how they identify regarding their ethnic and racial background and heritage. Counselors should also support youth in experiences of discrimination and oppression and advocate when needed. Cabral and Smith (2011) found that the counselor does not need to have the same ethnic or racial background as their client to have effective conversations about ethnic and racial identity. In our experience, regardless of background, the counselor's inquiry about ethnic and racial identity can send an important message to children and adolescents that their ethnic and racial identity is important. We propose the guidelines below when facilitating conversations about identity.

The Role of the Counselor in Identity Development

During counseling sessions, it is important for the counselor to demonstrate an affirming attitude toward diverse identities and allow adolescents space to process their thoughts and feelings about their identity without judgment. We recommend that counselors provide space for adolescents to independently explore their identity without significant direction from them unless requested. Adolescents may need assistance recruiting support from their family when they are ready to disclose their gender and/or sexual identity, and counselors can be a resource for helping children to practice phrasing their disclosure to their parents or guardians.

Counselors have an especially important role in establishing a supportive environment for adolescents who identify as gender minorities or sexual minorities. Counselors at times will need to advocate for an LGBTQQIA-supportive and -affirming atmosphere in the communities in which they reside. Counselors may also need to advocate for adolescents and adolescents who experience discrimination and oppression because of their ethnic and racial background.

Conclusion

Adolescence is a transitional stage marked by tremendous neurophysiological growth and development. The hormonal changes and rapid development of the limbic system and striatum that occur during adolescence enhance the emotional experiences and sensation-seeking impulses of teenagers before they have the ability to control them cognitively. As youth approach older adolescence, stronger connections are forged between the prefrontal cortex and the subcortical limbic regions, which assists them in better managing these emotions and moods. Adolescents also become more aware of themselves and others in their environment and form close relational bonds with peers. Counselors working with adolescents should support their emerging independence and problem-solving abilities, help to scaffold executive functioning (such as long-term planning), provide support during explorations of identity development, and normalize the moods and physiological changes that occur during adolescence.

Quiz Questions

1. Which of the following is correct about pubertal development?
   a. Estrogen supports female development only, and testosterone supports male development only
   b. The average age of pubertal onset is 10–12 years
   c. Children who are obese have a late onset of puberty
2. Oxytocin is secreted in . . .
   a. Higher amounts in females during sexual intercourse
   b. Reduced amounts as a sexual relationship continues over a 6-month period
   c. Increased amounts in the months following a breakup
3. The striatum and nucleus accumbens develop significantly during adolescence, which is associated with increased
   a. Sleepiness and fatigue
   b. Motivation to seek out novel experiences and conditioned rewards
   c. Intense emotional experiences and fear responses

References

Albert, D., Chein, J., & Steinberg, L. (2013). Peer influences on adolescent decision making. *Current Directions in Psychological Science, 22*(2), 114–120. https://doi.org/10.1177/0963721412471347

Arain, M., Haque, M., Johal, L., Mathur, P., Nel, W., Rais, A., . . . Sharma, S. (2013). Maturation of the adolescent brain. *Neuropsychiatric Disease and Treatment, 9,* 449–461. doi:10.2147/NDT.S39776

Baca-Garcia, E., Diaz-Sastre, C., Ceverino, A., Perez-Rodriguez, M. M., Navarro-Jimenez, R., Lopez-Castroman, J., . . . Oquendo, M. A. (2010). Suicide attempts among women during low estradiol/low progesterone states. *Journal of Psychiatric Research, 44,* 209–214. doi:10.1016/j.jpsychires.2009.08.004

Baker, K. D., Bisby, M. A., & Richardson, R. (2016). Impaired fear extinction in adolescent rodents: Behavioural and neural analyses. *Neuroscience & Biobehavioral Reviews, 70,* 59–73. doi:10.1016/j.neubiorev.2016.05.019

Balzer, B. W., Duke, S. A., Hawke, C. I., & Steinbeck, K. S. (2015). The effects of estradiol on mood and behavior in human female adolescents: A systematic review. *European Journal of Pediatrics, 174,* 289–298. doi:10.1007/s00431-014-2475-3

Belsky, J., Ruttle, P. L., Boyce, W. T., Armstrong, J. M., & Essex, M. J. (2015). Early adversity, elevated stress physiology, accelerated sexual maturation, and poor health in females. *Developmental Psychology, 51,* 816–822. doi:10.1037/dev0000017

Benmansour, S., Weaver, R. S., Barton, A. K., Adeniji, O. S., & Frazer, A. (2012). Comparison of the effects of estradiol and progesterone on serotonergic function. *Biological Psychiatry, 71,* 633–641. doi:10.1016/j.biopsych.2011.11.023

Bowker, J. C., Spencer, S. V., Thomas, K. K., & Gyoerkoe, E. A. (2012). Having and being an other-sex crush during early adolescence. *Journal of Experimental Child Psychology, 111,* 629–643. doi:10.1016/j.jecp.2011.11.008

Cabral, R. R., & Smith, T. B. (2011). Racial/ethnic matching of clients and therapists in mental health services: A meta-analytic review of preferences, perceptions, and outcomes. *Journal of Counseling Psychology, 58,* 537–554. doi:10.1037/a0025266

Calzo, J. P., Antonucci, T. C., Mays, V. M., & Cochran, S. D. (2011). Retrospective recall of sexual orientation identity development among gay, lesbian, and bisexual adults. *Developmental Psychology, 47,* 1658–1673. doi:10.1037/a0025508

Carmichael, M. S., Warburton, V. L., Dixen, J., & Davidson, J. M. (1994). Relationships among cardiovascular, muscular, and oxytocin responses during human sexual activity. *Archives of Sexual Behavior, 23,* 59–79. doi:10.1007/BF01541618

Casey, B. J. (2015). Beyond simple models of self-control to circuit-based accounts of adolescent behavior. *Annual Review of Psychology, 66,* 295–319. doi:10.1146/annurev-psych-010814-015156

Casey, B. J., Getz, S., & Galvan, A. (2008). The adolescent brain. *Developmental Review, 28,* 62–77. doi:10.1016/j.dr.2007.08.003

Casey, B. J., & Jones, R. M. (2010). Neurobiology of the adolescent brain and behavior: Implications for substance use disorders. *Journal of the American Academy of Child & Adolescent Psychiatry, 49,* 1189–1201. doi:10.1016/j.jaac.2010.08.017

Casey, B. J., Jones, R. M., & Hare, T. A. (2008). The adolescent brain. *Annals of the New York Academy of Sciences, 1124,* 111–126. doi:10.1196/annals.1440.010

Cheung, B. Y., Chudek, M., & Heine, S. J. (2011). Evidence for a sensitive period for acculturation: Younger immigrants report acculturating at a faster rate. *Psychological Science, 22,* 147–152. doi:10.1177/0956797610394661

Collins, W. A., Welsh, D. P., & Furman, W. (2009). Adolescent romantic relationships. *Annual Review of Psychology, 60,* 631–652. doi:10.1146/annurev.psych.60.110707.163459

Colvin, C. W., & Abdullatif, H. (2013). Anatomy of female puberty: The clinical relevance of developmental changes in the reproductive system. *Clinical Anatomy, 26,* 115–129. doi:10.1002/ca.22164

Council for Accreditation of Counseling and Related Educational Programs. (2015). *2016 CACREP standards.* Alexandria, VA: Author.

Fast, A. A., & Olson, K. R. (2018). Gender development in transgender preschool children. *Child Development, 89,* 620–637. doi:10.1111/cdev.12758

Fortenberry, J. D. (2013). Puberty and adolescent sexuality. *Hormones and Behavior, 64,* 280–287. doi:10.1016/j.yhbeh.2013.03.007

Galván, A. (2017). *The neuroscience of adolescence.* New York, NY: Cambridge University Press.

Galván, A., Hare, T. A., Parra, C. E., Penn, J., Voss, H., Glover, G., & Casey, B. J. (2006). Earlier development of the accumbens relative to orbitofrontal cortex might underlie risk-taking behavior in adolescents. *Journal of Neuroscience, 26,* 6885–6892. doi:10.1523/JNEUROSCI.1062-06.2006

Ganna, A., Verweij, K. J., Nivard, M. G., Maier, R., Wedow, R., Busch, A. S., . . . Lundström, S. (2019, August 30). Large-scale GWAS reveals insights into the genetic architecture of same-sex sexual behavior. *Science, 365,* eaat7693. doi:10.1126/science.aat7693

Gonzaga, G. C., Turner, R. A., Keltner, D., Campos, B., & Altemus, M. (2006). Romantic love and sexual desire in close relationships. *Emotion, 6,* 163–179. doi:1037/1528-3542.6.2.163

Gross, J. J., & Jazaieri, H. (2014). Emotion, emotion regulation, and psychopathology: An affective science perspective. *Clinical Psychological Science, 2,* 387–401. doi:10.1177/2167702614536164

Guyer, A. E., Silk, J. S., & Nelson, E. E. (2016). The neurobiology of the emotional adolescent: From the inside out. *Neuroscience & Biobehavioral Reviews, 70,* 74–85. doi:10.1016/j.neubiorev.2016.07.037

He, J., & Crews, F. T. (2007). Neurogenesis decreases during brain maturation from adolescence to adulthood. *Pharmacology Biochemistry and Behavior, 86,* 327–333. doi:10.1016/j.pbb.2006.11.003

Heylens, G., De Cuypere, G., Zucker, K. J., Schelfaut, C., Elaut, E., Bossche, H. V., . . . T'Sjoen, G. (2012). Gender identity disorder in twins: A review of the case report literature. *Journal of Sexual Medicine, 9,* 751–757. doi:10.1111/j.1743-6109.2011.02567.x

Hurlemann, R., & Scheele, D. (2016). Dissecting the role of oxytocin in the formation and loss of social relationships. *Biological Psychiatry, 79,* 185–193. doi:10.1016/j.biopsych.2015.05.013

Johnson, M. H., & de Haan, M. (2015). *Developmental cognitive neuroscience: An introduction* (4th ed.). Hoboken, NJ: Wiley-Blackwell.

Katz, M. G., & Vollenhoven, B. (2000). The reproductive endocrine consequences of anorexia nervosa. *British Journal of Obstetrics & Gynaecology, 107,* 707–713. doi:10.1111/j.1471-0528.2000.tb13329.x

Lanzenberger, R., Mitterhauser, M., Kranz, G. S., Spindelegger, C., Wadsak, W., Stein, P., . . . Kasper, S. (2011). Progesterone level predicts serotonin-1a receptor binding in the male human brain. *Neuroendocrinology, 94,* 84–88. doi:10.1159/000328432

Masten, C. L., Eisenberger, N. I., Borofsky, L. A., McNealy, K., Pfeifer, J. H., & Dapretto, M. (2011). Subgenual anterior cingulate responses to peer rejection: A marker of adolescents' risk for depression. *Development and Psychopathology, 23*(1), 283–292. doi:10.1017/S0954579410000799

McRae, K., Gross, J. J., Weber, J., Robertson, E. R., Sokol-Hessner, P., Ray, R. D., . . . Ochsner, K. N. (2012). The development of emotion regulation: An fMRI study of cognitive reappraisal in children, adolescents and young adults. *Social Cognitive and Affective Neuroscience, 7,* 11–22. doi:10.1093/scan/nsr093

Meeus, W. (2011). The study of adolescent identity formation 2000–2010: A review of longitudinal research. *Journal of Research on Adolescence, 21,* 75–94. doi:10.1111/j.1532-7795.2010.00716.x

Montoya, E. R., Terburg, D., Bos, P. A., & van Honk, J. (2012). Testosterone, cortisol, and serotonin as key regulators of social aggression: A review and theoretical perspective. *Motivation and Emotion, 36,* 65–73. doi:10.1007/s11031-011-9264-3

National Center for Health Statistics. (2017). *Key statistics from the National Survey of Family Growth—S listing.* https://www.cdc.gov/nchs/nsfg/key_statistics/s.htm

Negriff, S., Saxbe, S. E., & Trickett, P. K. (2015). Childhood maltreatment, pubertal development, HPA axis functioning, and psychosocial outcomes: An integrative biopsychosocial model. *Developmental Psychobiology, 57,* 984–993. doi:10.1002/dev.21340

Nelson, E. E., Jarcho, J. M., & Guyer, A. E. (2016). Social re-orientation and brain development: An expanded and updated view. *Developmental Cognitive Neuroscience, 17,* 118–127. doi:10.1016/j.dcn.2015.12.008

Noll, J. G., Trickett, P. K., Long, J. D., Negriff, S., Susman, E. J., Shalev, I., . . . Putnam, F. W. (2017). Childhood sexual abuse and early timing of puberty. *Journal of Adolescent Health, 60,* 65–71. doi:10.1016/j.jadohealth.2016.09.008

Nomi, J. S., & Uddin, L. Q. (2015). Face processing in autism spectrum disorders: From brain regions to brain networks. *Neuropsychologia, 71,* 201–216. doi:10.1016/j.neuropsychologia.2015.03.029

Olson, K. R., Key, A. C., & Eaton, N. R. (2015). Gender cognition in transgender children. *Psychological Science, 26,* 467–474. doi:10.1177/0956797614568156

Pahl, K., & Way, N. (2006). Longitudinal trajectories of ethnic identity among urban Black and Latino adolescents. *Child Development, 77,* 1403–1415. doi:10.1111/j.1467-8624.2006.00943.x

Pelphrey, K. A., Shultz, S., Hudac, C. M., & Vander Wyk, B. C. (2011). Research review: Constraining heterogeneity: The social brain and its development in autism spectrum disorder. *Journal of Child Psychology and Psychiatry, 52,* 631–644. doi:10.1111/j.1469-7610.2010.02349.x

Quinn, P. C., Yahr, J., Kuhn, A., Slater, A. M., & Pascalis, O. (2002). Representation of the gender of human faces by infants: A preference for female. *Perception, 31,* 1109–1121. doi:10.1068/p3331

Reisner, S. L., Vetters, R., Leclerc, M., Zaslow, S., Wolfrum, S., Shumer, D., & Mimiaga, M. J. (2015). Mental health of transgender youth in care at an adolescent urban community health center: A matched retrospective cohort study. *Journal of Adolescent Health, 56,* 274–279. doi:10.1016/j.jadohealth.2014.10.264

Sacher, J., Okon-Singer, H., & Villringer, A. (2013). Evidence from neuroimaging for the role of the menstrual cycle in the interplay of emotion and cognition. *Frontiers in Human Neuroscience, 7,* 374. doi:10.3389/fnhum.2013.00374

Sanchez-Garrido, M., & Tena-Sempere, M. (2013). Metabolic control of puberty: Roles of leptin and kisspeptins. *Hormones and Behavior, 64,* 187–194. doi:10.1016/j.yhbeh.2013.01.014

Sanders, A. R., Beecham, G. W., Guo, S., Dawood, K., Rieger, G., Badner, J. A., . . . Martin, E. R. (2017). Genome-wide association study of male sexual orientation. *Scientific Reports, 7,* 16950. doi:10.1038/s41598-017-15736-4

Sanders, A. R., Martin, E. R., Beecham, G. W., Guo, S., Dawood, K., Rieger, G., . . . Duan, J. (2015). Genome-wide scan demonstrates significant linkage for male sexual orientation. *Psychological Medicine, 45,* 1379–1388. doi:10.1017/S0033291714002451

Scherf, K. S., Luna, B., Avidan, G., & Behrmann, M. (2011). "What" precedes "which": Developmental neural tuning in face-and place-related cortex. *Cerebral Cortex, 21,* 1963–1980. doi:10.1093/cercor/bhq269

Schneiderman, I., Zagoory-Sharon, O., Leckman, J. F., & Feldman, R. (2012). Oxytocin during the initial stages of romantic attachment: Relations to couples' interactive reciprocity. *Psychoneuroendocrinology, 37,* 1277–1285. doi:10.1016/j.psyneuen.2011.12.021

Sebastian, C., Viding, E., Williams, K. D., & Blakemore, S. J. (2010). Social brain development and the affective consequences of ostracism in adolescence. *Brain and Cognition, 72,* 134–145. doi:10.1016/j.bandc.2009.06.008

Shirtcliff, E. A., Allison, A. L., Armstrong, J. M., Slattery, M. J., Kalin, N. H., & Essex, M. J. (2012). Longitudinal stability and developmental properties of salivary cortisol levels and circadian rhythms from childhood to adolescence. *Developmental Psychobiology, 54,* 493–502. doi:10.1002/dev.20607

Shumer, D. E., Nokoff, N. J., & Spack, N. P. (2016). Advances in the care of transgender children and adolescents. *Advances in Pediatrics, 63,* 79–102. doi:10.1016/j.yapd.2016.04.018

Silk, J. S., Siegle, G. J., Lee, K. H., Nelson, E. E., Stroud, L. R., & Dahl, R. E. (2013). Increased neural response to peer rejection associated with adolescent depression and pubertal development. *Social Cognitive and Affective Neuroscience, 9,* 1798–1807. doi:10.1093/scan/nst175

Soares, C. N., & Zitek, B. (2008). Reproductive hormone sensitivity and risk for depression across the female life cycle: A continuum of vulnerability? *Journal of Psychiatry & Neuroscience, 33,* 331–343. Retrieved from http://jpn.ca/wp-content/uploads/2014/04/33-4-331.pdf

Spear, L. P. (2009). *The behavioral neuroscience of adolescence.* New York: W. W. Norton.

Spear, L. P. (2013). Adolescent neurodevelopment. *Journal of Adolescent Health, 52,* 7–13. doi:10.1016/j.jadohealth.2012.05.006

Stennes, L. M., Burch, M. M., Sen, M. G., & Bauer, P. J. (2005). A longitudinal study of gendered vocabulary and communicative action in young children. *Developmental Psychology, 41,* 75–88. doi:10.1037/0012-1649.41.1.75

Tyborowska, A., Volman, I., Smeekens, S., Toni, I., & Roelofs, K. (2016). Testosterone during puberty shifts emotional control from pulvinar to anterior prefrontal cortex. *Journal of Neuroscience, 36,* 6156–6164. doi:10.1523/JNEUROSCI.3874-15.2016

Umaña-Taylor, A. J., Quintana, S. M., Lee, R. M., Cross, W. E., Jr., Rivas-Drake, D., Schwartz, S. J., . . . Ethnic and Racial Identity in the 21st Century Study Group. (2014). Ethnic and racial identity during adolescence and into young adulthood: An integrated conceptualization. *Child Development, 85,* 21–39. doi:10.1111/cdev.12196

van den Bos, W., van Dijk, E., Westenberg, M., Rombouts, S. A., & Crone, E. A. (2011). Changing brains, changing perspectives: The neurocognitive development of reciprocity. *Psychological Science, 22,* 60–70. doi:10.1177/0956797610391102

van Wingen, G. A., Ossewaarde, L., Bäckström, T., Hermans, E. J., & Fernández, G. (2011). Gonadal hormone regulation of the emotion circuitry in humans. *Neuroscience, 191,* 38–45. doi:10.1016/j.neuroscience.2011.04.042

Weinstein, S. M., & Mermelstein, R. (2007). Relations between daily activities and adolescent mood: The role of autonomy. *Journal of Clinical Child and Adolescent Psychology, 36,* 182–194. doi:10.1080/15374410701274967

Chapter 9

Problems of Adolescence

Key Concepts

- Adolescent depression and suicidality
- Nonsuicidal self-injury
- Generalized and social anxiety
- Posttraumatic stress
- Eating disorders
- Substance use
- Addiction and the dopaminergic system (ventral tegmental area; mesocorticolimbic projection, mesolimbic pathway, mesocortical pathway; nigrostriatal pathway)

Aligned 2016 CACREP Standards

Standard 2.F.3.c. Theories of normal and abnormal personality development

Standard 2.F.3.d. Theories and etiology of addictions and addictive behaviors

Standard 2.F.3.e. Biological, neurological, and physiological factors that affect human development, functioning, and behavior

Standard 2.F.3.f. Systemic and environmental factors that affect human development, functioning, and behavior

Standard 2.F.3.g. Effects of crisis, disasters, and trauma on diverse individuals across the life span

Standard 2.F.7.c. Procedures for assessing risk of aggression or danger to others, self-inflicted harm, or suicide
Standard 2.F.7.d. Procedures for identifying trauma and abuse and for reporting abuse
Standard 2.F.7.e. Use of assessments for diagnostic and intervention planning purposes
Standard 2.F.7.l. Use of assessment results to diagnose developmental, behavioral, and mental disorders
Standard 2.F.7.m. Ethical and culturally relevant strategies for selecting, administering, and interpreting assessment and test results

• • •

This chapter examines problems and disorders of adolescence, in particular depression, nonsuicidal self-injury (NSSI) and suicidality, social and generalized anxieties, panic attacks, posttraumatic stress disorder (PTSD), eating disorders, and substance use and addictions. We review characteristics often seen with these disorders, along with the neurological etiologies of these disorders. The chapter concludes with an in-depth case study of Brooke along with an application of the transdiagnostic approach to supporting her.

Depression

One of the primary areas of concern when working with adolescents is depression. Major depression is a fairly common problem, experienced by 4% to 5% of adolescents (Thapar, Collishaw, Pine, & Thapar, 2012). Depression and hopelessness are associated with significant risk for suicide. Along with substance use, depression and hopelessness each double the risk for death by suicide (Hawton, Casañas i Comabella, Haw, & Saunders, 2013). The only factor that is associated with a higher risk for suicide is a history of prior suicide attempts, which confers a fourfold risk of death by suicide (Hawton et al., 2013). For more than 20 years, suicide has been the third leading cause of death among 15- to 24-year-olds, and in 2011 it became the second leading cause of death (Drapeau & McIntosh, 2015). The counselor's assessment, identification, and treatment of adolescent depressive symptoms along with suicidal ideation is thus crucial.

Characteristics

Although major depression can manifest differently among individuals, common symptoms of depression are a feeling of sadness for most of the day, a lack of interest in things one used to enjoy (anhedonia), an inability to sleep or excessive sleeping (insomnia and hypersomnia, respectively), hypoactivity or agitation, unintentional losing or gaining of weight, an inability to focus or concentrate, low energy, thoughts of dying, and cognitive distortions such as unwarranted feelings of guilt (American Psychiatric Association [APA], 2013). The *Diagnostic and Statistical Manual of Mental Disorders* (5th ed.; *DSM-5*) notes that depression is indicated when five or more symptoms are evident during a 2-week period (APA, 2013). Depressive symptoms can present differently in children. Symptoms of irritability, boredom, and difficulty concentrating in an academic setting are more common than low energy. In our experience, children and adolescents may have little awareness of these mood changes. Referrals to counseling for depression are therefore often initiated by others in their environment (e.g., school counselors, parents and guardians). Depression in adolescents often coexists with anxiety, substance use, or disruptive behavior (Thapar et al., 2012). Assessment for depression should include an inquiry about social problems in multiple settings (home, school, community, and work). Because several physical health conditions, such as vitamin D deficiency, can cause depression, we recommend that counselors require their adolescent clients to contact their primary care physician to schedule a lab panel to rule out a biological cause for their symptoms.

Etiology

As noted in Chapter 8, on neurophysiological and social development during adolescence, the brain grows and changes functionally and structurally throughout adolescence. Depression during adolescence has been associated with hyperemotionality, rejection sensitivity, and increased activity in the amygdala and anterior cingulate cortex (Guyer, Silk, & Nelson, 2016; Masten et al., 2011; Weinstein & Mermelstein, 2007). Yet depression is difficult to diagnose, as there are no biomarkers (Jentsch et al., 2015). In the absence of biological markers, five theoretical approaches have been developed to provide a neural explanation for depressive symptoms (Field, Beeson, Luke, Ghoston, & Golubovic, 2019).

The monoamine theory is perhaps the best known neuroscientific theory for depression. This theory was proposed following research that connected reduced self-reported depressive symptoms with increased serotonin neurotransmission via reuptake inhibition as a result of taking imipramine (Schildkraut, 1965). Because of these results, serotonin deficits were believed to be a neurobiological explanation of depression (Mulinari, 2012). Over the past several decades, deficits in the neurotransmission of other monoamines (e.g., dopamine, norepinephrine) have also been linked to self-reported depression through drug studies that increased the amount of these monoamines in the synaptic cleft through reuptake inhibition (Liu, Liu, Wang, Zhang, & Li, 2017).

The neuroplasticity theory moved away from the monoamine perspective and focused on epigenetic changes to gene expression following a person's exposure to environmental stressors (McEwen, 2012; Pittenger & Duman, 2008). In previous chapters (specifically Chapter 3, on epigenetics), we articulated this theory through descriptions of the metaplasticity hypothesis and hypercortisolism. The glutamate theory is similar to the neuroplasticity theory, in that it focuses on the role of long-term depression and volumetric changes in the development of depression. You may recall that glutamate is an excitatory neurotransmitter in the brain that responds to two specific groups of receptors: ionotropic glutamate receptors and metabotropic glutamate receptors (Palucha & Pilc, 2005). Trullas and Skolnick (1990) found evidence that modifications to glutamertergic N-methyl-D-aspartate receptors were associated with depression. Because glutamate influences the frequency of neurotransmission, reductions in the production and secretion of glutamate result in synaptic loss and reduced numbers of new synapses.

Depression can also be caused by structural and functional abnormalities and other medical conditions. Head injuries, concussions, and strokes can result in damage and atrophy in the hippocampus, amygdala, and prefrontal cortex (Rolls, 2016). Adolescent participation in contact sports and bike riding presents the risk for head injury. Perhaps because males participate more in dirt bike racing and contact sports, the incidence of head injury is far higher in males compared to females, with a 21:1 ratio reported (Habelt, Hasler, Steinbrück, & Majewski, 2011). Rates of concussions in both male and female athletes have been rising (Lincoln et al., 2011). High school football injuries appear to significantly alter the default mode network, which is a risk factor for depression (Abbas et al., 2015). Medical conditions such as vitamin deficiencies and hormone changes can also cause depression (Dayan & Panicker, 2013; Parker, Brotchie, & Graham, 2017). Consider Reflection Question 9.1.

The prevalence of adolescent depression varies by biological sex, with a 2:1 ratio in females versus males (Hyde, Mezulis, & Abramson, 2008). Greater rates of depression in females seem to be due to several factors, such as differing impacts of gonadal hormone secretion; circulating cortisol; increased incidences of physical and sexual assault and abuse; and gender role socialization resulting in excessive cognitive rumination, especially about body image (Hyde et al., 2008; Shirtcliff et al., 2012; Soares & Zitek, 2008). The rate of depression is even higher in lesbian, gay, bisexual, transgender, nonbinary, queer, questioning, intersex, and/or asexual populations (Reisner et al., 2015).

Reflection Question 9.1

Imagine an adolescent asks you, "What is happening in my brain that I feel so depressed?" What explanation might you give?

A preponderance of tools exist for screening for depression, several of which have been developed and normed on adolescent populations. The second edition of the Reynolds Adolescent Depression Scale (Reynolds, 2002) was normed on adolescents ages 11 through 19, and a T score of 65 (+1.5 *SD*) correctly identified more than 90% of adolescents with major depression (Ortuño-Sierra et al., 2017). The scale has strong test-retest reliability and takes 5 minutes to administer. The second edition of the Beck Depression Inventory is another popular screening tool that was normed on adolescents and adults ages 13 and older (Beck, Steer, & Brown, 1996). Like the Reynolds Adolescent Depression Scale–2, the Beck Depression Inventory appears to correctly identify more than 90% of adolescents with major depression (Dolle et al., 2012). The test appears better able to identify mild and moderate symptoms of depression in adolescents compared to severe forms of depression (Dolle et al., 2012). Assessments also exist that measure adolescent suicidality, such as the Columbia–Suicide Severity Rating Scale (Posner et al., 2011). Although no perfect measure exists for predicting suicide attempts, a higher score on suicidal ideation predicts a higher odds of a suicide attempt on the Columbia scale (Posner et al., 2011).

As we will explore in a subsequent chapter, inquiring about an adolescent's sleep patterns and habits is important when assessing for depression. Sleep deprivation is typical during adolescence and can induce depression and anxiety (Babson, Trainor, Feldner, & Blumenthal, 2010).

NSSI

NSSI is defined as injury purposely inflicted on oneself without the intention of causing harm or committing suicide (APA, 2013). Furthermore, NSSI is not socially acceptable like other forms of body modification (i.e., tattooing and body piercing; Lloyd-Richardson, Perrine, Dierker, & Kelley, 2007). NSSI is listed as a condition under further study in the *DSM-5* and is not a codable diagnosis at this time. Adolescent NSSI is becoming more common (Zetterqvist, Lundh, Dahlström, & Svedin, 2013). In a sample of more than 3,000 adolescents with equal representation of males and females, approximately one third reported an episode of NSSI during the past year, with nearly 7% reporting five or more episodes in the past year (required for the proposed diagnosis in the *DSM-5;* Zetterqvist et al., 2013). In the Zetterqvist et al. (2013) study, females were 5 times more likely than males to meet the criterion of having five or more episodes of NSSI in the same year.

Characteristics

NSSI is different from a suicide attempt in that the adolescent does not intend to die when engaging in the behavior. Instead, adolescents tend to engage in these behaviors as a way of coping and dealing with stress, depression, and frustration. They frequently use NSSI to manage feelings related to interpersonal problems (APA, 2013). NSSI behaviors, such as making superficial cuts to the skin, can look similar to suicidal behaviors and may be mistakenly interpreted as suicide attempts. Like suicidal ideation, NSSI is associated with greater severity of depression and hopelessness (Stanley et al., 2010). In addition, although rare, some NSSI behaviors, such as cutting (if the cuts are deep enough to reach a vein or artery) or ingesting chemicals such as bleach, can cause significant damage and even risk of death. Adolescents may also ruminate about the self-injurious behavior when they are not engaging in the act (APA, 2013). Although NSSI is different from a suicide attempt, Muehlenkamp and Brausch (2019) found that NSSI was a robust predictor of future suicide attempts even when they controlled for protective factors such as life satisfaction and subjective happiness.

Etiology

Emerging evidence from samples of cerebrospinal fluid suggests that NSSI is associated with reduced levels of endorphins, such as beta-endorphins and metenkephalin, an opioid growth factor (Stanley et al., 2010). Endorphins are neuropeptides that are produced and secreted by the pituitary gland. Endorphins block pain signals in the nervous system and may also cause feelings of euphoria (Stanley et al., 2010). NSSI does not appear to be associated with abnormalities in the dopaminergic and serotonergic systems, as previously believed (Stanley et al., 2010). The primary function of NSSI appears to be regulating strong emotions such as emotional pain (Brausch & Muehlenkamp, 2018). NSSI is predictably less effective at managing interpersonal conflicts (Brausch & Muehlenkamp, 2018).

The following questions can be helpful to ask yourself when working with an adolescent who meets the criteria for NSSI: (a) What is the function of this behavior? (b) What alternative coping methods could help this adolescent meet these needs? (c) Have I properly assessed for suicidal ideation? (d) How might I ensure that the adolescent does not have a plan for suicide?

Generalized and Social Anxiety

In Chapter 8, we introduced rejection sensitivity and social anxiety that can emerge during adolescence. Anxiety is the most common condition during adolescence, with nearly one third of all adolescents struggling with anxiety (Merikangas et al., 2010). For context, this is double the prevalence of mood disorders (Merikangas et al., 2010). The age of onset for anxiety is much younger than for mood or substance use issues. In a study of 10,000 children and adolescents, the median age of onset for anxiety was 6 years compared to 13 years for mood issues (depression, bipolar disorder) and 15 years for substance use (Merikangas et al., 2010).

Characteristics

There are several different types of anxiety. *Generalized anxiety* is defined as persistent worry that exists across settings (e.g., home, school, community) and across situations (i.e., the worry is not triggered by a specific event). Symptoms of generalized anxiety include muscle tension, restlessness, edginess and irritability, impaired concentration, and sleep disturbance (APA, 2013). Symptoms of sleep disturbance and impaired concentration are shared with depression, and the diagnosis often co-occurs with major depression.

Symptoms of social anxiety include fears of negative evaluation and embarrassment in social contexts, such as performance situations (e.g., giving a speech) or social situations (e.g., parties; APA, 2013). These fears of embarrassment result in the adolescent attempting to avoid those situations. Social anxiety at school can create significant problems with attendance and truancy, similar to separation anxiety.

Etiology

Anxiety is associated with reduced connectivity between the frontal lobe (i.e., the orbitofrontal cortex and ventrolateral prefrontal cortex) and limbic structures such as the amygdala (Hahn et al., 2011; Monk et al., 2008). Reduced connectivity impairs top-down control over anxiety, worry, and fear responses, resulting in an overactive amygdala (Hahn et al., 2011). Attachment issues with caregivers appear to affect the likelihood of developing anxiety, as oxytocin attenuates amygdala activity to fear (Labuschagne et al., 2010). Deficits in the neurotransmission of gamma-aminobutyric acid, the main inhibitory neurotransmitter, have also been associated with anxiety (Möhler, 2012).

Posttraumatic Stress

PTSD is a cognitive, behavioral, emotional, and neurophysiological response to a traumatic event (Asalgoo, Jahromi, Meftahi, & Sahraei, 2015). A *traumatic event* is defined as direct exposure to or witnessing of threatened or actual injury, violence, or death, such as sexual assault, natural disaster, a car accident, or assault. The traumatic event(s) can happen directly to the adolescent, or the adolescent can observe this event indirectly as it affects a peer, family member, or even someone in the community.

Characteristics

Symptoms of PTSD are categorized by intrusion, avoidance, alterations in cognitions and mood, and arousal or reactivity (APA, 2013).

Intrusion symptoms are unwanted experiences related to the traumatic event that the child or adolescent cannot control, such as distressing dreams or memories and dissociative symptoms such as flashbacks. These intrusive symptoms are so aversive that the child or adolescent avoids them through intentional blocking of thoughts and memories related to the event and avoidance of any reminders. The child or adolescent may withdraw from relationships as a result and feel detached from others and the world around them. Being exposed to a traumatic event can cause cognitive distortions about oneself, others, or the world and a persistent state of fear, anger, guilt, or shame. The overactive threat response system in PTSD can also create a constant state of alertness (hypervigilance) and restless sleep, a strong reflexive startle response, and explosive episodes of anger (APA, 2013).

Etiology

As with the chronic stress pathway, a traumatic event can trigger a series of neurophysiological changes associated with cortisol and adrenaline production and secretion that engender the symptoms noted above. The longitudinal study by Trickett, Noll, and Putnam (2011) reviewed in Chapter 3, on epigenetics, provided evidence that children (specifically females) who were exposed to trauma early on in life had increased adrenocorticotropic hormone production in early childhood but decreased levels of this hormone in early adulthood. This study provides support for the longitudinal asymmetrical production and secretion of cortisol known as the *attenuation hypothesis* (Susman, 2006).

As we noted in earlier chapters, hypercortisolism is associated with long-term depression and a change in volume of the hippocampus. In addition, increased adrenaline receptor activity in the amygdala enhances reconsolidation of fear memories, making these memories resistant to extinction (Dębiec, Bush, & LeDoux, 2011). PTSD thus causes disruptions to memory consolidation of a traumatic event, with fear-based memories being more easily recalled and more difficult to extinguish.

PTSD also causes other changes in the brain. Impaired circuitry between the medial prefrontal cortex and amygdala results in greater activation of the amygdala in response to threat and reduced inhibitory ability to mediate fear responses and regulate emotions (Stevens et al., 2013). Enhanced circuitry between the amygdala and insula creates an exaggerated and perpetual state of physiological arousal that persists even in the absence of perceived threats in the environment (Rabinak et al., 2011; Sripada et al., 2012). Enhanced activation of the anterior cingulate cortex and impaired top-down control in the dorsolateral prefrontal cortex are associated with an inability to regulate hyperarousal and control unwanted thoughts, memories, and images (Akiki, Averill, & Abdallah, 2017).

Because traumatic stress is a complex problem and is often underreported, we recommend that counselors screen for traumatic stress using a psychometric instrument such as the Trauma Symptom Checklist for Children (Briere, 1996). This instrument was normed on more than 3,000 children, and separate profiles are available for children (8–12 years) and adolescents (13–16 years). The Trauma Symptom Checklist for Children contains 54 questions and is relatively quick to administer. It contains validity scales that measure over- and underresponding to maximize the accuracy of the test. Furthermore, an alternative version is available that excludes questions about sexual matters, for situations when it would be inappropriate to ask a child about their sexual history and behavior.

Eating Disorders

Eating disorders are often severe and life-threatening conditions that can emerge during adolescence. The low body weight seen in anorexia nervosa is associated with an elevated mortality rate. Death can occur as a result of heart complications attributed to malnutrition (Westmoreland, Krantz, & Mehler, 2016). There are several types of eating disorders: anorexia nervosa, bulimia nervosa, and binge eating.

Characteristics

Adolescents with anorexia are significantly underweight, with a body mass index less than 17 (APA, 2013). Low body weight in anorexia can occur through strict dieting; excessive exercise; and purging behavior, such as forced vomiting and use of rectal suppositories. The adolescent with anorexia may also binge eat, which is typically followed by either purging the food or burning the calories through exercise immediately afterward. Alongside low body weight, adolescents with anorexia tend to develop cognitive distortions about their body image, perceiving themselves as weighing more than they actually do. They may also deny the seriousness of their low body weight. The symptoms of bulimia are similar to those of anorexia, except that the adolescent does not have a low body mass index. Binge eating is marked by bingeing episodes only.

Low body weight has several detrimental physiological effects. Adolescents with anorexia are at elevated risk for fractures because of low bone mineral density (APA, 2013). Adolescents with anorexia also have reduced estrogen levels, and amenorrhea (i.e., the absence of menstruation) can occur (APA, 2013). Anorexia is linked to an underproduction of leptin and dysregulated thyroid function (Westmoreland et al., 2016). Purging is also associated with health effects, such as the erosion of teeth enamel from the acidity in bile (Westmoreland et al., 2016).

Etiology

The exact cause of eating disorders can vary among individuals. Family dynamics, gender role stereotypes related to body image, and preexisting anxiety have all been proposed as potential precipitants of eating disorders (APA, 2013; Klump, 2013; Westmoreland et al., 2016). It is notable that eating disorders are much more common in females than males (Klump, 2013). Klump, Keel, Sisk, and Burt (2010) found in a twin study that higher levels of estradiol were associated with eating disorders, which suggests a genetic predisposition toward disordered eating. Early female pubertal maturation is also a risk factor for eating disorders (Klump, 2013). As we learned in Chapter 8, anorexia can also slow down pubertal maturation because of reduced adipose tissue and depleted energy stores (Katz & Vollenhoven, 2000).

Anorexia is associated with atrophy and reductions in volume in the anterior cingulate cortex and cerebellum (Amianto et al., 2013). The anterior cingulate cortex is associated with conditioned learning. People with anorexia and bulimia also appear to have increased volume in the somatosensory regions, which are linked to bodily sensations and mental representations of body image (Amianto et al., 2013). The right amygdala also appears to be overactive, with alterations to food reward sensitivity and disgust (Joos et al., 2011).

The Minnesota Starvation Study (Keys, Brožek, Henschel, Mickelsen, & Taylor, 1950) provided insights into how starvation impacts the brain and body. During the study, participants experienced semistarvation. As a result, their basal metabolic rate (the energy needed when the body is in a state of rest) was reduced (Keys et al., 1950). Study participants demonstrated repetitive, compulsive behaviors that are sometimes associated with anorexia, such as compulsive food preparation and intake, food rituals, and hoarding (Keys et al., 1950).

Eating disorders are complex conditions that have behavioral, cognitive, emotional, motivational, and physiological components. Addressing these conditions requires a specialized approach, especially in the case of more severe forms of these disorders. Treatment centers for eating disorders tend to focus on instilling healthy eating habits and logging daily food intake while also working through cognitive distortions related to body weight and body image. Assessing eating disorders is complex, as the adolescent's body mass index must be determined in addition to other symptoms mentioned previously.

Substance Use and Addiction

Experimenting with substances is common during adolescence. As we noted previously, most substance use problems emerge during adolescence, at a median age of 15 years (Merikangas et al., 2010). A high percentage of 12th graders have tried various substances:

68% have tried alcohol, 46% have used cannabis, and 25% have used an illicit drug other than cannabis (Johnston, O'Malley, Miech, Bachman, & Schulenberg, 2014). Alcohol appears to be consumed fairly regularly, with approximately 50% of 10th graders and 66% of 12th graders reporting having consumed alcohol in the past month (Patrick & Schulenberg, 2014). The adolescent's peer group has a strong impact on their initiation of substance use. In a study by Mundt (2011), adolescents were more likely to consume alcohol if they had more popular friends, had friends three steps removed, and had more friends who themselves consumed alcohol. After controlling for confounding variables, the researchers found that the likelihood of an adolescent using alcohol increased 34% for each additional friend who consumed alcohol (Mundt, 2011).

Characteristics

Substance use is characterized as the excessive use of a substance that impacts the brain's reward system and behaviors (APA, 2013). A substance use disorder tends to include physiological, cognitive, and behavioral symptoms such as craving, tolerance, withdrawal, and continued use despite negative consequences (APA, 2013). Continued use has negative social effects. The adolescent may fail to follow through with typical expectations, such as attending school regularly. The adolescent may continue to use substances despite losing friends or having disagreements with parental and authority figures. The adolescent may also withdraw from activities that they previously enjoyed (e.g., sports).

Etiology

In Chapter 8, on adolescent neurophysiological and social development, we reviewed the neurophysiological basis for adolescent proclivities toward substance use. In brief, the striatum develops at a faster rate than the prefrontal cortex during adolescence. The striatum is associated with motivational drives and conditioned learning to rewards. This sensitizes youth toward novel rewards, risk taking, and sensation seeking. The striatum contains the nucleus accumbens, which has a vital role in the dopaminergic system, which is associated with motivation and reward. The dopaminergic system undergoes substantial development during adolescence (Sturman & Moghaddam, 2011).

Dopamine is developed and secreted by sets of neurons that are located in several pathways. The ventral tegmental area in the midbrain is a particularly notable structure, as it is a key site for dopamine production. The two pathways that are most associated with addiction are the mesocorticolimbic projection (composed of the mesolimbic pathway and mesocortical pathway) and the nigrostriatal pathway (Volkow & Morales, 2015). The mesolimbic pathway transmits dopamine between the ventral tegmental area and the ventral striatum in the limbic region, which includes the nucleus accumbens. The mesocortical pathway transmits dopamine from the ventral tegmental area to the prefrontal cortex. The mesolimbic pathway is implicated in a person's motivation to seek out the rewarding properties of a drug, whereas the mesocortical pathway is implicated in the person's decision making, impulse control, and planned behavior. The nigrostriatal pathway transmits dopamine from the substantia nigra in the midbrain to the dorsal striatum (i.e., the caudate nucleus and putamen, structures in the basal ganglia). The nigrostriatal pathway is known for its role in learned associations (i.e., situations that are linked to drug use, reward prediction).

On receiving a pleasurable and rewarding substance, the mesolimbic system begins to anticipate future rewards, a process known as *reward prediction* (Nieh, Kim, Namburi, & Tye, 2013). The mesolimbic system is so sensitive that dopamine will begin to be released in anticipation of the drug, and this excitement often feels powerful to the adolescent (Volkow & Morales, 2015). Some adolescents will experience ruminations about using the substance in anticipation of its effects. Over time, anticipating these rewards has impacts on the mesocortical pathway, which is associated with planning behavior around future use of the drug (Volkow & Morales, 2015). As substances continue to be introduced into the body, the reward circuit becomes saturated and the person develops tolerance for the substances (Koob, Arends, & Le Moal, 2014). When this occurs, the adolescent may try to avoid withdrawal symptoms by continuing to use the substance.

Differentiating an adolescent's normal or typical experimentation with substances from substance use problems and addiction can be a challenge. Counselors should inquire about any symptoms of tolerance or withdrawal and listen closely for indications that the adolescent is making lifestyle changes (e.g., losing friends, being truant, getting into conflicts with parents) because of their substance use. Because children often learn to drive motor vehicles during adolescence, counselors should be especially concerned about indications that the adolescent has been driving while intoxicated. Psychometric instruments such as the adolescent version of the Substance Abuse Subtle Screening Inventory, now in its second edition, could be potentially useful (Miller, Miller, & Lazowski, 2013). Like the Trauma Symptom Checklist for Children, the Substance Abuse Subtle Screening Inventory has validity scales to maximize test accuracy.

Transdiagnostic Application: The Case of Brooke

Problems that emerge during adolescence can be challenging to differentiate. We now introduce an in-depth case study to illustrate the use of the transdiagnostic model for identifying cross-cutting symptoms that help the counselor select an appropriate counseling approach (see Case Vignette 9.1). Thom uses first-person narrative to describe the

Case Vignette 9.1 Brooke, Part 1

Brooke was a 17-year-old biracial cisgender female (her father was Euro-American, and her mother was African American) who initially presented with a flat facial expression, lack of eye contact, and reduction in speech. Brooke was silent during most of the first session, mostly picking at her clothing and appearing bored. Her parents filled in most of the information.

Brooke's parents reported multiple problem behaviors, such as self-injury (cutting) and food restriction. Her parents had a vast liquor cabinet and did not mind her drinking in their presence because "she is discovering herself." The parents wondered whether Brooke was sexually active. They had recently found birth control pills in her bathroom. Her parents did not take her to the doctor, and Brooke refused to talk about it. At the end of the first session, the parents suggested that Brooke attend the next session alone, as she might feel more comfortable without them there. I ensured that Brooke's parents understood that they were not to pressure Brooke or her counselor for information moving forward, as it would impede therapeutic progress.

The first 20 minutes of the second session consisted of surface-level chit-chat about high school and peers. Eventually I asked directly about what Brooke would not tell her parents, if she felt comfortable sharing. Brooke sighed deeply before hesitantly telling me that 2 years ago she had been gang-raped at a party by (she thought) four men whom she did not know. She had become pregnant and elected to have an abortion. She recalled vivid details of sitting in the waiting room and watching four young girls entering a room. When it was Brooke's turn, she reported, "My memory blanks out at that point . . . I can't remember anything." Brooke added, "When I think about what happened to me, I feel sick to my stomach."

Brooke's choice to get an abortion left her with significant feelings of guilt and shame. Ever since the assault, she had been consuming large amounts of alcohol, especially at parties. Her self-injury seemed to be a form of coping and was not an intentional suicidal gesture. Brooke reported that she did not feel suicidal, though she did want the pain to stop. She decided to take birth control to prevent future pregnancies "just in case something bad happens again." Her parents were unaware of the assault. Toward the close of the session, I told Brooke that it took a lot of courage

(Continued)

Case Vignette 9.1 *(Continued)*

to share that information with me. I also asked what name she had given to her child before the abortion. Brooke replied, "Irene Carter." She then asked quizzically how I knew she had already named the baby.

• • •

counseling process. Note that this case study contains some information that may be distressing for some readers.

Brooke's presentation included symptoms of depression and posttraumatic stress. After experiencing not one but two traumatic events (per her self-report), she felt an overwhelming sense of guilt and shame. It is worth mentioning here that abortions do not typically seem to be associated with symptoms of posttraumatic stress. A large research study of more than 800 women found no significant difference in symptoms of posttraumatic stress between women who had had an abortion and those who had not (Biggs, Rowland, McCulloch, & Foster, 2016). Brooke's symptoms in response to her abortion would therefore be unusual.

Brooke had taken measures to prevent and avoid further traumatic experiencing, such as taking birth control. Her flat affect, lack of eye contact, and reduced speech further suggest posttraumatic stress alongside potential depression. Chronically high circulating cortisol is often a symptom of traumatic stress and could have been causing subsequent brain changes associated with depression. She had been attempting to cope with these symptoms through self-injury (private events) and alcohol (social events). In subsequent sessions, Thom would need to gather more information about Brooke's restricted eating patterns, as there was some evidence of a possible eating disorder. Similarly, the extent of Brooke's substance use would also need to be assessed.

Brooke's disclosure during the second session is somewhat remarkable. It is often difficult for an adolescent to be able to talk about traumatic events in counseling, and trust must typically be established first. Brooke also disclosed information about sexual assault with a counselor of the opposite sex, which could have felt uncomfortable. As the counselor, Thom checked in with Brooke during the next session to explore whether Brooke felt that she had shared too much, too soon. It is vital that clients feel a sense of control over when and how they disclose information about traumatic experiences. This control reduces the potential that the client will become overwhelmed and drop out of counseling prematurely. Consider Reflection Question 9.2.

Reflection Question 9.2

What are the counselor's ethical obligations in Brooke's case?

Conclusion

The intense emotions and motivational drives of adolescence may increase the risk of developing mental health conditions such as anxiety, depression, and substance use problems. Unlike some of the childhood diagnoses we explored (e.g., autism), many of these conditions can resolve through counseling and do not necessarily persist throughout the life span.

Quiz Questions

1. Which five neuroscience conceptualizations of depression were described in this chapter?
   a. Monoamine, neuroplasticity, glutamate, structural or functional abnormality, medical conditions
   b. Serotonin, dopamine, norepinephrine, melatonin, cortisol
   c. Amygdala, hippocampus, hypothalamus, medial prefrontal cortex, orbitofrontal cortex
2. NSSI is associated with reduced levels of
   a. Dopamine
   b. Endorphins
   c. Serotonin
3. Substance use proneness during adolescence is associated with the _____ system.
   a. Dopaminergic
   b. Serotonergic
   c. Corticotropic

References

Abbas, K., Shenk, T. E., Poole, V. N., Breedlove, E. L., Leverenz, L. J., Nauman, E. A., . . . Robinson, M. E. (2015). Alteration of default mode network in high school football athletes due to repetitive subconcussive mild traumatic brain injury: A resting-state functional magnetic resonance imaging study. *Brain Connectivity, 5,* 91–101. doi:10.1089/brain.2014.0279

Akiki, T. J., Averill, C. L., & Abdallah, C. G. (2017). A network-based neurobiological model of PTSD: Evidence from structural and functional neuroimaging studies. *Current Psychiatry Reports, 19,* 81. doi:10.1007/s11920-017-0840-4

American Psychiatric Association. (2013). *Diagnostic and statistical manual of mental disorders* (5th ed.). Arlington, VA: Author.

Amianto, F., Caroppo, P., D'Agata, F., Spalatro, A., Lavagnino, L., Caglio, M., . . . Mortara, P. (2013). Brain volumetric abnormalities in patients with anorexia and bulimia nervosa: A voxel-based morphometry study. *Psychiatry Research: Neuroimaging, 213,* 210–216. doi:10.1016/j.pscychresns.2013.03.010

Asalgoo, S., Jahromi, G. P., Meftahi, G. H., & Sahraei, H. (2015). Posttraumatic stress disorder (PTSD): Mechanisms and possible treatment. *Neurophysiology, 47,* 482–489. doi:10.1007/s11062-016-9559-9

Babson, K. A., Trainor, C. D., Feldner, M. T., & Blumenthal, H. (2010). A test of the effects of acute sleep deprivation on general and specific self-reported anxiety and depressive symptoms: An experimental extension. *Journal of Behavior Therapy and Experimental Psychiatry, 41,* 297–303. doi:10.1016/j.jbtep.2010.02.008

Beck, A. T., Steer, R. A., & Brown, G. K. (1996). *Beck Depression Inventory–II.* San Antonio, TX: Psychological Corporation.

Biggs, M. A., Rowland, B., McCulloch, C. E., & Foster, D. G. (2016). Does abortion increase women's risk for post-traumatic stress? Findings from a prospective longitudinal cohort study. *BMJ Open, 6,* e009698. doi:10.1136/bmjopen-2015-009698

Brausch, A. M., & Muehlenkamp, J. J. (2018). Perceived effectiveness of NSSI in achieving functions on severity and suicide risk. *Psychiatry Research, 265,* 144–150. doi:10.1016/j.psychres.2018.04.038

Briere, J. (1996). *Trauma Symptom Checklist for Children.* Lutz, FL: Psychological Assessment Resources.

Council for Accreditation of Counseling and Related Educational Programs. (2015). *2016 CACREP standards.* Alexandria, VA: Author.

Dayan, C. M., & Panicker, V. (2013). Hypothyroidism and depression. *European Thyroid Journal, 2,* 168–179. doi:10.1159/000353777

Dębiec, J., Bush, D. E., & LeDoux, J. E. (2011). Noradrenergic enhancement of reconsolidation in the amygdala impairs extinction of conditioned fear in rats—a possible mechanism for the persistence of traumatic memories in PTSD. *Depression and Anxiety, 28,* 186–193. doi:10.1002/da.20803

Dolle, K., Schulte-Körne, G., O'Leary, A. M., von Hofacker, N., Izat, Y., & Allgaier, A. K. (2012). The Beck Depression Inventory-II in adolescent mental health patients: Cut-off scores for detecting depression and rating severity. *Psychiatry Research, 200,* 843–848. doi:10.1016/j.psychres.2012.05.011

Drapeau, C. W., & McIntosh, J. L. (2015). *U.S.A. suicide: Official final data.* Washington, DC: American Association of Suicidology.

Field, T. A., Beeson, E. T., Luke, C., Ghoston, M., & Golubovic, N. (2019). Neuroscience conceptualizations of depression by counselors. *Journal of Mental Health Counseling, 41,* 260–279. doi:10.17744/mehc.41.3.05

Guyer, A. E., Silk, J. S., & Nelson, E. E. (2016). The neurobiology of the emotional adolescent: From the inside out. *Neuroscience & Biobehavioral Reviews, 70,* 74–85. doi:10.1016/j.neubiorev.2016.07.037

Habelt, S., Hasler, C. C., Steinbrück, K., & Majewski, M. (2011). Sport injuries in adolescents. *Orthopedic Reviews, 3,* e18. doi:10.4081/or.2011.e18

Hahn, A., Stein, P., Windischberger, C., Weissenbacher, A., Spindelegger, C., Moser, E., . . . Lanzenberger, R. (2011). Reduced resting-state functional connectivity between amygdala and orbitofrontal cortex in social anxiety disorder. *Neuroimage, 56,* 881–889. doi:10.1016/j.neuroimage.2011.02.064

Hawton, K., Casañas i Comabella, C., Haw, C., & Saunders, K. (2013). Risk factors for suicide in individuals with depression: A systematic review. *Journal of Affective Disorders, 147,* 17–28. doi:10.1016/j.jad.2013.01.004

Hyde, J. S., Mezulis, A. H., & Abramson, L. Y. (2008). The ABCs of depression: Integrating affective, biological, and cognitive models to explain the emergence of the gender difference in depression. *Psychological Review, 115,* 291–313. doi:10.1037/0033-295X.115.2.291

Jentsch, M. C., Van Buel, E. M., Bosker, F. J., Gladkevich, A. V., Klein, H. C., Oude Voshaar, R. C., . . . Schoevers, R. A. (2015). Biomarker approaches in major depressive disorder evaluated in the context of current hypotheses. *Biomarkers in Medicine, 9,* 277–297. doi:10.2217/bmm.14.114

Johnston, L. D., O'Malley, P. M., Miech, R. A., Bachman, J. G., & Schulenberg, J. E. (2014). *Monitoring the Future national results on drug use: 1975-2013: Overview, key findings on adolescent drug use.* Ann Arbor: The University of Michigan, Institute for Social Research.

Joos, A. A., Saum, B., van Elst, L. T., Perlov, E., Glauche, V., Hartmann, A., . . . Zeeck, A. (2011). Amygdala hyperreactivity in restrictive anorexia nervosa. *Psychiatry Research: Neuroimaging, 191,* 189–195. doi:10.1016/j.pscychresns.2010.11.008

Katz, M. G., & Vollenhoven, B. (2000). The reproductive endocrine consequences of anorexia nervosa. *British Journal of Obstetrics & Gynaecology, 107,* 707–713. doi:10.1111/j.1471-0528.2000.tb13329.x

Keys, A., Brožek, J., Henschel, A., Mickelsen, O., & Taylor, H. L. (1950). *The biology of human starvation* (Vol. 1). Minneapolis: University of Minnesota Press.

Klump, K. L. (2013). Puberty as a critical risk period for eating disorders: A review of human and animal studies. *Hormones and Behavior, 64,* 399–410. doi:10.1016/j.yhbeh.2013.02.019

Klump, K. L., Keel, P. K., Sisk, C., & Burt, S. A. (2010). Preliminary evidence that estradiol moderates genetic influences on disordered eating attitudes and behaviors during puberty. *Psychological Medicine, 40,* 1745–1753. doi:10.1017/S0033291705006653

Koob, G. F., Arends, M. A., & Le Moal, M. (2014). *Drugs, addiction, and the brain*. Waltham, MA: Elsevier.

Labuschagne, I., Phan, K. L., Wood, A., Angstadt, M., Chua, P., Heinrichs, M., . . . Nathan, P. J. (2010). Oxytocin attenuates amygdala reactivity to fear in generalized social anxiety disorder. *Neuropsychopharmacology, 35,* 2403–2413. doi:10.1038/npp.2010.123

Lincoln, A. E., Caswell, S. V., Almquist, J. L., Dunn, R. E., Norris, J. B., & Hinton, R. Y. (2011). Trends in concussion incidence in high school sports: A prospective 11-year study. *American Journal of Sports Medicine, 39,* 958–963. doi:10.1177/0363546510392326

Liu, B., Liu, J., Wang, M., Zhang, Y., & Li, L. (2017). From serotonin to neuroplasticity: Evolvement of theories for major depressive disorder. *Frontiers in Cellular Neuroscience, 11,* 305. doi:10.3389/fncel.2017.00305

Lloyd-Richardson, E. E., Perrine, N., Dierker, L., & Kelley, M. L. (2007). Characteristics and functions of non-suicidal self-injury in a community sample of adolescents. *Psychological Medicine, 37,* 1183–1192. doi:10.1017/S003329170700027X

Masten, C. L., Eisenberger, N. I., Borofsky, L. A., McNealy, K., Pfeifer, J. H., & Dapretto, M. (2011). Subgenual anterior cingulate responses to peer rejection: A marker of adolescents' risk for depression. *Development and Psychopathology, 23,* 283–292. doi:10.1017/S0954579410000799

McEwen, B. S. (2012). Brain on stress: How the social environment gets under the skin. *Proceedings of the National Academy of Sciences, USA, 109,* 17180–17185. doi:10.1073/pnas.1121254109

Merikangas, K. R., He, J. P., Burstein, M., Swanson, S. A., Avenevoli, S., Cui, L., . . . Swendsen, J. (2010). Lifetime prevalence of mental disorders in US adolescents: Results from the National Comorbidity Survey Replication–Adolescent Supplement (NCS-A). *Journal of the American Academy of Child & Adolescent Psychiatry, 49,* 980–989. doi:10.1016/j.jaac.2010.05.017

Miller, F. G., Miller, G. A., & Lazowski, L. E. (2013). *Adolescent Substance Abuse Subtle Screening Inventory–A2*. Springfield, IN: The SASSI Institute.

Möhler, H. (2012). The GABA system in anxiety and depression and its therapeutic potential. *Neuropharmacology, 62,* 42–53. doi:10.1016/j.neuropharm.2011.08.040

Monk, C. S., Telzer, E. H., Mogg, K., Bradley, B. P., Mai, X., Louro, H. M., . . . Pine, D. S. (2008). Amygdala and ventrolateral prefrontal cortex activation to masked angry faces in children and adolescents with generalized anxiety disorder. *Archives of General Psychiatry, 65,* 568–576. doi:10.1001/archpsyc.65.5.568

Muehlenkamp, J. J., & Brausch, A. M. (2019). Protective factors do not moderate risk for past-year suicide attempts conferred by recent NSSI. *Journal of Affective Disorders, 245,* 321–324. doi:10.1016/j.jad.2018.11.013

Mulinari, S. (2012). Monoamine theories of depression: Historical impact on biomedical research. *Journal of the Histories of the Neurosciences, 21,* 366–392. doi:10.1080/0964704X.2011.623917

Mundt, M. P. (2011). The impact of peer social networks on adolescent alcohol use initiation. *Academic Pediatrics, 11,* 414–421. doi:10.1016/j.acap.2011.05.005

Nieh, E. H., Kim, S-Y., Namburi, P., & Tye, K. M. (2013). Optogenetic dissection of neural circuits underlying emotional valance and motivated behaviors. *Brain Research, 1511,* 73–92. http://dol.org/10.1016/j.brainres.2012.11.001

Ortuño-Sierra, J., Aritio-Solana, R., Inchausti, F., Chocarro de Luis, E., Lucas Molina, B., Pérez de Albéniz, A., & Fonseca-Pedrero, E. (2017). Screening for depressive symptoms in adolescents at school: New validity evidences on the short form of the Reynolds Depression Scale. *PLoS ONE, 12,* e0170950. doi:10.1371/journal.pone.0170950

Palucha, A., & Pilc, A. (2005). The involvement of glutamate in the pathophysiology of depression. *Drug News Perspectives, 18,* 262–268. doi:10.1358/dnp.2005.18.4.908661

Parker, G. B., Brotchie, H., & Graham, R. K. (2017). Vitamin D and depression. *Journal of Affective Disorders, 208,* 56–61. doi:10.1016/j.jad.2016.08.082

Patrick, M. E., & Schulenberg, J. E. (2014). Prevalence and predictors of adolescent alcohol use and binge drinking in the United States. *Alcohol Research: Current Reviews, 35,* 193–200.

Pittenger, C., & Duman, R. S. (2008). Stress, depression, and neuroplasticity: A convergence of mechanisms. *Neuropsychopharmacology, 33,* 88–109. doi:10.1038/sj.npp.1301574

Posner, K., Brown, G. K., Stanley, B., Brent, D. A., Yershova, K. V., Oquendo, M. A., . . . Mann, J. J. (2011). The Columbia–Suicide Severity Rating Scale: Initial validity and internal consistency findings from three multisite studies with adolescents and adults. *American Journal of Psychiatry, 168,* 1266–1277. doi:10.1176/appi.ajp.2011.10111704

Rabinak, C. A., Angstadt, M., Welsh, R. C., Kennedy, A., Lyubkin, M., Martis, B., & Phan, K. L. (2011). Altered amygdala resting-state functional connectivity in post-traumatic stress disorder. *Frontiers in Psychiatry, 2,* 62. doi:10.3389/fpsyt.2011.00062

Reisner, S. L., Vetters, R., Leclerc, M., Zaslow, S., Wolfrum, S., Shumer, D., & Mimiaga, M. J. (2015). Mental health of transgender youth in care at an adolescent urban community health center: A matched retrospective cohort study. *Journal of Adolescent Health, 56,* 274–279. doi:10.1016/j.jadohealth.2014.10.264

Reynolds, W. M. (2002). *Reynolds Adolescent Depression Scale* (2nd ed.). Lutz, FL: Psychological Assessment Resources.
Rolls, E. T. (2016). Pattern separation, completion, and categorisation in the hippocampus and neocortex. *Neurobiology of Learning and Memory, 129,* 4–28. doi:10.1016/j.nlm.2015.07.008
Schildkraut, J. J. (1965). The catecholamine hypothesis of affective disorders: A review of supporting evidence. *American Journal of Psychiatry, 122,* 509–522.
Shirtcliff, E. A., Allison, A. L., Armstrong, J. M., Slattery, M. J., Kalin, N. H., & Essex, M. J. (2012). Longitudinal stability and developmental properties of salivary cortisol levels and circadian rhythms from childhood to adolescence. *Developmental Psychobiology, 54,* 493–502. doi:10.1002/dev.20607
Soares, C. N., & Zitek, B. (2008). Reproductive hormone sensitivity and risk for depression across the female life cycle: A continuum of vulnerability? *Journal of Psychiatry & Neuroscience, 33,* 331–343.
Sripada, R. K., King, A. P., Garfinkel, S. N., Wang, X., Sripada, C. S., Welsh, R. C., & Liberzon, I. (2012). Altered resting-state amygdala functional connectivity in men with posttraumatic stress disorder. *Journal of Psychiatry & Neuroscience, 37,* 241–249. doi:10.1503/jpn.110069
Stanley, B., Sher, L., Wilson, S., Ekman, R., Huang, Y. Y., & Mann, J. J. (2010). Non-suicidal self-injurious behavior, endogenous opioids and monoamine neurotransmitters. *Journal of Affective Disorders, 124,* 134–140. doi:10.1016/j.jad.2009.10.028
Stevens, J. S., Jovanovic, T., Fani, N., Ely, T. D., Glover, E. M., Bradley, B., & Ressler, K. J. (2013). Disrupted amygdala-prefrontal functional connectivity in civilian women with posttraumatic stress disorder. *Journal of Psychiatric Research, 47,* 1469–1478. doi:10.1016/j.jpsychires.2013.05.031
Sturman, D. A., & Moghaddam, B. (2011). The neurobiology of adolescence: Changes in brain architecture, functional dynamics, and behavioral tendencies. *Neuroscience and Behavioral Reviews, 35,* 1704–1712. doi:10.1016/j.neubiorev.2011.04.003
Susman, E. J. (2006). Psychobiology of persistent antisocial behavior: Stress, early vulnerabilities and the attenuation hypothesis. *Neuroscience & Biobehavioral Reviews, 30,* 376–389. doi:10.1016/j.neubiorev.2005.08.002
Thapar, A., Collishaw, S., Pine, D. S., & Thapar, A. K. (2012). Depression in adolescence. *The Lancet, 379,* 1056–1067. doi:10.1016/S0140-6736(11)60871-4
Trickett, P. K., Noll, J. G., & Putnam, F. W. (2011). The impact of sexual abuse on female development: Lessons from a multigenerational, longitudinal research study. *Development and Psychopathology, 23,* 453–476. doi:10.1017/S0954579411000174

Trullas, R., & Skolnick, P. (1990). Functional antagonists at the NMDA receptor complex exhibit antidepressant actions. *European Journal of Pharmacology, 185,* 1–10. doi:10.1016/0014-2999(90)90204-J

Volkow, N., & Morales, M. (2015). The brain on drugs: From reward to addiction. *Cell, 162,* 712–725. doi:10.1016/j.cell.2015.07.046

Weinstein, S. M., & Mermelstein, R. (2007). Relations between daily activities and adolescent mood: The role of autonomy. *Journal of Clinical Child & Adolescent Psychology, 36,* 182–194. doi:10.1080/15374410701274967

Westmoreland, P., Krantz, M. J., & Mehler, P. S. (2016). Medical complications of anorexia nervosa and bulimia. *American Journal of Medicine, 129,* 30–37. doi:10.1016/j.amjmed.2015.06.031

Zetterqvist, M., Lundh, L. G., Dahlström, Ö., & Svedin, C. G. (2013). Prevalence and function of non-suicidal self-injury (NSSI) in a community sample of adolescents, using suggested *DSM-5* criteria for a potential NSSI disorder. *Journal of Abnormal Child Psychology, 41,* 759–773. doi:10.1007/s10802-013-9712-5

Chapter 10

Counseling Approaches III: Cognitive Behavior Therapies

Key Concepts

- Neuroscience-informed cognitive behavior therapy
- Collaborative goal setting
- Psychoeducation and neuroeducation
- Self-efficacy
- Self-monitoring
- Behavioral chain analysis
- Cognitive restructuring
- Schema
- Mindfulness
- Nonjudgmental acceptance
- Identified patient
- Homeostasis
- Surrogate parenting

Aligned 2016 CACREP Standards

Standard 2.F.5.a. Theories and models of counseling
Standard 2.F.5.f. Counselor characteristics and behaviors that influence the counseling process
Standard 2.F.5.j. Evidence-based counseling strategies and techniques for prevention and intervention
Standard 2.F.8.b. Identification of evidence-based counseling practices

• • •

In Chapter 8, on adolescent neurophysiological and social development, we learned that subcortical development outpaces cortical development during adolescence. Adolescents therefore experience intense emotions without the circuitry yet to fully process and regulate them (Casey, Jones, & Hare, 2008; Tyborowska, Volman, Smeekens, Toni, & Roelofs, 2016). We also learned that the nucleus accumbens within the striatum develops faster than the prefrontal cortex. The nucleus accumbens is a key structure in the dopaminergic system, and dopamine production increases significantly during adolescence (Galván et al., 2006). This helps us understand why adolescents have stronger motivational drives toward reward seeking and risk taking (Baker, Bisby, & Richardson, 2016). Issues such as identifying emotions, managing intense emotions, and anticipating the long-term consequences of short-term rewards are perhaps best addressed through cognitive behavior therapy (CBT).

There are now a proliferation of CBT theories, interventions, and protocols. Perhaps the most popular at the time of this writing are third-wave CBTs that incorporate aspects of mindfulness practice, such as acceptance and commitment therapy, dialectical behavior therapy, and mindfulness-based cognitive therapy, among others. These approaches assist adolescents with experiencing and accepting their emotional experiences without rejecting them or attempting to avoid them. Some pioneers of these approaches reject the notion that these therapies are forms of CBT (e.g., acceptance and commitment therapy; Hayes, Levin, Plumb-Vilardaga, Villatte, & Pistorello, 2013), though there are common themes in how the approaches are applied.

A neuroscience-informed CBT (nCBT) model also exists. The nCBT model differentiates interventions based on a person's response to threats in the environment (Field, Beeson, & Jones, 2015). Initial interventions target a process known as *Wave1,* whereby rapid activation of the hypothalamic-pituitary-adrenal and sympathetic-adrenal-medullary axes results in the secretion of cortisol and adrenaline that prime a person for action outside of conscious awareness. Once a person becomes aware of their activation during a process called *Wave2,* subsequent interventions seek to help the person make sense of their experiences (Field et al., 2015).

The nCBT model was developed after multiple failed attempts to help children change their cognitions in response to threats in their environment. Children typically became activated before they could change their thinking patterns, at which point their ability to think rationally was impaired. In nCBT, the adolescent first implements techniques such as mindfulness along with therapeutic lifestyle change, biofeedback, and neurofeedback (which we explore in Chapter 11). These techniques both help the adolescent prevent unnecessary sympathetic activation and assist them in coping with sympathetic activation automatically when activation does occur.

In this chapter, we propose a three-phase model for implementing cognitive behavior interventions that is grounded in third-wave mindfulness-based CBTs and nCBT (Beeson, Field, Jones, & Miller, 2017; Field et al., 2015). We apply the CBT model to the case of Brooke, which was introduced in Chapter 9.

Phase 1: Collaborative Goal Setting and Psychoeducation

CBTs are fairly directive approaches. At the beginning of the counseling process, the client collaboratively forms goals with the counselor to address the current problem. From there, the counselor teaches new skills to the client, such as coping strategies and cognitive restructuring of negative cognitions. The counselor and client then identify action plans (i.e., homework) to be completed in between sessions with the goal of reviewing and reinforcing progress. Making progress toward goals helps to foster self-efficacy, or the client's belief in their ability to make progress and complete tasks.

Identifying goals can be complicated when working with adolescents. In many cases, children and adolescents are brought into counseling by third parties, such as school counselors and parents or guardians. They therefore often present as mandated clients rather than self-referred clients. When working with adolescents who do not particularly want to attend counseling (to put it mildly), it can help to identify and align with goals that the adolescents already possess. In inpatient and residential settings, it is common for adolescents to have the primary goal of being discharged from the facility and ending mental health treatment as quickly as possible! In such cases, the counselor could build rapport through a statement such as "It's clear that you don't want to be here and want to leave as soon as possible. I'm wondering if you would like my help with that. I could help you identify the kinds of behaviors that would demonstrate you are ready to be discharged and help you work toward those. I also think it might be helpful if we figured out what you'd need to do to avoid coming back here again." In short, working *with* rather than *against* client resistance is a very useful technique for establishing counseling goals.

Psychoeducation

Psychoeducation is a core component of CBT and involves providing information to clients with the goal of helping them develop a better understanding of their current issues. Sharing neuroscience information with clients is called *neuroeducation* (Miller, 2016). The technical nature of neuroscience terminology requires a slightly different approach to delivery than is typical for psychoeducation. In Chapter

12, we provide a three-step procedure for delivering neuroeducation to child and adolescent clients.

The nCBT model contains one example of how to integrate neuroeducation into CBT. During the first few sessions of nCBT, the counselor provides information to the client about brain processing models called *Wave1* and *Wave2* (Field et al., 2015). These two processes describe how people typically experience threat response. In Wave1 processing, the person is unaware of their neurophysiological response to threats in the environment. Any preconscious identification of threat through sensory input (e.g., sounds, smells) or implicit (i.e., preconscious) memories results in messages being sent quickly from information processing structures within the brain (i.e., the thalamus) to glands within the endocrine system to release hormones that prepare a person for action to respond to the threat. This can result in neurophysiological consequences of adrenaline and cortisol secretion, such as increased heart rate. During Wave2 processing, the person eventually becomes aware of their neurophysiological activation and decides how to respond next. Wave2 thoughts and actions generate subsequent neurophysiological responses (e.g., accepting one's current experience and engaging in deep breathing and activating parasympathetic activation to reduce stress response, or becoming angry at oneself for being activated and sustaining one's current degree of activation). Neuroeducation can help clients understand why they are struggling to control their neurophysiological responding (automatic threat responses) and methods for reducing neurophysiological activation when it occurs (e.g., acceptance of experience, deep breathing).

Phase 2: Coping With Symptoms

Many adolescents enter counseling in distress. They are experiencing significant symptoms that they are looking to better manage or resolve. Symptoms such as anxiety, depression, flashbacks, panic attacks, and sleep disturbance are aversive experiences that people wish to quell. Often goal setting initially focuses on reducing or managing these symptoms. The interventions below can help adolescents cope with their current symptoms.

Self-Monitoring

During counseling, people may be unaware of the context for their distressing symptoms. They may not know how often their symptoms occur, how long they last, what precipitates their occurrence, and so on. An initial task in coping with these symptoms is thus helping clients begin monitoring their behavior more closely. Tracking these experiences is useful to conducting a behavioral chain analysis, which connects antecedents and consequences to the behaviors and symptoms a person is experiencing.

Tracking behavior can itself be a mechanism of change. When we pay more attention to our habits (e.g., diet, spending), we tend to change them by default. The same principle works for mental health symptoms. Adolescents who begin to track behaviors such as self-injury, substance use, and suicidal ideation tend to experience reductions in these behaviors as a result.

Self monitoring interventions are common across CBTs. When using self-monitoring interventions, we recommend asking adolescents to bring in their diaries to discuss during sessions so they can review their progress. Reviewing a diary often yields more specific information than asking an adolescent at the start of a session to review their week. Over time, the adolescent learns to recognize patterns (e.g., rejection fears prompt self-injury, screen time at night impairs sleep duration) and can adjust accordingly by using different coping skills.

Coping Skills

Alongside self-monitoring, identifying strategies for coping with mental health symptoms is very useful to symptom management. Many adolescents struggle with problematic forms of coping and can benefit from review and training in different coping methods. When providing coping skills training, a few principles are useful.

Identify the Function of Problematic Coping

Most coping skills training needs to initially identify and address coping attempts by the adolescent that are problematic or maladaptive, such as self-injury, substance use, withdrawal from others, and so on. As we learned from Chapter 6, on behavior modification, it is critical to identify the function of a behavior before introducing a replacement behavior. There are a variety of reasons why an adolescent might engage in a specific behavior. For example, an adolescent might consume alcohol because they like the experience of getting intoxicated (i.e., hedonic sensation seeking) or may become intoxicated to reduce anxiety and stress. Replacement behaviors for problematic drinking behavior will thus differ by the function of the behavior. The dialectical behavior therapy skills training module on distress tolerance features a review of the function of coping behaviors (e.g., distraction, self-soothing, improving the moment).

Reinforce Current Adaptive Coping Strategies

We recommend that counselors ask about adolescents' current coping strategies before teaching new ones. We have found that it is a lot easier for adolescents to increase the use of coping skills they already possess than to learn new skills. Reinforcing existing skills also helps adolescents build self-efficacy (i.e., belief in their ability to master problems).

Provide Several Options for New Coping Strategies

When introducing new coping strategies, it can be helpful to have a list of potential strategies for the adolescent to choose from (see Reflection Question 10.1). Counselors can develop handouts to review with the client. The nCBT model (Beeson et al., 2017) contains several

Reflection Question 10.1

Imagine you are creating a list of coping skills for use with adolescents. Which skills would be on your list and why? Which would you exclude and why?

considerations for coping skills. Skills should be portable, accessible, socially acceptable, available for repetitive practice, and salient or attractive to the adolescent. For example, listening to music is fairly portable, accessible, available for repetitive practice, and in most cases socially acceptable (except when one is talking to someone else or in class). In contrast, soaking in a bath is not as easily accessed or available for repetitive practice. Repetitive practice is important so that the adolescent learns to use the skill in stressful situations automatically.

Mindfulness

Alongside coping skills training, mindfulness practice can be a very useful strategy for managing and coping with distressing symptoms. Meta-analyses have substantiated the effectiveness of mindfulness for addressing anxiety and depression (Hofmann, Sawyer, Witt, & Oh, 2010; Khoury et al., 2013). Mindfulness is a practice derived from Eastern traditions such as Buddhism that fosters awareness of the present moment and acceptance of one's thoughts, feelings, and physiological sensations (Hofmann et al., 2010; Tang, Hölzel, & Posner, 2015). Mindfulness appears to be as effective as CBT and, as mentioned earlier, is often integrated into more recent models of CBT (Khoury et al., 2013). For example, mindfulness is a core component of acceptance and commitment therapy, dialectical behavior therapy, and mindfulness-based cognitive therapy. Mindfulness practice can assist adolescents in identifying their thoughts and feelings, acknowledging and accepting them without judgment, and allowing these experiences to eventually pass rather than ruminating on them.

Daily mindfulness practice has strong neurophysiological impacts. A meta-analysis on mindfulness practice found changes to the activity and structure of the anterior cingulate cortex, which is associated with attentional control (Tang et al., 2015). Mindfulness also strengthens prefrontal cortex control over limbic structures such as the amygdala and thus enhances capacity for emotional regulation (Tang et al., 2015). Mindfulness also appears to increase gray matter density in the hippocampus and structures associated with the default mode network and self-referential awareness (Hölzel et al., 2011; Tang et al., 2015).

We now apply the practices of self-monitoring, coping skills training, and mindfulness to the case of Brooke (see Case Vignette 10.1). Thom uses first-person narrative to describe the counseling process.

Case Vignette 10.1 Brooke, Part 2

During the early stages of counseling, I worked with Brooke to explore the function of her coping behavior. Together we learned that Brooke's self-injury and substance use served to help her manage the emotional pain she was experiencing subsequent to her sexual assault and loss of a child. Her food restriction helped her feel a sense of control that she felt had been taken from her. Her self-injury had another, more pernicious function of inflicting the pain that she believed she deserved. She acknowledged feelings of self-disgust and shame. Brooke could acknowledge that these coping methods were not the most effective but also added that they had helped her get through the past few months. She was open to developing alternative coping behaviors, though she knew this would be difficult, as she considered her self-injury to be a form of addiction.

Brooke began to self-monitor her self-injury, suicidality, substance use, and food restriction using a diary card. Her suicidality waxed and waned throughout the week, though her urge to self-injure remained constant. A precipitant to her suicidal ideation was reminders of the sexual assault. For example, one of her peers taunted her at school about being a "skinny girl," which made her recall something that one of her attackers had said to her during the rape. I helped Brooke self-advocate by teaching her how to approach the peer and ask her to use an alternative phrase because "skinny girl" was triggering for her. Brooke was proud of herself for taking this action.

We identified several coping resources that Brooke started using in place of her self-injury, substance use, and food restriction. Brooke developed a daily mindfulness practice that she found helpful. Her mindfulness practice helped her to acknowledge her intense feelings without becoming overwhelmed by them. I taught Brooke to identify when she felt overwhelmed by her emotions. During these times, we practiced diaphragmatic breathing techniques to help her become grounded and centered. (More on these techniques in Chapter 11.) Once ready, Brooke was encouraged to verbally describe her emotional and physiological activation by giving voice to her experiences ("If your body could talk, what would it say?"). Brooke then deliberately worked to accept these experiences without judgment and without trying to avoid them. Sitting with her feelings of disgust and shame was very difficult for her at first. I

(Continued)

Case Vignette 10.1 *(Continued)*

used neuroscience information to explain how Brooke's hypothalamic-pituitary-adrenal and sympathetic-adrenal-medullary axes had become dysregulated. I shared that the oversecretion of adrenaline and cortisol had ensuing effects in the amygdala, which explained why her emotions felt so intense. With ongoing mindfulness practice, Brooke was able to be kinder to herself and recognize that such feelings were somewhat expected and understandable, considering the trauma she had experienced.

Brooke also wanted something tactile that felt relieving. She began rubbing a soothing skin cream over her skin when she felt like cutting. She also began attending weaving classes and learned to make her own bracelets. She eventually learned to weave using a loom. She was often proud of her work and would showcase it in my office. I learned several years later that she had opened her own online store and was selling her weavings professionally. Her greatest coping challenge was attempting parties that her friends attended and drinking in moderation. She identified a concrete number of alcoholic drinks that she felt was a healthy amount and by and large was able to stick to her goal. Her food restriction remained problematic until we worked through her schematic cognitions.

• • •

Phase 3: Cognitive Restructuring

Once the adolescent's symptoms have stabilized, the counselor can work through deeper underlying causes of the symptoms through cognitive restructuring. During cognitive restructuring, the counselor works with the adolescent to identify and transform cognitive distortions and irrational beliefs so that they become more adaptive, realistic, and rational. In CBT, a person's core self-beliefs are called *schemata*. Schematic thoughts such as "I am unlovable" are believed to precipitate and perpetuate automatic thoughts, emotions, and behaviors that are associated with depression (Beck, Rush, Shaw, & Emery, 1987).

When exploring an adolescent's thought patterns, it is important to inquire about their life context. Thoughts such as "Everyone is out to get me" and "The world is a cruel place where people act primarily for self-preservation" might be typical and expected of an adolescent who has been raised in a dangerous community where violent acts occur regularly and criminal acts (e.g., stealing, theft, drug dealing) are common survival behaviors. In such an environment, the adolescent may need to be wary of the motives of others. Seeking merely to restructure these cognitions would miss the point. Instead, what the adolescent would need most is an example of a caring relationship that demonstrates interest, respect, and validation in which the adolescent can develop trust and vulnerability without fearing reprisal. The counseling relationship is thus at times an important restructuring technique in and of itself.

Some thinking patterns are distorted and require the counselor to use more active restructuring methods. In third-wave CBTs, the counselor emphasizes the client's mindful awareness of these thought patterns when they occur and moves toward nonjudgmental acceptance of those patterns while also balancing them with counterthoughts.

We now return to the example of Brooke (see Case Vignette 10.2) to demonstrate the application of this technique. Thom uses first-person narrative to describe the counseling process.

As this case illustrates, the counseling relationship is central to all counseling approaches, including CBT. Disclosure of deeply personal thoughts and feelings such as self-disgust and shame following sexual assault can only occur when the adolescent has developed a deep trust in the counselor and in the therapeutic process. It is therefore important that the counselor attend to the relationship first and foremost when applying CBT techniques. Brooke needed to feel heard, understood, and validated initially. When Thom provided cognitive restructuring, he reinforced the fact that Brooke's experiences of self-disgust and shame made sense and should be acknowledged and accepted as part of her experience rather than rejected. By validating these experiences, Thom avoided sending the message to Brooke that she just needed to "think positive," which is often perceived by clients as disingenuous. Through this validation of her experience, Brooke came to understand and accept her self-experiences, which then modified her schematic beliefs. Consider Reflection Question 10.2.

Parent and Guardian Involvement and Family Intervention

Even though adolescence is known for increases in peer-focused socialization, parent-child interaction remains important during adolescence (Guyer, Silk, & Nelson, 2016). Parental warmth appears to have beneficial effects for the development of the striatum and limbic system during adolescence (Morgan, Shaw, & Forbes, 2014; Whittle et al., 2014). Parental warmth also protects against an adolescent's rumination and internalized self-criticism during periods when the parent is upset about another matter in the environment that is unrelated to the adolescent (Lee, Siegle, Dahl, Hooley, & Silk, 2014). Adolescents remain sensitive to the opinions of their parents and guardians, and caregiver appraisal and criticism of their behavior is still emotionally

Case Vignette 10.2 Brooke, Part 3

Brooke's symptoms of depression, traumatic stress, suicidal ideation, self-injury, and substance use were all associated with her self-concept as a damaged and unlovable person following her sexual assault. During counseling, Brooke was able to identify that she felt disgust toward herself and believed she deserved the pain and scars she self-inflicted. Brooke could acknowledge that such thinking was a distortion based on her experience.

After Brooke became better able to manage her symptoms (with the exception of her food restriction), I transitioned the focus of therapy to help her restructure these core cognitions by disputing through experience. I first sought to understand the context of these schematic thoughts of feeling she deserved to be punished. We discussed Brooke's place in a patriarchal system that objectified women and placed them at risk for victimization. Brooke began to understand that her assault had occurred in the context of larger social trends that stripped women of basic rights. Brooke's anger turned outward, and she began to express her rage at her assailants. Brooke also expressed an interest in exploring her multiracial ethnic identity at this time, which was a healthy step toward identity formation.

The next step in restructuring Brooke's belief about being fundamentally damaged in the eyes of others was to help her rekindle her love for herself and her physical body. We used Brooke's prior experiences to dispute her self-hatred. Brooke was able to identify positive traits that she loved about herself, such as being able to start up conversations with strangers, being able to make friends easily, and being a supportive and dependable friend. She could also identify parts of her body that she considered beautiful. Brooke also used her experiences in counseling to dispute her self-hatred through identifying that she was proud of herself for overcoming her problems and learning healthier ways of coping. Over time, we were eventually able to restructure her cognitions around self-hate and feeling that she deserved self-inflicted pain to "I hate what happened to me. I love myself in spite of what happened to me." This change in her schematic thought was crucial to the outcome of therapy.

• • •

Reflection Question 10.2

If you were counseling Brooke, which aspects of the CBT approach would you want to use? What would you do differently?

salient (i.e., important) to them. Furthermore, parental warmth is also associated with an adolescent's ability to respond adaptively to peer criticism. Warm parenting, described as supportive and noncritical, has been associated with attenuation in striatum activity in response to peer rejection, whereas critical parenting attenuates activity of the striatum in response to peer acceptance (Guyer et al., 2015; Tan et al., 2014). This means that warm and supportive parenting assists an adolescent in better regulating their emotions through appreciating peer acceptance and adapting to peer rejection. Parenting thus has a crucial role in supporting an adolescent's emotional regulation relative to peer relationships, which themselves are so crucial during adolescence.

Reducing unnecessary parental criticism is an important cognitive behavior intervention during adolescence. In a study by Lee and colleagues (2014), adolescent brain activation during maternal criticism of neutral events such as the weather was associated with increased subcortical limbic activity, such as activation of the insula, and reduced activation of the dorsolateral prefrontal cortex and anterior cingulate cortex. This suggests that adolescents struggle with regulating their emotions when exposed to parental criticism.

General Principles for Family Intervention

Several CBTs that have been developed for adolescents contain parent modules. We propose 10 principles for integrating parent and guardian involvement into CBT for adolescents based on our practice experience: (a) Remain neutral and unbiased, (b) Respect the uniqueness of each family system, (c) Respect the dignity of each family member, (d) Identify and work within existing power structures, (e) Acknowledge multiple perspectives and perceptions of the same event, (f) Closely observe interactions between family members, (g) Facilitate improved interactions between family members, (h) Explain homeostasis, (i) Ensure that all relevant family members attend sessions, and (j) Avoid surrogate parenting.

Remain Neutral and Unbiased

Family counseling can often bring with it power struggles as various family members jostle for position. It is quite common for members of a family to seek to recruit the counselor to their perspective and position. The counselor must therefore be wary of such efforts and attempt to be as neutral as possible. Taking sides with a parent or guardian will marginalize a child or adolescent and vice versa. Taking sides also removes an opportunity for the family to work through their problems without an outsider deciding for them. Remaining neutral is especially important when a family member is not present in session. Counselors should work hard to avoid aligning against family members whom they have not yet met.

Many children and adolescents are brought into counseling as the *identified patient* (Gehart, 2017). In systems theory, this term is used to denote that the child or adolescent is shouldering the blame for dysfunction that is occurring in the family system (i.e., the child or adolescent is not solely responsible for their family's dysfunction). During the first few sessions, the counselor must therefore work to establish neutrality by requiring the parents to participate in the initial sessions (see Chapter 1 for more information). This sends an important message to the child or adolescent that the counselor does not necessarily believe that they are the problem within the family system.

Respect the Uniqueness of Each Family System

Every family is unique and has its own set of rules and norms (Gehart, 2017). Families are complex systems, and it is important to bracket assumptions and withhold clinical judgment until you have gotten to know the rules and norms of the family. Work hard to avoid imposing your own values and beliefs on what you believe is functional and optimal. This is an especially important principle for working with parents. Differences in parenting choices are not necessarily dysfunctional or problematic. For example, imagine a spectrum of parental discipline from harshly punitive on one end to permissively placating on another. The extremes of this spectrum are unhealthy. The disciplinary approach of most parents will reside somewhere toward the middle. If a parent is more strict or lenient than you might be, this does not necessarily mean the parent is not responding appropriately.

Respect the Dignity of Each Family Member

Counselors should be thoughtful when sharing information in front of all family members. When the counselor is providing parent education, children should typically be excused from the conversation. Parents may become embarrassed or defensive when being educated about parenting in front of their child, and the child may also feel bad for the parent being given feedback.

Identify and Work Within Existing Power Structures

Although counselors should attempt to be neutral, they should also follow Salvador Minuchin's advice to work with the existing power structures of the family to make changes (Gehart, 2017). For example, the family will likely not adhere to assignments such as out-of-session tasks (i.e., homework) if the parents or guardians do not approve of them. In addition, parents or guardians may have goals and expectations for counseling that need to be addressed at the beginning of the process.

Acknowledge Multiple Perspectives and Perceptions of the Same Event

Family members will perceive the same family event differently. This is normal and can be expected. The family should eventually learn to respect the multiple perspectives within the family, which can best be taught through the counselor's own ability to manage and respect multiple perspectives during sessions.

Closely Observe Interactions Between Family Members

To understand the functioning of a family, we strongly recommend closely observing interactions during sessions. Counselors can internally ask themselves questions such as "What are the seating arrangements, and is there a significance to them?" "Who controls the dialogue?" "How does each family member respond to the other members of the family in regard to body language and verbal communication?" Facilitating an enactment (Gehart, 2017), such as replaying a recent conflict in session, can be helpful for observing the dynamics of family interaction.

Facilitate Improved Interactions Between Family Members

A primary goal of family intervention during CBT is to help each family member develop active listening skills so that each member of the family feels heard and understood. As we have mentioned in prior chapters, parents must make the transition during adolescence to becoming active listeners rather than problem solvers, and so developing these skills is particularly important for ongoing relationship building between adolescents and their caregivers. CBT's focus on skills training is tremendously useful for helping parents or guardians and adolescents develop active listening skills. We recommend a specific procedure to facilitate caregiver-child active listening training.

Active Listening Training Procedure for Adolescents and Their Caregivers

Step 1: Inform the adolescent and their caregiver that they are going to take turns listening closely to the other and trying to understand the other's perspective without trying to change it or fix it.

Step 2: Ask who would like to play the listener role first.

Step 3: Instruct the listener to attend closely and try to bracket their own beliefs and biases about the topic to understand the other person. After hearing the other person, the listener should be prepared to (a) give a short summary of what the other person has said, (b) check for accuracy, and (c) ask a follow-up question that has the intent of trying to better understand the other person.

Step 4: Ask any observers to observe closely and give feedback following the interaction.

Step 5: During the interaction, watch the listener closely and ensure that they are following the procedure in Step 3 without interjecting questions that insinuate a bias (e.g., "Don't you think . . .?"). Remind the listener about the procedure and prompt them with a follow-up question that has the intent of trying to better understand the other person.

Step 6: After 20–25 minutes or so, once a natural stopping point is reached, have the adolescent and caregiver switch roles and repeat Steps 3, 4, and 5.

Explain Homeostasis

CBT is predicated on the importance of making necessary changes that enhance a person's functioning and quality of life (Beck et al., 1987). Making changes within a family system is often a challenge. Family systems tend to resist change and seek to maintain current homeostasis (i.e., adherence to established rules and roles). Homeostasis can hamper an adolescent's attempt to change their thoughts and actions. We have observed that families often become more open to change once they become aware of this tendency. Small changes in family interactions can often result in much larger changes, so working through resistance is important to building momentum for larger change.

Ensure That All Relevant Family Members Attend Sessions

In our experience, it is common for family members to insist that they cannot attend family sessions. Often these family members are a key part of the adolescent's problems, and their lack of attendance will stymy the work. When this occurs, the dialogue can quickly devolve to complaining about the family member who is not in the room. Even discussing how best to address issues with the family member is largely unproductive. It is therefore crucial that counselors emphasize that family counseling will only be successful if all relevant family members attend sessions.

Avoid Surrogate Parenting

Counselors can possess many biases about the parents they are working with and may at times feel the allure of aligning with the child or adolescent against the caregiver. There are two main dangers to aligning with youth against their caregivers. First, the schism between the adolescent and caregiver will widen, and the rupture will worsen. Second, the counselor will likely become increasingly pulled into a caregiving role, such as managing the child or adolescent's feelings toward the caregiver rather than helping them express their feelings directly to the caregiver.

In situations when the child is clearly upset about their relationship with the parent, the best course of action is to try to repair the relationship between the caregiver and child (as best as possible). The active listening procedure described previously is an excellent technique for gradually repairing caregiver-child ruptures. It is also important to recognize when parental behaviors are creating problems and are in need of intervention and to provide parent education without the child or adolescent present.

Counselors should withhold judgment when caregivers make mistakes and assist caregivers in using these mistakes as learning experiences. Parenting does not have to be perfect. A parent or guardian's response after a mistake is more important than the mistake itself. If a parent becomes reactive and regrets their actions, apologizing to the adolescent and asking for forgiveness can demonstrate important modeling for how to repair a rupture. In short, adolescents do not need to learn how to be perfect. Adolescents learn vicariously through their parents and guardians and need to learn how to repair mistakes they have made. The counselor's ability to bracket their biases and help the caregiver repair ruptures is thus crucial to forging closer caregiver-child relationships.

We now apply these family intervention principles to the case of Brooke (see Case Vignette 10.3). Thom uses first-person narrative to describe the counseling process.

Conclusion

Adolescents experience faster development of subcortical systems associated with emotional experiencing and reward prediction than cortical systems associated with emotional regulation and predicting long-term consequences of short-term actions. As adolescents gain more sophisticated self-awareness and verbal abilities associated with both cortical and subcortical development, they may benefit from insight-oriented approaches that help them cope with stressors and symptoms and restructure root problems such as distorted schematic thoughts. Family counseling approaches are important to consider when providing CBT to adolescents who are experiencing barriers to family support or problems that emerge from family dynamics. Finally, neuroscience is already being formally integrated into CBT models. In this chapter, we integrated concepts from nCBT to demonstrate nCBT approaches.

Case Vignette 10.3 Brooke, Part 4

During my work with Brooke, it became apparent that several issues within the caregiver-child relationship needed to be addressed. Her parents had unusual oversight over her behavior, becoming upset that she was taking birth control even though she was an older adolescent. At the same time, they had enabled her drinking behavior. In addition, Brooke had yet to tell them about her assault and the subsequent abortion. I wondered why she had decided not to disclose to them. Brooke mentioned that her parents tended to become reactive and criticize her when a negative event occurred, even if it was not her fault. She feared that her parents would blame her for the event, such as for drinking on the night of the assault, which would have been too much for her to bear.

It took Brooke a long time to feel comfortable enough to invite her parents into session. After a lot of coaching, Brooke felt ready to tell her parents about what had occurred. During the first session with her parents present, I spent 10 to 15 minutes setting the stage for her disclosure. I informed the parents that Brooke had something important to tell them that would be upsetting and would require them to manage their own emotions to support their daughter. I explained that Brooke needed to feel supported by her parents rather than criticized by them. I then outlined the active listening procedure described earlier in the chapter, and Brooke began to tell her story. Her parents were tearful and shaken by Brooke's disclosure but worked hard to listen to their daughter and show support. They were open to my feedback on providing active listening rather than problem-solving. At the end of the session, the parents hugged Brooke and told her they were so glad she had told them what had happened. Brooke looked relieved. The parents agreed to practice active listening rather than criticizing their daughter. Brooke continued to attend counseling for the next few months and eventually felt ready to conclude counseling.

• • •

Quiz Questions

1. Replacing problematic coping behavior with alternative coping methods is most effective when it
   a. Considers the function of the behavior
   b. Starts small and builds slowly
   c. Uses sensory-based coping methods

2. To work through underlying root problems that are causing emotional and behavioral problems, cognitive restructuring is most effective when it addresses
   a. Automatic thoughts
   b. Schematic thoughts
   c. Negative thoughts
3. In active listening training, the listener should be instructed to
   a. Give their feedback to the speaker
   b. Demonstrate that they already know what the speaker thinks about this issue
   c. Seek to understand the speaker

References

Baker, K. D., Bisby, M. A., & Richardson, R. (2016). Impaired fear extinction in adolescent rodents: Behavioural and neural analyses. *Neuroscience & Biobehavioral Reviews, 70,* 59–73. doi:10.1016/j.neubiorev.2016.05.019

Beck, A. T., Rush, A. J., Shaw, B. F., & Emery, G. (1987). *Cognitive therapy of depression.* New York, NY: Guilford Press.

Beeson, E. T., Field, T. A., Jones, L. K., & Miller, R. (2017). *nCBT: A semi-structured treatment manual.* Boise, ID: Boise State University.

Casey, B. J., Jones, R. M., & Hare, T. A. (2008). The adolescent brain. *Annals of the New York Academy of Sciences, 1124,* 111–126. doi:10.1196/annals.1440.010

Council for Accreditation of Counseling and Related Educational Programs. (2015). *2016 CACREP standards.* Alexandria, VA: Author.

Field, T. A., Beeson, E. T., & Jones, L. K. (2015). The new ABCs: A practitioner's guide to neuroscience-informed cognitive-behavioral therapy. *Journal of Mental Health Counseling, 37,* 206–220. doi:10.17744/mehc.37.3.02

Galván, A., Hare, T. A., Parra, C. E., Penn, J., Voss, H., Glover, G., & Casey, B. J. (2006). Earlier development of the accumbens relative to orbitofrontal cortex might underlie risk-taking behavior in adolescents. *Journal of Neuroscience, 26,* 6885–6892. doi:10.1523/JNEUROSCI.1062-06.2006

Gehart, D. R. (2017). *Theory and treatment planning in family therapy: A competency-based approach.* Boston, MA: Cengage.

Guyer, A. E., Jarcho, J. M., Pérez-Edgar, K., Degnan, K. A., Pine, D. S., Fox, N. A., & Nelson, E. E. (2015). Temperament and parenting styles in early childhood differentially influence neural response to peer evaluation in adolescence. *Journal of Abnormal Child Psychology, 43,* 863–874. doi:10.1007/s10802-015-9973-2

Guyer, A. E., Silk, J. S., & Nelson, E. E. (2016). The neurobiology of the emotional adolescent: From the inside out. *Neuroscience & Biobehavioral Reviews, 70,* 74–85. doi:10.1016/j.neubiorev.2016.07.037

Hayes, S. C., Levin, M. E., Plumb-Vilardaga, J., Villatte, J. L., & Pistorello, J. (2013). Acceptance and commitment therapy and contextual behavioral science: Examining the progress of a distinctive model of behavioral and cognitive therapy. *Behavior Therapy, 44,* 180–198. doi:10.1016/j.beth.2009.08.002

Hofmann, S. G., Sawyer, A. T., Witt, A. A., & Oh, D. (2010). The effect of mindfulness-based therapy on anxiety and depression: A meta-analytic review. *Journal of Consulting and Clinical Psychology, 78,* 169–183. doi:10.1037/a0018555

Hölzel, B. K., Carmody, J., Vangel, M., Congleton, C., Yerramsetti, S. M., Gard, T., & Lazar, S. W. (2011). Mindfulness practice leads to increases in regional brain gray matter density. *Psychiatry Research: Neuroimaging, 191,* 36–43. doi:10.1016/j.pscychresns.2010.08.006

Khoury, B., Lecomte, T., Fortin, G., Masse, M., Therien, P., Bouchard, V., . . . Hofmann, S. G. (2013). Mindfulness-based therapy: A comprehensive meta-analysis. *Clinical Psychology Review, 33,* 763–771. doi:10.1016/j.cpr.2013.05.005

Lee, K. H., Siegle, G. J., Dahl, R. E., Hooley, J. M., & Silk, J. S. (2014). Neural responses to maternal criticism in healthy youth. *Social Cognitive and Affective Neuroscience, 10,* 902–912. doi:10.1093/scan/nsu133

Miller, R. (2016). Neuroeducation: Integrating brain-based psychoeducation into clinical practice. *Journal of Mental Health Counseling, 38,* 103–115. doi:10.17744/mehc.38.2.02

Morgan, J. K., Shaw, D. S., & Forbes, E. E. (2014). Maternal depression and warmth during childhood predict age 20 neural response to reward. *Journal of the American Academy of Child & Adolescent Psychiatry, 53,* 108–117. doi:10.1016/j.jaac.2013.10.003

Tan, P. Z., Lee, K. H., Dahl, R. E., Nelson, E. E., Stroud, L. J., Siegle, G. J., . . . Silk, J. S. (2014). Associations between maternal negative affect and adolescent's neural response to peer evaluation. *Developmental Cognitive Neuroscience, 8,* 28–39. doi:10.1016/j.dcn.2014.01.006

Tang, Y. Y., Hölzel, B. K., & Posner, M. I. (2015). The neuroscience of mindfulness meditation. *Nature Reviews Neuroscience, 16,* 213–225. doi:10.1038/nrn3916

Tyborowska, A., Volman, I., Smeekens, S., Toni, I., & Roelofs, K. (2016). Testosterone during puberty shifts emotional control from pulvinar to anterior prefrontal cortex. *Journal of Neuroscience, 36,* 6156–6164. doi:10.1523/JNEUROSCI.3874-15.2016

Whittle, S., Simmons, J. G., Dennison, M., Vijayakumar, N., Schwartz, O., Yap, M. B., . . . Allen, N. B. (2014). Positive parenting predicts the development of adolescent brain structure: A longitudinal study. *Developmental Cognitive Neuroscience, 8,* 7–17. doi:10.1016/j.dcn.2013.10.006

Chapter 11

Counseling Approaches IV: Biofeedback, Neurofeedback, and Therapeutic Lifestyle Change

Key Concepts

- Biofeedback
- Diaphragmatic breathing
- Peripheral galvanic skin temperature
- Neurofeedback
- Electroencephalography
- Quantitative electroencephalography
- Brain waves (alpha, beta, delta, gamma, theta)
- The impact of technology on helping processes
- Specialty credentialing for biofeedback and neurofeedback
- Therapeutic lifestyle change
- Sleep-wake phase delay

Aligned 2016 CACREP Standards

Standard 2.F.5.e. The impact of technology on the counseling process

Standard 2.F.5.j. Evidence-based counseling strategies and techniques for prevention and intervention

Standard 2.F.8.b. Identification of evidence-based counseling practices

Standard 2.F.8.i. Analysis and use of data in counseling

• • •

Throughout the text, we have emphasized that the brain and body are highly adaptive to the environment. Events in a person's environment can trigger epigenetic changes, create new neurons and synaptic connections, and strengthen existing neural pathways. In this chapter, we describe three approaches that intentionally seek to alter aspects of a person's neurophysiology: biofeedback, neurofeedback, and therapeutic lifestyle change. The first two approaches use feedback (i.e., environmental events) and behavioral principles of reinforcement and reward. However, although neurofeedback is grounded in classical and operant conditioning principles, most behaviorists would not classify the approach as a behavioral intervention. Thus, we describe operant conditioning in Chapter 6. The three major classes of interventions described in this chapter can be used with both child and adolescent populations, though some interventions (e.g., therapeutic lifestyle change) are most applicable for adolescents.

The information in this chapter, especially regarding neurofeedback, is fairly technical. For a more comprehensive introduction to these topics, we recommend the following texts, which informed our writing: *Technical Foundations of Neurofeedback* by Collura (2017) and *Neurotherapy and Neurofeedback: Brain-Based Treatment for Psychological and Behavioral Problems* by Chapin and Russell-Chapin (2014). Like other counseling approaches described in Chapters 6 and 7, biofeedback and neurofeedback require specialty training and certification to practice proficiently.

Biofeedback

In prior chapters, we identified the pernicious influence of chronic stress and hypercortisolism on a person's physical and mental health (Guerry & Hastings, 2011; Hulme, Jones, & Abraham, 2013; Vose & Stanton, 2017). For example, hypercortisolism (a) overstimulates and degrades cells, resulting in apoptosis or programmed cell death (Sapolsky, 2000a), and (b) inhibits glutamate receptors and downregulates brain-derived neurotrophic factor (BDNF; Numakawa, Odaka, & Adachi, 2017), (c) resulting in fewer neurons, fewer synaptic connections, and reduced volumetric density, in particular in the amygdala and hippocampus (Malykhin & Coupland, 2015; Pagliaccio et al., 2014). (d) Reduced regulatory control (e.g., reduced hippocampal function) over the stress response system creates a dysregulated negative feedback loop and further increases chronically high levels of cortisol (Sapolsky, 2000b) so that (e) over time, chronically high levels of circulating cortisol cause immunosuppression, susceptibility to disease (notably cancer), metabolic problems (such as obesity and type 2 diabetes), and major depression (Dhabhar, 2009; Harris et al., 2017; Malykhin & Coupland, 2015; van der Valk, Savas, & van Rossum, 2018). Chronic stress and hypercortisolism can therefore be conceptualized as a potential root problem that is causing presenting symptoms. Like the root of a weed in the garden (to use a metaphor), chronic stress should be addressed for the client to make progress on their presenting issues.

Interventions that seek to directly target the stress response system are therefore especially important to consider when working with children who are experiencing the effects of chronic or traumatic stress. You may recall from earlier chapters that the parasympathetic branch of the autonomic nervous system helps a person to return to baseline following activation of the sympathetic nervous system and the secretion of hormones such as cortisol and adrenaline. In this section, we review interventions that intentionally seek to activate the parasympathetic branch of the autonomic nervous system and reduce cortisol secretion through initiating the negative feedback loop of the hypothalamic-pituitary-adrenal axis. Experts such as Bessel van der Kolk (2015) have proposed that conditions such as developmental trauma can be addressed through mind-body interventions that facilitate parasympathetic activation.

Biofeedback consists of a group of interventions that share common principles (Chapin & Russell-Chapin, 2014). In biofeedback, a person receives feedback on their neurophysiological functioning with the intention of enhancing parasympathetic activation. This feedback is typically delivered through technology that uses biometrics as the foundation for the feedback (e.g., provides feedback on heart rate). In this section, we review diaphragmatic breathing training and forms of technology that are used to provide feedback on the effect of deep breathing practice (heart rate and peripheral skin temperature training). We should also note that heart rate variability training is another popular biofeedback intervention that we decided not to cover in this chapter.

Diaphragmatic Breathing

Deep breathing from the diaphragm (rather than the upper chest) has a role in enhancing parasympathetic activation and reducing cortisol levels (Ma et al., 2017). Deep breathing stimulates the vagus nerve, which in turn activates parasympathetic recovery and the negative feedback loop that reduces cortisol secretion (Ma et al., 2017). A randomized controlled study examined the effect of diaphragmatic breathing on saliva cortisol levels (Ma et al., 2017). The intervention group received 20 group sessions over the course of 8 weeks and had significant reductions in cortisol levels compared to the control group (Ma et al., 2017). Diaphragmatic breathing is a ubiquitous intervention and is used in modalities that include mindfulness-based stress reduction, progressive muscle relaxation, yoga, and so on.

There are many variations on deep breathing procedures for children. One of the diaphragmatic breathing techniques that we prefer using with children is the four-square technique, also known as *box breathing*. In the four-square technique, children time their inhalation and exhalation by sketching a square in the air with their finger. As they sketch the first side of the square, they inhale slowly. For the second side, they hold their breath. For the third side, they exhale slowly. They hold their breath for the fourth side. We like this technique because it prompts children to hold their breath in between inhaling and exhaling and also provides a visual image to guide their breathing.

Prior to engaging in this technique for the first time, children may benefit from identifying the difference between diaphragmatic breathing and upper chest breathing. We sometimes ask children to lie on their back and hold their belly while inhaling deeply to demonstrate belly breathing (i.e., diaphragmatic breathing). We have also used visual images, such as Figure 11.1, to help children differentiate diaphragmatic breathing from upper chest breathing.

Feedback via Heart Rate and Peripheral Skin Temperature

Diaphragmatic breathing training can be enhanced through technology. We have used mobile wristbands (e.g., FitBit bands) and pulse oximeters that measure heart rate to help children observe the effects of this intervention. When a child engages in deep breathing,

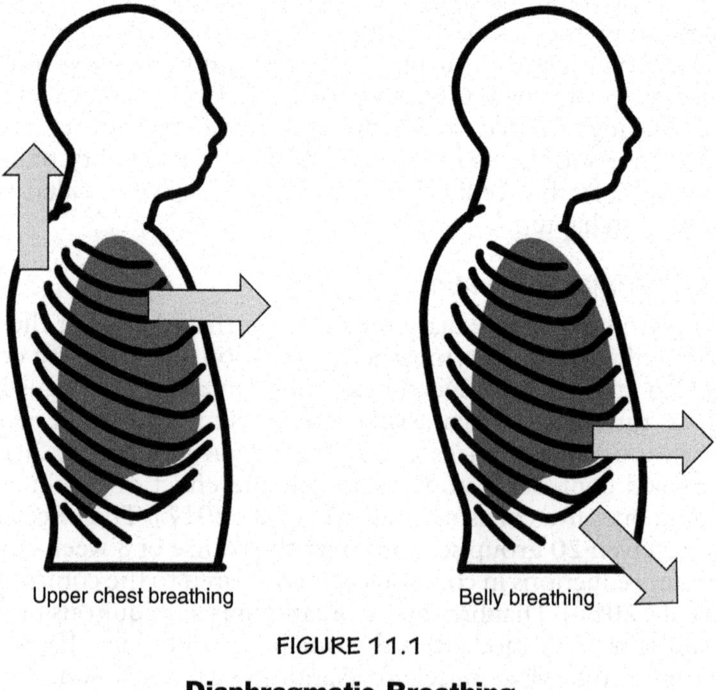

FIGURE 11.1

Diaphragmatic Breathing

Note. From Rachel Chaney, illustrator. Used by permission.

their heart rate tends to decrease. This reduction in heart rate is an important proxy for parasympathetic activation, as an increased heart rate is associated with adrenaline secretion.

When using mobile technology, we first train children to get a baseline reading of their pulse when in a relaxed, resting state. We then initiate diaphragmatic breathing and assist children in observing small reductions in heart rate when already in a resting state. When they are activated, we teach children to identify changes in their heart rate from baseline. A change in heart rate likely indicates that they are in a state of sympathetic activation. We then teach children to take a break when they notice this activation and to engage in diaphragmatic breathing until their heart rate approximates their resting rate. This can take 20 minutes or so, typically. Children may find it difficult to disengage from conflict when physiologically activated and soothe through breathing. Seeing the benefits of diaphragmatic breathing in real time can provide sufficient motivation to follow the protocol.

Measuring peripheral skin temperature can also be helpful during diaphragmatic breathing. In peripheral skin temperature training, the child uses a skin thermometer to measure galvanic temperature at the fingertips (i.e., peripheral extremities). A higher temperature is typically associated with a relaxed state, because more blood is flowing to the extremities rather than localized at the organs (an indication of sympathetic activation). Guidelines provided by Chapin and Russell-Chapin (2014) suggest that a galvanic skin temperature of 85 to 90 degrees Fahrenheit suggests a relaxed state, and a galvanic skin temperature of less than 85 degrees Fahrenheit suggests tension and potential sympathetic activation. As with the heart rate training, children receive feedback on the effects of diaphragmatic breathing by observing changes in skin temperature. Consider Reflection Question 11.1.

Neurofeedback

Neurofeedback is a type of biofeedback that uses electroencephalography (EEG). EEG measures electrical activity in the brain, such as action potentials and electrical charge within neurons. Neurofeedback was first used to reduce seizure activity (Collura, 2017). Neurofeedback trains the client to increase or reduce certain brain waves through technology-guided feedback (Chapin & Russell-Chapin, 2014; Collura, 2017). In neurofeedback, a child's or adolescent's brain activity is measured via

Reflection Question 11.1

> Which challenges can you anticipate when using feedback systems to monitor physiological activation? How might these be overcome?

electrode sensors at different sites on the scalp that detect electrical activity within and between neurons. This electrical activity is aggregated at each electrode site on the scalp to produce a composite measure of electrical activity. These waveforms are measured by their amplitude (i.e., the height of peaks and troughs) and tonal frequency in hertz (Hz). Figure 11.2 provides a graphic depiction of this process.

An amplifier receives data on EEG waveforms, and they are processed in a computer where they are often analyzed against the electrical activity of children or adolescents in a norm group sample. This is known as *quantitative EEG*. The counselor identifies areas of the brain that seem to be under- or overactivated and develops a protocol that rewards the child or adolescent for increasing electrical activity in underactivated brain areas or reducing electrical activity in overactivated brain areas. The child or adolescent receives feedback on their activation through a screen. For example, a child or adolescent might be watching a movie that either stops playing or dims the screen when optimal electrical activity is out of range. A child or adolescent might also play a race car video game in which the car speeds up when electrical activity is in the desired range and slows down when electrical activity is outside of the desired range. The child or adolescent is thus encouraged to voluntarily alter their brain activity to receive the reward (operant conditioning) in addition to receiving the reward involuntarily (classical conditioning). Figure 11.3 depicts the feedback loop involved in the neurofeedback treatment process.

Electrical activity has been classified into five major types of waveforms (Chapin & Russell-Chapin, 2014; Collura, 2017). Delta waves (0–4 Hz) are the slowest brain waves and are typically present when a person is sleeping, such as in Stage IV sleep. Theta waves (4–8 Hz) indicate drowsiness or fatigue and are observed in Stage I sleep. Alpha waves (8–12 Hz) occur when a person is in a reflective or rested state, such as during mindful meditation. Beta waves (12–25 Hz) are

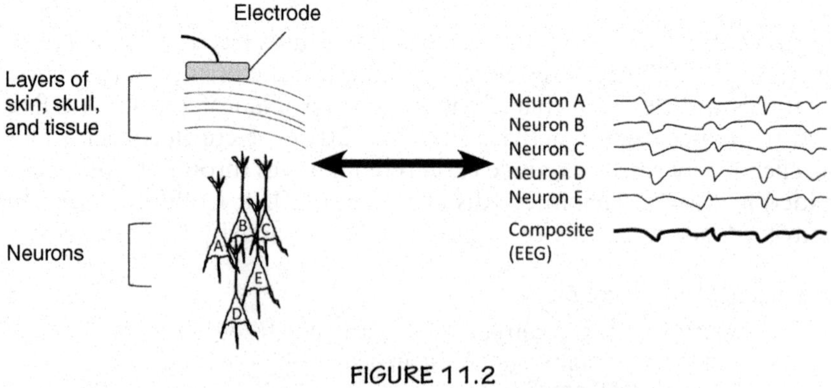

FIGURE 11.2

Electroencephalography (EEG)

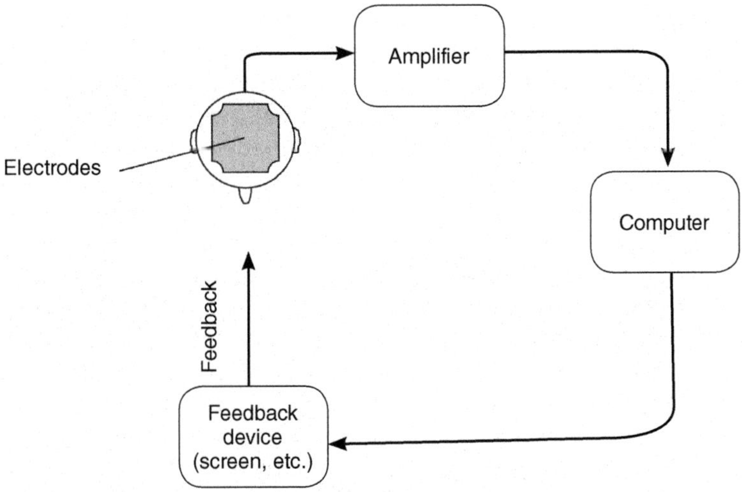

FIGURE 11.3

Feedback Loops in Neurofeedback

associated with mental activity and an active brain state. High beta waves (25–35 Hz) are associated with more focused concentration and anxiety or worry. Gamma waves (35–50 Hz) are the fastest brain waves and are associated with even greater mental activity, such as problem-solving and preconscious processing. Beta and gamma waves typically occur during REM sleep. These waveforms are depicted in Figure 11.4.

Brain waves are measured at the surface of the scalp for different cortex sites. Sites associated with the frontal lobe are called *F* (frontal) or *Fp* (frontal polar) sites. Parietal lobe sites are designated by

Brain Wave	Hertz Range	Associations	Waveform
Gamma	35–50	Problem solving	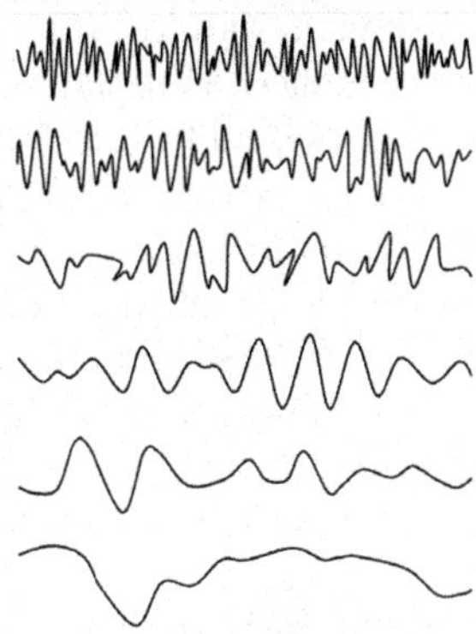
High beta	25–35	Focused concentration	
Beta	12–25	Mental activity	
Alpha	8–12	Reflective and meditative	
Theta	4–8	Drowsiness and fatigue	
Delta	0–4	Deep sleep	

FIGURE 11.4

Brain Waves on Electroencephalography

P, temporal lobe sites by *T*, and occipital sites by *O*. Neurofeedback also addresses the sensorimotor cortex, designated by *C*. If a site is near the midline of the cortex, a descriptor of *z* is added. You may recall from earlier chapters that the frontal lobes are associated with attention, executive functioning, and planned behavior and have a role in downregulating activation of the amygdala. The parietal lobes are associated with navigating in space (proprioception) and receiving input from touch sensors. The temporal lobes are associated with memory because of their proximity to the hippocampus. The occipital lobe processes visual stimuli. The sensorimotor cortex, which is typically associated with the parietal lobe, is associated with visual control of muscle movement. Neurofeedback protocols often attempt to target cerebral lobe sites in which the person is under- or overactivated. For example, a child with attention-deficit/hyperactivity disorder (ADHD) might have an overactivated sensorimotor cortex (i.e., hyperkinetic motor movement) but an underactive frontal lobe (i.e., inattention). Figure 11.5 provides a visual depiction of these electrode placement sites with a key that describes the location and function of these sites. Note that two sites (A1 and A2) are reference points at the ear lobes only, and electrical activity at these sites is not the direct target of training protocols.

Considerations When Providing Neurofeedback

Neurofeedback is a generally safe intervention that collects information about electrical activity *from* the brain and does not provide electrical current *to* the brain. From discussions with experienced neurofeedback practitioners, we have learned that children and adolescents are typically curious about the games involved in neurofeedback rather than frightened by the equipment. Explaining the equipment beforehand can help to assuage any anxiety about the use of EEG technology. For example, when setting up a neurofeedback session, the clinician typically must apply a gel to the scalp for the electrical sensors to adequately measure electrical activity on the scalp. The child or adolescent should be informed about this practice before the conductive gel is applied. Watching a video of a neurofeedback session beforehand can also be helpful for children and adolescents.

We recommend that when providing a technology-based intervention such as neurofeedback, counselor still attend to the therapeutic relationship. We recommend that in addition to clearly explaining how neurofeedback works before starting training sessions, counselors spend time in each session discussing progress and processing after the training session. Without such an intentional focus on building the relationship, adolescents may perceive the counselor as an insincere and detached technician.

Effectiveness

The strongest evidence for the efficacy of neurofeedback is in treating ADHD, with several rigorous research studies indicating that

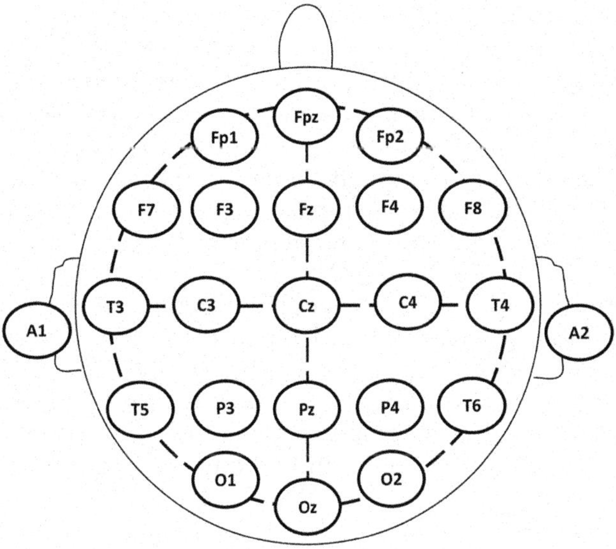

KEY	
Lobes and Sites	**Function**
Frontal	
Fpz, Fp1, Fp2, Fz, F3, F4, F7, F8	Attention, executive functioning, planning, cognitive control of amygdala
Sensorimotor	
Cz, C3, C4	Voluntary control of muscle movement
Parietal	
Pz, P3, P4	Naming objects, spatial awareness, touch sensitivity
Temporal	
T3, T4, T5, T6	Proximity to the hippocampus; receptive language, facial recognition, recall
Occipital	
Oz, O1, O2	Visual processing

FIGURE 11.5

Electrode Placement Sites

Note. A1 and A2 are reference points (left and right ear lobes) rather than brain regions.

neurofeedback reduces symptoms of inattention, impulsivity, and hyperactivity in children (Arns, Heinrich, & Strehl, 2014). Three protocols appear to have empirical evidence of their effectiveness: the theta/beta ratio, slow cortical potentials, and sensorimotor rhythm. The theta/beta ratio protocol aims to balance theta and beta brain waves by decreasing overactivity of theta waves (associated with fatigue and drowsiness) and underactivity of beta waves (associated with attention and concentration). The slow cortical potentials protocol assists a child in predicting and shifting brain waves in anticipation of reinforcement. For example, a child may anticipate a light changing to green and thus shift their brain wave activity so that the light changes to green on their own volition. In the sensorimotor rhythm protocol, hyperkinetic motor activity is reduced. Although one might imagine that neurofeedback for ADHD is most effective when it targets the prefrontal cortex and sensorimotor areas, critics have postulated that more evidence is needed for the specific actions of neurofeedback at certain electrode sites (Thibault & Raz, 2017). Neurofeedback appears to be most effective when paired with learning theory, such as positively reinforcing the child for achieving certain electrical activity (Arns et al., 2014).

The typical length of neurofeedback treatment is 30 to 40 sessions, though improvement can be seen in approximately 15 to 20 sessions (Chapin & Russell-Chapin, 2014; Collura, 2017). At the time of this writing, neurofeedback is not covered as an approved mental health treatment by insurance companies and thus cannot be directly billed for reimbursement. Consider Reflection Question 11.2.

Training

In our experience, neurofeedback requires substantially more training than most biofeedback modalities. Neurofeedback equipment can also be expensive, with hardware and software packages ranging from $5,000 to $15,000. Counselors who wish to specialize in neurofeedback will thus likely need to make a significant commitment to learning the practice. If you are interested, we suggest you explore the websites of the International Society for Neurofeedback and Research (www.isnr.org) and the Association for Applied Psychophysiology and Biofeedback (www.aapb.org). Furthermore, we encourage counselors who wish to specialize in neurofeedback to pursue board certification in neurofeedback (BCN) through the Biofeedback Certification International Alliance.

Therapeutic Lifestyle Change

Lifestyle habits have important roles in child and adolescent development. In particular, adequate sleep duration and quality and regular exercise support mental health as well as hormonal and cell functioning. In this section, we review the importance of sleep and exercise and provide guidance for implementing therapeutic lifestyle change (Ivey, Ivey, & Zalaquett, 2017). Although we focus primarily on applications with adolescents, the information in this section is also applicable to children.

Reflection Question 11.2

What information might a child need to know about neurofeedback before starting the treatment?

Sleep Duration and Quality

Sleep during adolescence promotes neurophysiological development (Galván, 2017). Yet during adolescence, several factors prevent adequate sleep from occurring. Adolescents can struggle with meeting the demands of homework, friendships, dating relationships, extracurricular activities, and going to bed in time to get sufficient sleep. In addition, adolescents experience a neurophysiological phenomenon known as *sleep-wake phase delay* that is caused by later nighttime release of melatonin, the chemical associated with preparing the body for the onset of sleep (Crowley, Acebo, & Carskadon, 2007). This later release of melatonin creates a circadian rhythm preference for later bedtimes and wake times (Carskadon, 2011). This phenomenon has been observed in several countries around the world (Galván, 2017). Unfortunately, school start times remain early, so adolescents are often forced into a pattern of sleep deprivation that has led some public health leaders to push for later high school start times (Galván, 2017). Adolescents perform better academically when school start times are later in the morning, even when researchers control for socioeconomic status and mental health symptomatology (Carrell, Maghakian, & West, 2011).

Thus, the vast majority (a staggering 90%) of adolescents are sleep deprived (Basch, Basch, Ruggles, & Rajan, 2014). Adolescents may attempt to compensate by sleeping longer on the weekends, which creates a jet lag effect (Crowley & Carskadon, 2010) that has impacts on mental health (Galván, 2017). Anxiety and depression can be induced through sleep deprivation (Babson, Trainor, Feldner, & Blumenthal, 2010), which is notable considering that both anxiety and depression increase substantially around the time of puberty.

Sleep deprivation also impairs learning and academic performance. Sleep loss impairs hippocampal function associated with initial encoding and long-term memory storage and retrieval (Abel, Havekes, Saletin, & Walker, 2013). Sleep deprivation also impairs working memory and attention (Lim & Dinges, 2010). Even one night of sleep loss can impair executive functioning and learning ability (Lim & Dinges, 2010). Finally, sleep deprivation also has metabolic effects, such as affecting various areas of the hypothalamus and immune system (Fifel Meijer, & Deboer, 2018) and decreasing the satiety hormone leptin while increasing the hunger-stimulating hormone ghrelin (Hanlon & Van Cauter, 2011; Schmid, Ricci, & Leitzmann, 2015; Spiegel, Tasali, Leproult, & Van Cauter, 2009). Sleep deprivation is thus linked to a risk for weight gain (Spiegel et al., 2009).

As part of a standard intake assessment procedure, we recommend that counselors ask adolescents about their sleep habits and whether they obtain the recommended 8.5 to 9.5 hours of sleep per night (Galván, 2017). In addition to advocating for later school start times, counselors can recommend a variety of sleep hygiene techniques that can enhance sleep quality and duration, such as establishing a predictable bedtime routine, refraining from using alcohol and stimulants (e.g., caffeine) close to bedtime, refraining from exercising close to bedtime, and establishing the discipline of stopping using technology (especially blue-light technology) in the hour leading up to bedtime. Increasing the use of blue-light technology (e.g., tablets, smartphones, laptops) close to bedtime is problematic because it blocks melatonin secretion and further impacts the quality and onset of sleep (Chellappa et al., 2013). In our experience, assisting adolescents in refraining from using technology at bedtime can be challenging, as teens may want to communicate with their peers late into the night.

There are a variety of methods for tracking sleep duration and quality. Several mobile applications that measure sleep quality can detect different stages of sleep (i.e., Stages I, II, III, IV) and track sleep over the course of days and weeks. These monitoring systems can be integrated into counseling sessions by asking the adolescent to share their weekly sleep duration and quality via a review of the app data. As with typical self-monitoring interventions, counselors can ask adolescents to also keep a daily sleep diary that documents any precipitating habits or events associated with better sleep quality and duration.

Physical Exercise

Physical exercise has multiple health benefits. Researchers have found that a single dose of physical exercise increases BDNF, which you may remember is associated with neurogenesis (Venezia, Quinlan, & Roth, 2017). It appears that the gene sequence associated with the FNDC5 muscle protein is associated with enhanced BDNF expression (Wrann et al., 2013). FNDC5 is a precursor to irisin. Irisin increases cell proliferation via the STAT3 gene transcription factor alongside BDNF, especially in the hippocampus, leading to increased hippocampal volume (Moon, Dincer, & Mantzoros, 2013). Figure 11.6 depicts the irisin-BDNF/STAT3-hippocampus pathway. Physical exercise is thus associated with improved working memory, a key ingredient in academic performance. Irisin also increases energy expenditure by browning white adipose fat tissue (Rodrigues et al., 2018). Through these processes, physical exercise and the associated release of irisin are believed to be protective factors against obesity and even type 2 diabetes (Rodrigues et al., 2018). Physical exercise also stimulates activation of catecholamines, such as dopamine, norepinephrine, and serotonin, and thus has antidepressant properties (Schuch et al., 2016).

Lifestyle change interventions that involve physical activity need to be carefully planned. If the adolescent has any medical conditions, those need to inform any exercise plan that they develop. Because adolescents often have a full schedule, counselors should also be careful not to promote physical exercise at the expense of sleep.

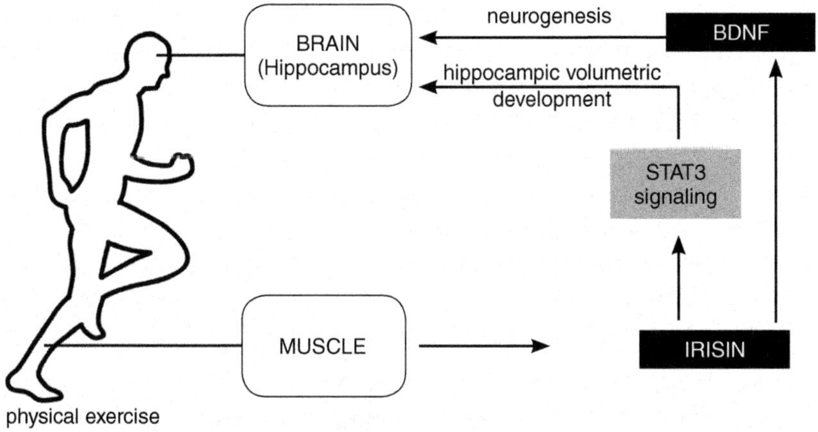

FIGURE 11.6

Irisin, Physical Exercise, and Neuroplasticity

Note. From Rachel Chaney, illustrator. Used by permission. BDNF = brain-derived neurotropic factor.

Conclusion

Children and adolescents may have clinical problems with a strong neurophysiological basis, such as chronic stress and sleep disruption. Traditional talk therapy interventions do not directly address these issues (e.g., reliably reducing cortisol). Counselors should therefore consider integrating interventions that directly address these issues, such as biofeedback, neurofeedback, and therapeutic lifestyle change. Although several of the interventions described in this chapter can be implemented with fairly minimal training (e.g., therapeutic lifestyle change, diaphragmatic breathing), neurofeedback requires substantial training and equipment to practice proficiently.

Quiz Questions

1. Pulse oximeters are included in diaphragmatic breathing training to
   a. Ensure that the child does not have an abnormal heartbeat during diaphragmatic breathing
   b. Provide feedback to the child about the impact of diaphragmatic breathing
   c. Increase the heart rate of a child during diaphragmatic breathing
2. Neurofeedback trains children to alter their electrical activity through
   a. Voluntary control
   b. Involuntary control
   c. Both voluntary and involuntary control

3. Sleep-wake phase delay is caused by later nighttime release of
   a. Testosterone
   b. Oxytocin
   c. Melatonin

References

Abel, T., Havekes, R., Saletin, J. M., & Walker, M. P. (2013). Sleep, plasticity and memory from molecules to whole-brain networks. *Current Biology, 23,* R774–R788. doi:10.1016/j.cub.2013.07.025

Arns, M., Heinrich, H., & Strehl, U. (2014). Evaluation of neurofeedback in ADHD: The long and winding road. *Biological Psychology, 95,* 108–115. doi:10.1016/j.biopsycho.2013.11.013

Babson, K. A., Trainor, C. D., Feldner, M. T., & Blumenthal, H. (2010). A test of the effects of acute sleep deprivation on general and specific self-reported anxiety and depressive symptoms: An experimental extension. *Journal of Behavior Therapy and Experimental Psychiatry, 41,* 297–303. doi:10.1016/j.jbtep.2010.02.008

Basch, C. E., Basch, C. H., Ruggles, K. V., & Rajan, S. (2014). Prevalence of sleep duration on an average school night among 4 nationally representative successive samples of American high school students, 2007-2013. *Preventing Chronic Disease, 11,* E216, 1–5. doi:10.5888/pcd11.140383

Carrell, S. E., Maghakian, T., & West, J. E. (2011). A's from Zzzz's? The causal effect of school start time on the academic achievement of adolescents. *American Economic Journal: Economic Policy, 3,* 62–81. doi:10.1257/pol.3.3.62

Carskadon, M. A. (2011). Sleep in adolescents: The perfect storm. *Pediatric Clinics, 58,* 637–647. doi:10.1016/j.pcl.2011.03.003

Chapin, T. J., & Russell-Chapin, L. A. (2014). *Neurotherapy and neurofeedback: Brain-based treatment for psychological and behavioral problems.* New York, NY: Routledge.

Chellappa, S. L., Steiner, R., Oelhafen, P., Lang, D., Götz, T., Krebs, J., & Cajochen, C. (2013). Acute exposure to evening blue-enriched light impacts on human sleep. *Journal of Sleep Research, 22,* 573–580. doi:10.1111/jsr.12050

Collura, T. F. (2017). *Technical foundations of neurofeedback.* New York, NY: Routledge.

Council for Accreditation of Counseling and Related Educational Programs. (2015). *2016 CACREP standards.* Alexandria, VA: Author.

Crowley, S. J., Acebo, C., & Carskadon, M. A. (2007). Sleep, circadian rhythms, and delayed phase in adolescence. *Sleep Medicine, 8,* 602–612. doi:10.1016/j.sleep.2006.12.002

Crowley, S. J., & Carskadon, M. A. (2010). Modifications to weekend recovery sleep delay circadian phase in older adolescents. *Chronobiology International, 27,* 1469–1492. doi:10.3109/07420528.2010.503293

Dhabhar, F. S. (2009). Enhancing versus suppressive effects of stress on immune function: Implications for immunoprotection and immunopathology. *Neuroimmunomodulation, 16,* 300–317. doi:10.1159/000216188

Fifel, K., Meijer, J. H., & Deboer, T. (2018). Long-term effects of sleep deprivation on neuronal activity in four hypothalamic areas. *Neurobiology of Disease, 109,* 54–63. doi:10.1016/j.nbd.2017.10.005

Galván, A. (2017). *The neuroscience of adolescence.* New York, NY: Cambridge University Press.

Guerry, J. D., & Hastings, P. D. (2011). In search of HPA axis dysregulation in child and adolescent depression. *Clinical Child and Family Psychology Review, 14,* 135–160. doi:10.1007/s10567-011-0084-5

Hanlon, E. C., & Van Cauter, E. (2011). Quantification of sleep behavior and of its impact on the cross-talk between the brain and peripheral metabolism. *Proceedings of the National Academy of Sciences, USA, 108,* 15609–15616. doi:10.1073/pnas.1101338108

Harris, M. L., Oldmeadow, C., Hure, A., Luu, J., Loxton, D., & Attia, J. (2017). Stress increases the risk of type 2 diabetes onset in women: A 12-year longitudinal study using causal modelling. *PLoS ONE, 12,* e0172126. doi:10.1371/journal.pone.0172126

Hulme, S. R., Jones, O. D., & Abraham, W. C. (2013). Emerging roles of metaplasticity in behaviour and disease. *Trends in Neurosciences, 36,* 353–362. doi:10.1016/j.tins.2013.03.007

Ivey, A. E., Ivey, M. B., & Zalaquett, C. P. (2017). *Intentional interviewing and counseling: Facilitating client development in a multicultural society* (9th ed.). Boston, MA: Cengage.

Lim, J., & Dinges, D. F. (2010). A meta-analysis of the impact of short-term sleep deprivation on cognitive variables. *Psychological Bulletin, 136,* 375–389. doi:10.1037/a0018883

Ma, X., Yue, Z. Q., Gong, Z. Q., Zhang, H., Duan, N. Y., Shi, Y. T., . . . Li, Y. F. (2017). The effect of diaphragmatic breathing on attention, negative affect and stress in healthy adults. *Frontiers in Psychology, 8,* 874. doi:10.3389/fpsyg.2017.00874

Malykhin, N. V., & Coupland, N. J. (2015). Hippocampal neuroplasticity in major depressive disorder. *Neuroscience, 309,* 200–213. doi:10.1016/j.neuroscience.2015.04.047

Moon, H. S., Dincer, F., & Mantzoros, C. S. (2013). Pharmacological concentrations of irisin increase cell proliferation without influencing markers of neurite outgrowth and synaptogenesis in mouse H19-7 hippocampal cell lines. *Metabolism: Clinical and Experimental, 62,* 1131–1136. doi:10.1016/j.metabol.2013.04.007

Numakawa, T., Odaka, H., & Adachi, N. (2017). Actions of brain-derived neurotrophic factor and glucocorticoid stress in neurogenesis. *International Journal of Molecular Sciences, 18,* 2312. doi:10.3390/ijms18112312

Pagliaccio, D., Luby, J. L., Bogdan, R., Agrawal, A., Gaffrey, M. S., Belden, A. C., . . . Barch, D. M. (2014). Stress-system genes and life stress predict cortisol levels and amygdala and hippocampal volumes in children. *Neuropsychopharmacology, 39,* 1245–1253. doi:10.1038/npp.2013.327

Rodrigues, K. C. D. C., Pereira, R. M., De Campos, T. D. P., De Moura, R. F., Da Silva, A. S. R., Cintra, D. E., . . . De Moura, L. P. (2018). The role of physical exercise to improve the browning of white adipose tissue via POMC neurons. *Frontiers in Cellular Neuroscience, 12,* 88. doi:10.3389/fncel.2018.00088

Sapolsky, R. M. (2000a). Glucocorticoids and hippocampal atrophy in neuropsychiatric disorders. *Archives of General Psychiatry, 57,* 925–935. doi:10.1001/archpsyc.57.10.925

Sapolsky, R. M. (2000b). The possibility of neurotoxicity in the hippocampus in major depression: A primer on neuron death. *Biological Psychiatry, 48,* 755–765. doi:10.1016/S0006-3223(00)00971-9

Schmid, D., Ricci, C., & Leitzmann, M. F. (2015). Associations of objectively assessed physical activity and sedentary time with all-cause mortality in US adults: The NHANES study. *PLoS ONE, 10,* e0119591. doi:10.1371/journal.pone.0119591

Schuch, F. B., Deslandes, A. C., Stubbs, B., Gosmann, N. P., da Silva, C. T. B., & de Almeida Fleck, M. P. (2016). Neurobiological effects of exercise on major depressive disorder: A systematic review. *Neuroscience & Biobehavioral Reviews, 61,* 1–11. doi:10.1016/j.neubiorev.2015.11.012

Spiegel, K., Tasali, E., Leproult, R., & Van Cauter, E. (2009). Effects of poor and short sleep on glucose metabolism and obesity risk. *Nature Reviews Endocrinology, 5,* 253–261. doi:10.1038/nrendo.2009.23

Thibault, R. T., & Raz, A. (2017). The psychology of neurofeedback: Clinical intervention even if applied placebo. *American Psychologist, 72,* 679–688. doi:10.1037/amp0000118

van der Kolk, B. A. (2015). *The body keeps the score: Brain, mind, and body in the healing of trauma.* East Rutherford, NJ: Penguin Books.

van der Valk, E. S., Savas, M., & van Rossum, E. (2018). Stress and obesity: Are there more susceptible individuals? *Current Obesity Reports, 7,* 193–203. doi:10.1007/s13679-018-0306-y

Venezia, A. C., Quinlan, E., & Roth, S. M. (2017). A single bout of exercise increases hippocampal BDNF: Influence of chronic exercise and noradrenaline. *Genes, Brain, and Behavior, 16,* 800–811. doi:10.1111/gbb.12394

Vose, L. R., & Stanton, P. K. (2017). Synaptic plasticity, metaplasticity, and depression. *Current Neuropharmacology, 15,* 71–86. doi:10.2174/1570159X14666160202121111

Wrann, C. D., White, J. P., Salogiannnis, J., Laznik-Bogoslavski, D., Wu, J., Ma, D., . . . Spiegelman, B. M. (2013). Exercise induces hippocampal BDNF through a PGC-1α/FNDC5 pathway. *Cell Metabolism, 18,* 649–659. doi:10.1016/j.cmet.2013.09.008

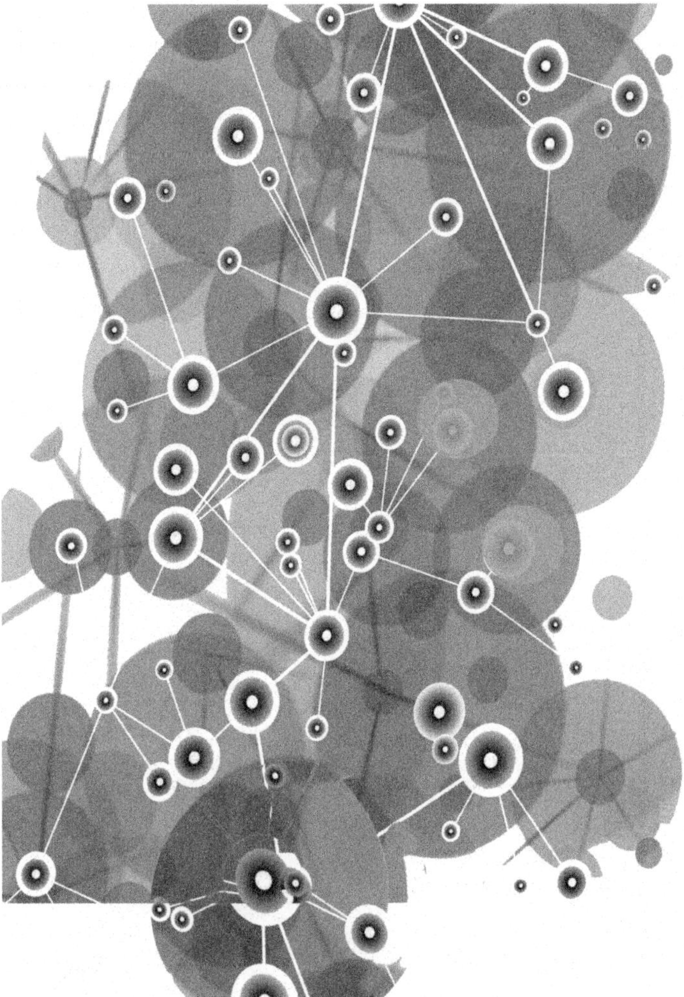

Section IV

Conclusion

Chapter 12

Delivering Neuroeducation to Children and Adolescents

Key Concepts

- Neuroeducation
- Three-step model of neuroeducation

Aligned 2016 CACREP Standards

Standard 2.F.5.f. Counselor characteristics and behaviors that influence the counseling process

• • •

Throughout this text, we have introduced neuroscience information pertinent to child and adolescent development. As the reader, you might be wondering which information you can share with children, adolescents, and their families and how to share this information appropriately. In this final chapter, we conclude this text with a three-step procedure for applying neuroscience information when working with children, adolescents, and families. We include an abridged case study of a client that Michelle worked with to provide further insight into the effective delivery of neuroscience information to both a child client and their guardian as part of a comprehensive treatment approach. In the case study, we demonstrate how to integrate various intervention approaches when working with children and adolescents.

Delivering Neuroeducation

The sharing with clients of neuroscience information about their development and problems they are experiencing has been called *neuroeducation* (Miller, 2016). Neuroeducation is similar to psychoeducation, although the technical nature of neuroscience terminology requires a slightly different approach to delivery. In this section, we describe a three-step procedure for delivering neuroeducation to child and adolescent clients.

Step 1: Validate and Explore

Counselors should first seek to understand and validate the experiences of children and adolescents before providing descriptions that help them better understand their experience. Rushing too quickly into explanation can feel invalidating, as if the counselor knows more about the client's experience than the client does. Instead, children and adolescents should first feel heard and understood by their counselor.

Similarly, if the child or adolescent asks a genuine question about why they are experiencing certain problems, the counselor should validate that question and seek to explore the reasons behind it. You may recall that in Chapter 9, on problems of adolescence, we posed a discussion prompt about how you might respond to an adolescent who asks you what is happening in their brain for them to feel so depressed. Adolescents could ask a question like this for a number of reasons. They could be genuinely curious about the brain. They could also be feeling discouraged or demoralized. They could also be asking this question with the hope that you will "fix" their depression. The kind of response you provide will be grounded in the rationale for their question. For example, an adolescent who is discouraged may need more processing of their lived experience rather than premature delivery of neuroeducation. An adolescent who is curious about the brain may want more descriptions of brain anatomy and function. Exploring reasons behind questions is therefore a crucial first step.

Step 2: Assess

Prior to providing neuroeducation, the counselor should assess the client's familiarity with neuroscience, level of comprehension, and interest in receiving neuroeducation. Children, adolescents, and families have different levels of familiarity with and comprehension of neuroscience concepts. A younger child such as Wayne (age 8; from Chapter 5) with a lower IQ (55–65) will need rudimentary descriptions of the brain, if any at all. An older child such as Brooke (age 17; from Chapter 9) with above-average intelligence may benefit from more in-depth descriptions of brain structures (e.g., amygdala, hippocampus) and function. Assessment can be fairly short, with a brief series of questions about the child's or adolescent's prior knowledge of the brain and body ("Do you know what cortisol is?"). Assessment should also address the child's or adolescent's interest in gaining knowledge of the brain ("Would you like to hear more about how cortisol works, or would you prefer to stay on topic?"). If the child or adolescent has no interest in receiving neuroeducation at this time, we do not recommend providing it!

Step 3: Effectively Deliver Information

Once you have validated the child's or adolescent's lived experience, understood the rationale behind their questions, and appraised their prior knowledge, comprehension, and interest, you are ready to provide neuroeducation information to the client. When delivering this information, you should consider three factors that are crucial to effective delivery.

Connect Information to the Problem

First, connect information to the current issue or problem. If the child or adolescent is struggling with posttraumatic stress, neuroeducation should focus on dysregulation of the hypothalamic-pituitary-adrenal axis and its effects (e.g., impaired hippocampal functioning and memory). If the child or adolescent has questions about sexual development, neuroeducation should target the hypothalamic-pituitary-gonadal axis.

Distill Without Diluting

Second, provide information that follows the principle of distilling without diluting. Select the most important concepts to share, and describe those in sufficient detail for the client's developmental age and understanding. Ensure that there is a connection between concepts, so that your description flows from one concept to another. Avoid describing concepts in a vague manner that lacks a grounding in neuroscience.

Facilitate Optimism and Hope

Third, provide information that facilitates optimism and hope for recovery. The brain is adaptive and plastic and capable of changing in response to repetitive practice. Avoid sharing information that discourages children or adolescents by proposing that their problems are outside of their control and destined to remain constant throughout their lives (unless this is factually correct). Counselors should also avoid sharing information that is overly reductionistic. For example, conceptualizing depression as merely a deficit in monoamine neurotransmission invalidates other factors that generate and sustain depression (e.g., life stressors, grief and loss).

Following are two examples (see Case Vignette 12.1) of how to describe the neurophysiology of trauma when working with Brooke, a case vignette that was described in Chapters 9 and 10. The first example effectively distils without diluting, whereas the second example is too vague.

Case Vignette 12.1
Neuroeducation Examples

Example 1

Our brain and body are very responsive to the environment around us. When a person feels extremely threatened and fears for their own safety, it results in the release of two important stress hormones called *cortisol* and *adrenaline*. These hormones prepare you for action, so you can address the threat facing you. Cortisol and adrenaline cause people to feel an increased heart rate, sweaty palms, and slow digestion. In most situations, the threat passes and the amount of cortisol and adrenaline in your blood decreases because your body stops secreting these hormones. In trauma, this system is impaired. The threat is so severe that the brain and body overlearn and wait in constant expectation of the threat returning. This means that cortisol and adrenaline may be secreted perpetually, at higher levels than normal. This creates a host of problems, such as having impaired memory, being emotionally reactive, distrusting others in your environment, always being vigilant of threat, and having difficulty settling for sleep at night. The good news is that we can improve your ability to reduce your stress levels through activities that help to reduce cortisol and adrenaline over time, such as diaphragmatic breathing. I would be happy to help teach you some diaphragmatic breathing techniques.

Example 2

When you get upset, parts of your brain get hijacked. You get activated very quickly, and you can't stop yourself from getting activated. As a result, you want to fight, flight, or freeze. Although there is nothing a person can do to change the past, I can help you to manage these symptoms.

• • •

The first example provides a clear description of how the brain and body respond to traumatic events using the stress hormones cortisol and adrenaline to define elevated and chronic stress response. Hearing terms like *hypothalamic-pituitary-adrenal axis* is perhaps less crucial to Brooke than understanding that these hormones have physiological effects that she can observe. These hormones are described as something she can alter through practices like diaphragmatic breathing. From this neuroeducation, Brooke has a rationale for why she is experiencing certain problems and a clear direction for how to address these problems.

In comparison, the second example contains vague information that is not directly connected to trauma (though it could easily be). Neuroscience information is lacking and feels diluted. For example, fight, flight, or freeze is a very general response that can easily be substantiated with descriptions of the hypothalamic-pituitary-adrenal axis system. Finally, and most important, this response could potentially discourage the client. The counselor emphasizes twice that the client has little control over their responding and only suggests at the end that the client can better manage their symptoms (rather than change them).

Next, we will focus on application of these neuroeducation concepts to the case of Makayla (see Case Vignette 12.2).

Case Conceptualization

Before applying neuroeducation, the counselor should first identify symptoms and conceptualize where these problems originated. Makayla displayed cross-cutting symptoms of anger outbursts, defiance, difficulty concentrating, irritability, restlessness, sleep disturbance, and nightmares. Like many children and adolescents with early life trauma, Makayla displayed symptoms that met some of the criteria for multiple mental disorders, and therefore her symptoms could not easily be categorized by a single diagnosis. For example, without formal psychological testing, it was difficult to determine whether Makayla's concentration problems and restlessness were symptoms of anxiety, attention-deficit/hyperactivity disorder, or both. As a result, Makayla had been previously diagnosed with five mental disorders.

Conceptualizing the genesis of a child's or adolescent's symptomatology can be challenging. Although there did not appear to be a family history of mental disorders, not enough information existed to rule out a genetic cause of her symptoms. An epigenetic basis for Makayla's symptoms was possible given that she displayed several symptoms associated with chronic activation of the stress response system (e.g., irritability and edginess, restlessness, sleep disturbance). Multiple situational factors could also have played a role in Makayla's problem behaviors (i.e., running away from home, having indiscriminate sex with peers, smoking cigarettes). These behaviors could have served a hedonic function (i.e., sensation seeking), met a need for social affiliation and acceptance, or been a method of coping with unresolved grief and loss related to her mother's death. It was also possible that her grandmother's medical problems had rekindled Makayla's fears of future loss of a major attachment figure. If so, Makayla's defiant behavior (e.g., running away) could have been a method of distancing herself from her grandmother as a form of self-protection against anticipated loss.

Case Vignette 12.2 Makayla

Makayla is an African American female who was 11 years old when I first met her. She was demonstrating aggressive behaviors (mostly verbal) toward her grandmother and authority figures at school. Makayla had been living with her grandmother ever since her mother had been killed when she was 4 years old. Makayla had participated in some form of counseling since age 5, when she had come to the attention of her school counselor. Before her mother's death, Makayla had met all developmental milestones and had demonstrated no evidence of an intellectual or developmental disability. Things began to shift for Makayla at the age of 4, when she lost the caregiver with whom she had developed a secure attachment.

Between ages 5 and 11, Makayla was in and out of foster care, her grandmother's home, acute hospitalization, and long-term residential care. Makayla had been diagnosed by prior counselors with the inattentive subtype of attention-deficit/hyperactivity disorder, along with oppositional defiant disorder, depression, and generalized and social anxiety. She displayed cross-cutting symptoms of anger outbursts, defiance, difficulty concentrating, irritability, restlessness, sleep disturbance, and nightmares. She had taken a series of psychotropic medications that included stimulants (methylphenidate/Ritalin), antidepressants (fluoxetine/Prozac), and atypical stimulants (e.g., clonidine/Catapres). These medications had seemed to help Makayla's academic performance but had not substantially modified her problematic behaviors.

Makayla had begun puberty slightly earlier than her peers at the age of 10. Almost immediately, Makayla had begun engaging in risky behaviors. By age 11, Makayla was running away from home, having indiscriminate sex with peers, and smoking cigarettes. She never tested positive for other drugs. Her grandmother reported that Makayla's behaviors began to change when she had learned that her grandmother was experiencing non-life-threatening medical problems. Makayla had no contact with her biological father, who himself had another family. Per the grandmother's report, Makayla's father seemed not to care about her. Makayla was able to admit when she made mistakes and showed remorse when confronted about her behavior by her grandmother. Yet she struggled to make appropriate decisions in the immediate moment and continued to run away from home

(Continued)

Case Vignette 12.2 *(Continued)*

and engage in other dysfunctional behaviors. Her typical saying was "Oh crap, I have messed up again!" Her overall participation in counseling was inconsistent. She would miss several sessions at a time and probably attended less than 50% of her scheduled appointments. Makayla indicated feeling tired of just talking to everyone about what had gone wrong in her life.

• • •

Several potential diversity factors and environmental influences in this case might have influenced how the root problems emerged as symptoms. Makayla's sexual development occurred early, and she may have been struggling with emotional lability (i.e., fluctuations) attributable to an active gonadal hormone system that was secreting estradiol and estrogen. Her early secondary sexual development may also have generated sexual interest from her peers, in particular older peers. Some of her behaviors, such as running away and smoking cigarettes, tended to be more common in adolescents than children. Thus, Makayla's early pubertal development may have impacted how others in the environment interacted with her. Makayla's racial and ethnic identity development could also have been a factor influencing her behavior (e.g., anger at experiences of oppression or discrimination).

Counseling Approach and Treatment Planning

Michelle selected a cognitive behavior approach to working with Makayla and used neuroeducation as part of a comprehensive treatment plan that also included integrating creative arts activities. Michelle sought to reduce Makayla's immediate problem behaviors and symptoms to stabilize her situation before addressing the root problems or issues that were causing these symptoms to occur. Michelle thus decided to address Makayla's problem behaviors of running away, having indiscriminate sex, and smoking cigarettes first before exploring more deeply rooted problems such as Makayla's response to her grandmother's health concerns.

Behavioral Chain Analysis

Michelle's first task was to address the symptoms that were causing significant dysfunction prior to working through Makayla's root problems. Makayla's most concerning problem behaviors were running away, having indiscriminate sex with peers, and smoking cigarettes. Michelle conducted a behavioral chain analysis to understand the antecedents to Makayla's running away, sexual behavior, and cigarette use. It became apparent that these behaviors occurred in response to interest and invitation from older high school peers ages 14 and 15. Makayla acknowledged that she yearned for peer validation and social affiliation. She met this need by hanging out with older peers. Makayla was able to process the quality of these interactions and over time realized that she was being used by these older peers. Because these peers were younger than 16, their sexual acts with Makayla did not meet the criteria for statutory rape in the state where Michelle was practicing.

Parent Education

Makayla's grandmother reported holding "traditional" values around the importance of a child respecting their elders and the guardian having the right to determine rules and limits without input from the child. Baumrind (1991) classified such beliefs, values, and actions as forms of authoritarian parenting. Baumrind classified parenting styles into four types: authoritarian, authoritative, passive, and uninvolved. According to Baumrind's model, parenting that is overly controlling (i.e., authoritarian), laissez-faire (i.e., permissive), or unresponsive (i.e., uninvolved) can cause problem behaviors in children, whereas democratic and collaborative parenting (i.e., authoritative parenting) is least likely to propagate child behavior problems.

In this case, the grandmother's authoritarian parenting style had likely prompted Makayla's defiant behavior. Michelle worked individually with the grandmother to educate her on the four parenting styles identified by Baumrind (1991). At first, the grandmother was resistant to feedback because she felt that Makayla should obey directives from her guardians without question. Over several sessions, Makayla's grandmother learned the benefits of collaboratively setting limits and developing a more authoritative style if she wanted Makayla to develop trust and rapport with her rather than resent her for imposing these limits.

Collaborative Problem-Solving

Following parent education, Michelle invited both Makayla and her grandmother into sessions to facilitate collaborative problem-solving regarding Makayla's problematic behavior of running away. The pair discussed the pattern of the grandmother repeatedly punishing Makayla for sneaking out after she went to bed. As a result of her grandmother's punishment, Makayla seemed to hate being at home. She wished to be left alone in her room or to go out with her friends.

To address this interactional pattern, Michelle assisted the pair in identifying a vehicle for Makayla meeting her needs for social affiliation within the grandmother's rules and limits. Makayla identified same-age peers whom her grandmother approved of that she could form closer bonds with. Makayla was allowed to ride her bike to these friend's houses on the condition that she attend school regularly, let her grandmother know where she was going, and be back home at the agreed-upon time. Makayla largely stuck to these expectations. Makayla's progress toward forming a more stable group of friends strengthened her relationship with her grandmother, as the pair began having more positive interactions rather than negative ones.

Neuroeducation

Several of Makayla's symptoms, such as difficulty sleeping, seemed to be caused by an overactive stress response system. Makayla's sleep problems were addressed through neuroeducation about sleep hygiene practices. Michelle addressed sleep hygiene issues by following the three-step neuroeducation model described earlier.

Step 1: Validate and explore. First, Michelle explored and validated Makayla's difficulty obtaining adequate sleep. Makayla acknowledged typically getting 6 hours of sleep and waking up several times during the night. She found it difficult to fall back asleep once she woke up. Makayla did not seem to have a predictable bedtime routine and typically texted friends on her iPhone until she fell asleep each night. Michelle validated Makayla's fatigue and frustrations with falling back asleep.

Step 2: Assess. The second step of the neuroeducation protocol was to assess Makayla and her grandmother's interest in and knowledge of neuroscience. Both Makayla and her grandmother were interested in learning more information. They both reported lacking foundational information about the brain and body (e.g., the role of melatonin in sleep initiation).

Step 3: Effectively deliver information. Effective delivery of information was the third step of the neuroeducation protocol. Michelle *connected information to the problem* by suggesting that improving the quality of her sleep might help to improve Makayla's symptoms of impaired academic performance related to working memory and attention and enhance her overall mood (i.e., reduce irritability). Michelle then provided neuroeducation to Makayla about the importance of a consistent bedtime routine and the role of blue-light technology in reducing melatonin secretion. To *distill without diluting*, Michelle provided brief descriptions of neuroscience information (e.g., the role of melatonin in sleep initiation) to avoid overwhelming Makayla and her grandmother. She used charts and graphics to emphasize basic concepts related to melatonin secretion and blue-light technology.

Michelle *facilitated optimism and hope* by helping Makayla to identify small changes that could impact the quality of her sleep. Makayla collaboratively identified an appropriate and consistent bedtime routine and agreed to refrain from using her cell phone 1 hour before bedtime. She also used a white noise machine in her room to reduce the potential for nighttime awakening due to her sensitivity to noise (i.e., her hyperstartle response). Makayla began to sleep better and had improved concentration at school. These gains helped Makayla to develop the self-efficacy that would be helpful for later interventions. Consider Reflection Question 12.1.

Addressing Root Problems

Michelle believed that Makayla's problem behaviors were influenced by Makayla's fears of reexperiencing the loss of a major attachment figure and her distancing herself emotionally as a form of self-protection. In neuroscience-informed cognitive behavior therapy, this is considered an avoidance response style (Beeson, Field, Jones, & Miller, 2017). Michelle believed that modifying this response style to approach rather than avoid the situation would benefit Makayla by enabling her to work through her fears of loss and foster a deeper bond with her grandmother. Michelle hoped that these changes would reduce Makayla's distancing (i.e., avoidant) behaviors.

In the fifth session, Michelle wondered aloud whether the grandmother's medical issues could be a cause of Makayla engaging in behaviors that would create distance with her grandmother, considering that these behaviors seemed to begin shortly after she had learned about her grandmother's condition. Makayla sat in silence on hearing this and, after a long pause, tearfully shared that she was afraid of losing her grandmother and could not stand the thought of losing another major attachment figure. Although she denied that these behaviors were intentionally defiant and means of initiating power struggles with her grandmother, she could see how these behaviors could create distance. Michelle led the discussion into the importance of Makayla joining with her grandmother rather than creating distance (i.e., approaching rather than avoiding) and ways in which Makayla could deepen her attachment and engagement with her grandmother rather than back away.

With time, Makayla became open to having her grandmother attend her sessions so she could work through her fears of her grandmother's passing. Through active listening training, Makayla's grandmother was able to be supportive of her during these discussions and came to understand why Makayla would fear future loss. Makayla even began to share that she missed her mother. During discussions of her mother's passing, it became apparent that Makayla held the schematic belief that her life was irreparably damaged following her mother's death. Through cognitive restructuring, Makayla came to understand that her

Reflection Question 12.1

What other neuroeducation topics could Michelle have addressed with Makayla?

mother would not want her to be defined by this loss. She could instead honor the memory of her mother by treating herself and her grandmother with kindness. Makayla and her grandmother decided to spend more time together in shared activities. They especially wanted to start cooking meals together, as Makayla liked her grandmother's recipes.

Creative Arts

To continue processing these deep-seated feelings after these joint sessions with her grandmother, Makayla engaged in creative arts activities during individual counseling sessions to further process her memories of her mother and her fears of losing another major attachment figure. Makayla enjoyed making collages, and Michelle asked Makayla to share her story of her relationship with her mother using visual images that Makayla cut out from magazines. After Makayla created the collage, Michelle asked her to explain the meaning of her composition. Over the course of several sessions that involved collage, Makayla disclosed how much she missed her mother and felt unwanted by her father. She also expressed fears of losing her grandmother. Makayla was also able to process her feelings of guilt related to how her behavior had created stress for her grandmother. As the counseling process reached closure a year later, Michelle made a binder for Makayla with her collages inside. Makayla reported that this was one of the most meaningful aspects of counseling for her.

Case Conclusion

Because Michelle was an African American female who was old enough to be Makayla's mother, she anticipated transference and countertransference during her work with Makayla. Michelle sought supervision and consultation throughout the counseling process to work through any countertransference and avoid surrogate parenting. At times, Michelle noticed that Makayla would engage in behaviors during session that elicited an urge to reprimand and discipline Makayla. Michelle used this countertransference to better understand the two-way dynamic of Makayla and her grandmother regarding their authoritarian pattern of disobedience and punishment. When the timing felt right, Michelle disclosed to Makayla her pull toward reprimanding her ("I've noticed at times that I feel drawn to reprimanding you for some of the actions you take, such as when you told me today that you plan to exact revenge on your grandmother by giving her the silent treatment") and wondered whether Makayla noticed her role in this dynamic ("It makes me wonder if you are aware that you elicit disciplinarian responses in others, responses that you despise and resent"). This disclosure helped Makayla to understand her role in the relational dynamic with her grandmother and her agency and ability to change the dynamic so that she did not elicit authoritarian parenting responses.

Michelle stayed in touch with Makayla throughout middle and high school as she episodically reinitiated brief bouts of counseling. The grandmother's health continued to decline, and this was one of Makayla's major stressors. Over time, Makayla became better able to cope with this stressor and became more comfortable sharing her fears of losing her grandmother. She often repeated the phrase "I know doc, I need to keep my brain charged and things regulated!" Makayla graduated from high school and lived independently as an adult. Consider Reflection Question 12.2.

Conclusion

In this chapter we introduced a three-step process for delivering neuroeducation to clients: (a) validating and exploring client experience; (b) assessing clients' interest in, familiarity with, and knowledge of neuroscience; and (c) effectively delivering neuroscience information that is matched to the client's developmental age and understanding. We applied this neuroeducation approach to the case of Makayla. In the case review, we described a comprehensive and integrated approach to case conceptualization and treatment planning that facilitated the counseling process by identifying root problems that were causing cross-cutting symptomatology. Michelle's work with Makayla emphasized the three general principles noted in Chapter 1 of this text: (a) Seek to know the person beyond the label, (b) Form effective working relationships, and (c) Address areas of personal and professional growth as a counselor.

Quiz Questions

1. Neuroeducation means
   a. Telling clients to make lifestyle changes so that they can avoid future brain damage
   b. Reviewing and explaining the results of clients' brain scans (e.g., electroencephalography, functional magnetic resonance imaging)

Reflection Question 12.2

What other approaches besides cognitive behavior therapy could Michelle have used with Makayla? How might you use these approaches to address symptom stabilization followed by addressing root problems?

   c. Sharing neuroscience information relevant to clients' presenting problems

2. In the three-step model for delivering neuroeducation, counselors follow the steps in a sequential order. Which of the following is the correct order?
   a. Validate and explore, assess, effectively deliver information
   b. Assess, validate and explore, effectively deliver information
   c. Validate and explore, effectively deliver information, assess
3. You are preparing to provide neuroeducation to an adolescent client about the effects of traumatic stress. What information would be most essential to share?
   a. Cognitive distortions
   b. Cortisol and adrenaline
   c. Cortical lobes

References

Baumrind, D. (1991). The influence of parenting style on adolescent competence and substance use. *Journal of Early Adolescence, 11,* 56–95. doi:10.1177/0272431691111004

Beeson, E. T., Field, T. A., Jones, L. K., & Miller, R. (2017). *nCBT: A semi-structured treatment manual.* Boise, ID: Boise State University.

Council for Accreditation of Counseling and Related Educational Programs. (2015). *2016 CACREP standards.* Alexandria, VA: Author.

Miller, R. (2016). Neuroeducation: Integrating brain-based psychoeducation into clinical practice. *Journal of Mental Health Counseling, 38,* 103–115. doi:10.17744/mehc.38.2.02

Neuroscience

Glossary

Acetylcholine. A neurotransmitter that has an excitatory effect on the sensory nervous system and an inhibitory effect on the autonomic nervous system (i.e., stimulates parasympathetic response).

Action potential. A polarized electrical charge that occurs following neurotransmission that may result in a neuron firing an electrical impulse from a cell's dendrites to an axon.

Adrenal gland. A gland composed of the adrenal cortex and medulla that releases cortisol and adrenaline. It is located above the kidneys.

Adrenaline. A hormone secreted from the adrenal gland above the kidneys. It is associated with preparation for action, such as increased heart rate, pupil dilation, and slowed digestion.

Adrenarche. The secretion of adrenal androgens during childhood that facilitates the development of pubic hair, body odor, and skin oil that can result in acne.

Adrenocorticotropic hormone (ACTH). A hormone secreted by the pituitary gland and sent to the adrenal gland to stimulate the release of glucocorticoid hormones, such as cortisol, from the adrenal cortex.

Afferent nerves. Nerves in the peripheral nervous system that carry messages to muscles, glands, and the senses. Efferent nerves carry messages from muscles, glands, and the senses.

Alpha waves. Waveforms on electroencephalography observed at 8–12 Hz. They are associated with a reflective or rested state, such as mindful meditation.

Amygdala. A limbic structure known for its role in processing emotions. The amygdala has an important function in threat detection and fear processing.

Androgens. Gonadal hormones, such as testosterone, associated with the development of secondary sex characteristics and the male reproductive system.

Anterior. A directional term meaning "toward the front."

Anterior cingulate cortex. A subcortical structure involved in emotional processing and regulation with linkages to the limbic regions and prefrontal cortex. It is implicated in conditioned learning.

Apoptosis. The programmed death of a cell, whereby the cell intentionally breaks apart and dies.

Asymmetrical stress response. The finding that people who experience extreme childhood stress have initially greater cortisol excretion during childhood and then blunted cortisol excretion during adulthood.

Attenuation hypothesis. See **asymmetrical stress response.**

Autonomic nervous system (ANS). A division of the peripheral nervous system. The autonomic nervous system has a self-regulatory capacity and controls involuntary functions. It is associated with the release of stress hormones (sympathetic activation) and return to baseline (parasympathetic activation).

Axon. The part of a neuron that signals with other nearby cells and releases neurotransmitters into the synaptic cleft.

Axon terminal buttons. The parts of a neuron that release neurotransmitters and other amino acids from vesicles in the axon into the synaptic cleft.

Basal ganglia. A group of structures located near the limbic region that includes the caudate nucleus, putamen, globus pallidus, and striatum. It is associated with smooth motor movement and planning, motivation, aversion, and conditioned learning (in particular in the striatum).

Beta waves. Waveforms on electroencephalography observed at 12–25 Hz. They are associated with mental activity and an active brain state.

Brain-derived neurotrophic factor (BDNF). A protein that stimulates the continual growth of new neurons (neurogenesis).

Brain stem. A structure that connects the brain to the spinal cord and the peripheral nervous system. The brain stem contains the medulla oblongata, midbrain, and pons.

Broca's area. A structure in the frontal lobe associated with speech production and comprehension.

Catecholamines. See **monoamine.**

Central nervous system (CNS). The structures and function of the brain and spinal cord.

Cerebellum. A brain structure located close to the brain stem and below the cerebrum. It has important roles in motor movement and coordination, cognition, and emotion.

Cerebrum. The largest structure of the brain. The cerebrum contains the subcortex, limbic region, and cerebral cortex.

Chromosomes. Tight packages of DNA molecules and histones.

Corticotropin-releasing hormone (CRH). A hormone secreted by the hypothalamus and sent to the pituitary gland to stimulate the release of adrenocorticotropic hormone.

Cortisol. A hormone secreted from the adrenal gland above the kidneys. It assists with controlling blood sugar and blood pressure, regulating metabolism, and reducing inflammation.

Cortisol trajectories. Differing levels of baseline cortisol secretion across childhood.

Cranial nerves. Twelve major groups of nerve fibers that extend from the spinal cord.

Cytokines. Proteins that have a crucial role in inflammatory responses, as they draw and recruit white blood cells to the site of infection or injury. Proinflammatory cytokines promote inflammation.

Default mode network (DMN). A group of brain structures associated with information processing when a person is in a resting state and not actively engaged in attention-demanding tasks. These structures include the medial prefrontal cortex and the posterior cingulate cortex.

Delta waves. Waveforms on electroencephalography observed at 0–4 Hz. These are the slowest brain waves and are typically present when a person is sleeping, such as in Stage IV sleep.

Dendrites. Parts of a neuron that contain receptors for neurotransmitters.

Deoxyribonucleic acid. See **DNA.**

DNA. A molecule made from hereditary material that is passed down from a person's parents. Parts of DNA contain genetic instructions for developing new proteins.

Dopamine. A neurotransmitter associated with motivation and reward prediction.

Dorsal. A directional term meaning "above."

Efferent nerves. Nerves in the peripheral nervous system that carry messages from muscles, glands, and the senses. Afferent nerves carry messages to muscles, glands, and the senses.

Electroencephalography (EEG). A test that measures electrical activity in the brain, such as ionic currents that create action potentials within neurons.

Endocrine system. A system composed of glands that release hormones (e.g., the pituitary gland).

Endorphins. Neuropeptides that are produced and secreted by the pituitary gland. Endorphins block pain signals in the nervous system and may also cause feelings of euphoria.

Enteric nervous system (ENS). A division of the autonomic nervous system that functions to send and receive messages related to the gastrointestinal system.

Epigenetics. The influence of chemical compounds on protein production by impacting of gene transcription. These chemical compounds are often effected by environmental events.

Epigenome. The entire composition of the genome and the chemical compounds that influence gene expression.

Estradiol. A gonadal hormone associated with the development of secondary sex characteristics and the female reproductive system. A type of estrogen.

Estrogen. A group of gonadal hormones associated with the development of secondary sex characteristics and the female reproductive system. There are three estrogens: estrone, estradiol, and estriol.

Excitatory neurotransmitters. Neurotransmitters that increase the likelihood of an action potential occurring.

Follicle-stimulating hormone. A hormone that stimulates the release of gonadal hormones associated with the initiation and development of secondary sex characteristics.

Frontal lobe. An area of the cortex that contains the primary motor cortex, the premotor cortex, the prefrontal cortex, and the orbitofrontal cortex.

Fusiform face area (FFA). A region of the fusiform gyrus that is strongly associated with face recognition.

Gametes. Reproductive cells that are formed from fertilized eggs and contain one set of chromosomes each from the egg and sperm.

Gamma-aminobutyric acid (GABA). An amino acid and form of neurotransmitter that is the most common inhibitory neurotransmitter in the central nervous system. It is associated with sleep and moderating anxiety.

Gamma waves. Waveforms on electroencephalography observed at 35–50 Hz. These are the fastest brain waves and are associated with intensive mental activity, such as problem-solving and preconscious processing.

Genetic predisposition. Possessing the genetic coding for certain characteristics, traits, and health problems. These genetic codes are derived from DNA passed to a child in the mother's egg and father's sperm. These genes must be transcribed and translated into proteins for these characteristics, traits, and health problems to be expressed.

Gene transcription. A process whereby enzymes called *RNA* read DNA information about protein development and copy it into molecules called *messenger RNA*.

Gene translation. A process whereby messenger RNA leaves the nucleus of a cell and enters the cytoplasm, where ribosomes read the precise chemical sequence that was copied earlier from DNA that the messenger RNA is carrying.

Genome. The entirety of genetic instructions in a person's DNA.

Glia. A group of cells (e.g., astrocytes, oligodendrocytes, and microglia) that support the functioning of neurons.

Glutamate. An amino acid that is the most common excitatory neurotransmitter in the central nervous system. It is associated with synaptogenesis (i.e., the growth of new synapses).

Gonadal hormones. Hormones associated with sexual maturation and function, such as estradiol, estrogen, progesterone, and adrenaline.

Gonadotropin-releasing hormone. A hormone sent by the hypothalamus to the pituitary gland that stimulates the release of luteinizing hormone. It has a role in the initiation and development of secondary sex characteristics.

Gray matter. Brain material that consists largely of neurons that have unmyelinated axons.

Gut colonization. A process of bacterial proliferation in the gut.

Gut microbiome. The complete collection of microorganisms in the gastrointestinal tract.

Gut microbiota. Microorganisms in the gastrointestinal tract. Also called *gut flora*.

Hippocampus. A limbic structure that has an important role in memory formation and consolidation and is involved in the processing of new memories.

Homeostasis. The body's balance of activation and recovery, as seen in sympathetic activation and parasympathetic recovery.

Human chorionic gonadotropin hormone. A hormone that reduces the mother's immune function so that the fetus is not rejected as a foreign organism. It also secretes human placental lactogen that prepares the mother's breasts for lactation.

Hypercortisolism. A process whereby chronically high levels of circulating cortisol impair the negative feedback system, resulting in even greater levels of circulating cortisol. Over time, chronically high cortisol can cause a series of changes that have damaging effects.

Hypothalamic-pituitary-adrenal (HPA) axis. A system that releases cortisol through messages sent among the hypothalamus, pituitary gland, and adrenal gland.

Hypothalamic-pituitary-gonadal axis. The system that releases gonadal hormones such as estrogen and testosterone through messages sent among the hypothalamus, pituitary gland, and gonads.

Hypothalamus. A limbic structure that sends messages to the pituitary gland, the master hormone gland of the brain.

Inhibitory neurotransmitters. Neurotransmitters that reduce the likelihood of an action potential occurring.

Insula. A subcortical structure that has a variety of functions, including emotional and sensory processing and higher order cognition, such as empathy.

Interoception. Conscious awareness of internal bodily sensations.

Ion channels. Dendritic receptor structures that affect the entry of molecules associated with an electrical charge into a cell. When the threshold of electrical charge is exceeded, an action potential is reached.

Irisin. A hormone that increases energy expenditure by browning white adipose fat tissue and also increases cell proliferation via the STAT3 gene transcription factor alongside brain-derived neurotrophic factor.

Knockout. Replacing genes with nongenetic DNA, most typically in animal studies.

Lateral prefrontal cortex. A frontal lobe structure associated with executive functioning and planned behavior, especially in unscripted, unpredictable, and open-ended situations.

Leptin. A hormone associated with hunger inhibition and satiation. Leptin levels climb just prior to the onset of puberty.

Leukocytes. A group of white blood cells in the immune system, also called *immune cells.* Leukocytes consist of basophils, eosinophils, lymphocytes, monocytes, and neutrophils.

Ligand-activated ionotropic receptors. Receptors that directly open ion channels.

Limbic system. A region of the subcortex that contains several important structures for processing sensory information, including the amygdala, hippocampus, and hypothalamus.

Long-term depression (LTD). A reduction in the number of neurons and synapses over time caused by an insufficient number of new cells being available to replace degraded cells.

Long-term potentiation (LTP). The continual growth of new neurons and synapses over time.

Luteinizing hormone. A hormone sent by the pituitary gland to the ovaries or testes to stimulate the release of gonadal hormones such as estrogen and testosterone. Luteinizing hormone has a role in the initiation and development of secondary sex characteristics.

Macrophages. Leukocytes (white blood cells) that engulf (i.e., eat) invading bacteria by phagocytosis.

Medial prefrontal cortex. A region of the prefrontal cortex that is associated with self-referential thought (dorsal) and emotional regulation (ventral), in particular of fear responses.

Medulla oblongata. A brain stem structure that is involved in cardiac functioning (e.g., blood pressure, heart rate) and respiratory functioning (e.g., breathing).

Meiosis. A process of cell division whereby DNA is split between the divided cells.

Melatonin. A neurotransmitter whose secretion is influenced by the exposure of light to the eyes. It has an established role in the circadian rhythm.

Menarche. The first occurrence of menstruation.

Mesocortical pathway. A neural pathway that projects (i.e., transmits) dopamine from the ventral tegmental area to the prefrontal cortex.

Mesocorticolimbic projection. Two pathways for dopamine transportation within the brain: the mesolimbic and mesocortical pathways.

Mesolimbic pathway. A neural pathway that projects (i.e., transmits) dopamine from the ventral tegmental area to the striatum and nucleus accumbens.

Metabotropic receptors. Receptors that do not directly open ion channels.

Metaplasticity. Lasting homeostatic change to baseline cortisol secretion caused by DNA methylation, elevated cortisol, downregulated glutamate and brain-derived neurotrophic factor, and long-term depression.
Methylation. The influence of methyl groups on protein production by binding to DNA and silencing the transcription of genetic material.
Microbiota-gut-brain axis. The interconnected functions of gut microbiota and the central nervous system.
Microcephaly. Reduced head size caused by in utero viral infection. Microcephaly is associated with severe neurodevelopmental abnormalities and intellectual disability.
Midbrain. A brain stem structure that regulates body temperature, sleep and wake cycles, and motor movement.
Mitosis. A process of cell division whereby each divided cell has identical DNA.
Monoamine. A class of neurotransmitters that includes dopamine, norepinephrine, and serotonin. Also known as *catecholamines.*
Monozygotic twins. Twins with identical DNA.
Motor neuron. The primary type of neuron in the peripheral nervous system (along with sensory neurons).
Myelination. A process whereby a myelin sheath is wrapped around an axon to form a tight membrane and insulate a cell. This enhances electrical conduction and transportation.
Negative feedback loop. Messages sent to stop the release of hormones such as glucocorticoids (e.g., cortisol).
Neural pathway. A collective series of synaptic connections.
Neural tube. The early structures of the brain and spinal cord in a first-trimester fetus.
Neurogenesis. The creation of new neurons.
Neurons. Nerve cells.
Neuroplasticity. The ability of the nervous system to create new synaptic connections.
Nigrostriatal pathway. A neural pathway that projects (i.e., transmits) dopamine from the substantia nigra in the midbrain to the dorsal striatum (i.e., caudate nucleus and putamen, structures in the basal ganglia).
Norepinephrine. A neurotransmitter related to epinephrine (adrenaline). It is associated with attention and concentration.
Nucleus. The command center of the cell. The nucleus produces and stores DNA and enzymes.
Nucleus accumbens. A striatum structure in the basal ganglia. It has a major role in the dopaminergic system and is associated with reward and conditioned learning.
Occipital lobe. A region of the cortex that processes visual stimuli and sensory information.
Orbitofrontal cortex. A frontal lobe structure that assists with emotional processing and regulation and impulse control, especially related to social conventions.

Oxytocin. A neuropeptide that facilitates close relationships and associated feelings of bonding, trust, intimacy, and empathy.

Pancreas. A gland in the endocrine system that excretes glucagon and insulin hormones, which regulate blood sugar level.

Parasympathetic branch. A branch of the autonomic nervous system that is associated with reducing sympathetic activation and returning stress hormone levels (e.g., cortisol) to baseline.

Parietal lobe. A region of the cortex that processes touch sensors on the skin. It also contains the somatosensory cortex, which is implicated in awareness of oneself in space and navigation.

Peripheral nervous system (PNS). Sets of nerve fibers that connect the central nervous system (brain and spinal cord) with the body's various glands, limbs, muscles, organs, and skin.

Pineal gland. A gland in the brain that produces and secretes melatonin.

Pituitary gland. The master hormone gland of the body. The pituitary gland sends messages to other hormone glands (e.g., the adrenal gland) to release other hormones.

Polypeptides. Collective amino acids developed through gene translation that eventually become proteins.

Pons. A brain stem structure that relays sensory signals to the thalamus and has a role in balance, bladder control, body posture, eye movement, and facial expressions and sensations.

Posterior. A directional term meaning "toward the back."

Posterior cingulate cortex (PCC). A subcortical structure associated with information processing. It is considered part of the default mode network.

Prefrontal cortex. A group of brain regions associated with executive functioning and conscious awareness. It includes the medial and lateral prefrontal cortexes.

Premotor cortex. A cortical structure that, with the primary motor cortex, directs voluntary movements by sending messages to the brain stem and spinal cord.

Primary motor cortex. A cortical structure that, with the premotor cortex, directs voluntary movements by sending messages to the brain stem and spinal cord.

Progesterone. A gonadal hormone associated with the development of secondary sex characteristics and the female reproductive system. It has an important role in pregnancy.

Projection. A series of neurotransmissions between neurons that transmit messages via neural pathways from one brain structure to another.

Pyramidal neuron. The primary type of neuron in the brain.

Reuptake. The reabsorption of neurotransmitters into the axon of the neuron that released them.

Ribonucleic acid. See **RNA.**

Ribosome. A type of organelle within a cell that creates proteins by translating genetic information that has been transcribed by RNA.

RNA. A molecule that works to code, decode, and regulate the expression of DNA. RNA transcribes (copies) information from DNA to eventually build amino acids into chains that become proteins.

Sensory nervous system. A division of the peripheral nervous system that contains groups of nerve fibers that carry messages to and from the five senses to the central nervous system.

Sensory neuron. The primary type of neuron in the peripheral nervous system (along with motor neurons).

Serotonin. A neurotransmitter associated with tryptophan and melatonin. It has a role in mood, appetite, and sleep.

Sleep-wake phase delay. The later nighttime release of melatonin during adolescence, which creates a circadian rhythm preference for later bedtimes and wake times.

Soma. The cell body, which directs the cell's functioning and includes the nucleus.

Somatosensory cortex. A region of the parietal lobe that is implicated in awareness of oneself in space and navigation, known as *proprioception.*

Subcortex. A region of the brain located dorsal to (i.e., above) the cerebellum and brain stem but ventral to (i.e., below) the surface of the cerebral cortex. The subcortex contains the limbic system, among other structures.

Sympathetic-adrenal-medullary axis. A system that releases adrenaline through messages sent among the hypothalamus, pituitary gland, and adrenal gland.

Sympathetic branch. A branch of the autonomic nervous system that is associated with increasing sympathetic activation and returning stress hormone levels (e.g., cortisol) to baseline.

Synaptic cleft. The space in between neurons where neurotransmitters and amino acids are released from the axon terminal buttons of the signaling neuron that bind to dendritic receptors of the receiving neuron.

Synaptic density. The number of synaptic connections between neurons.

Synaptic pruning. A process whereby synaptic connections that lose their usefulness are winnowed and removed.

Synaptogenesis. The creation of new synapses between neurons.

Telomeres. DNA found at the end of a chromosome that tie up the genetic material and stop it from unravelling.

Temporal lobe. A region of the cortex, proximal to the hippocampus, associated with visual object recognition and the consolidation, storage, and retrieval of long-term memories.

Testosterone. A gonadal hormone associated with the development of secondary sex characteristics and the male reproductive system.

Thalamus. A limbic structure that is the central relay center of the cerebrum. It sends messages to various parts of the subcortex and cortex.

Thelarche. Secondary breast development during puberty.

Thyroid gland. A gland that releases hormones such as thyroxine and triiodothyronine.

Transcription factors. Proteins, such as methyl groups, that bind to a gene to increase or reduce transcription of genetic material.

Transdiagnostic. An approach to case conceptualization and treatment planning that addresses symptoms that are cross-cutting and may not meet the threshold of a formal mental disorder.

Vagus nerve. The tenth cranial nerve (CN X), associated with parasympathetic activation.

Ventral. A directional term meaning "below."

Ventral tegmental area. A key site for dopamine production in the midbrain.

Wernicke's area. A temporal lobe structure involved in language comprehension.

White matter. Brain material that consists largely of neurons that have myelinated axons.

Answer Key to Quiz Questions

Chapter 1
General Principles for Counseling Children and Adolescents
1. c 2. a 3. b

Chapter 2
Structure and Function of the Nervous System
1. b 2. c 3. b

Chapter 3
Cellular Function and Epigenetics
1. a 2. c 3. a

Chapter 4
Neurophysiological and Social Development During Childhood
1. a 2. c 3. c

Chapter 5
Problems of Childhood
1. a 2. a 3. b

Chapter 6
Counseling Approaches I:
Behavior Modification and Behavior Analysis
1. c 2. a 3. b

Chapter 7
Counseling Approaches II:
Play Therapy and the Creative Arts
1. b 2. c 3. a

Chapter 8
Neurophysiological and Social Development
During Adolescence

1. b 2. a 3. b

Chapter 9
Problems of Adolescence

1. a 2. b 3. a

Chapter 10
Counseling Approaches III:
Cognitive Behavior Therapies

1. a 2. b 3. c

Chapter 11
Counseling Approaches IV:
Biofeedback, Neurofeedback, and Therapeutic Lifestyle Change

1. b 2. c 3. c

Chapter 12
Delivering Neuroeducation to Children and Adolescents

1. c 2. a 3. b

Index

Figures and tables are indicated by f and t following the page number.

A

(Continued)

(Continued)

D

E

F

G

H

I

J

K

O

R

S